D0845022

The ACC Basketball
Book of Fame

North Carolina's forward
Pete Brennan who played
from 1955–58
UNC ATHLETIC COMMUNICATIONS

THE
ACC
BASKETBALL
BOOK
OF
FAME

by Dan Collins

Foreword by Dave Odom

 JOHN F. BLAIR, PUBLISHER *Winston-Salem, North Carolina*

Also by Dan Collins

*Tales from the
Wake Forest Hardwood*

ACC Media Relations

Duke's Mike Gminski
DUKE SPORTS INFORMATION

North Carolina's Mitch Kupchak
UNC ATHLETIC
COMMUNICATIONS

Virginia's Ralph Sampson, Maryland's Albert King, and Virginia's Jeff Lamp
UNIVERSITY OF MARYLAND ARCHIVES

JOHN F. BLAIR,
PUBLISHER
1406 Plaza Drive
Winston-Salem, North Carolina 27103
www.blairpub.com

Library of Congress Cataloging-in-Publication Data

Collins, Dan, 1952-
  The ACC basketball book of fame / by Dan Collins ; foreword by Dave Odom.
      pages   cm
  Includes bibliographical references and index.
  ISBN 978-0-89587-606-5 (alk. paper) — ISBN 978-0-89587-607-2 (ebook) 1. Basketball—Tournaments—United States—History. 2. Atlantic Coast Conference—History. 3. Basketball—Records—United States—History. I. Title.
  GV885.49.A84C67 2013
  796.3230973—dc23
                        2013013545

10 9 8 7 6 5 4 3 2 1

Front cover image: ©Shutterstock.com / B. Calkins; background: psdgraphics.com
Design by Debra Long Hampton

To every player

who ever suited up for an ACC game,

and all of us who were there

to cheer and/or boo them on

North Carolina's
Billy Cunningham
UNC Athletic Communications

Christian Laettner, Duke's center from 1988–92

CONTENTS

Duke's Jeff Mullins (*left*) with teammates
DUKE SPORTS INFORMATION

FOREWORD

For six decades, the Atlantic Coast Conference has brought excitement, joy, and even an occasional tear to fans living within its geographic footprint. While ACC teams have excelled in nearly every sport, men's basketball has unquestionably been the league's beacon.

Growing up in eastern North Carolina, I learned early on that the best Christmas gift was a ticket to the legendary Dixie Classic, held in Reynolds Coliseum on the campus of North Carolina State University. It was there that I cheered the exploits of my heroes—Ronnie Shavlik, Lennie Rosenbluth, Len Chappell, Art Heyman—who were coached by some of the game's best—Everett Case, Frank McGuire, Bones McKinney, Vic Bubas—as their Tobacco Road teams conquered national powers daring to visit that historic event.

In the late 1960s, the landscape of college basketball changed, and the ACC found itself at the forefront for the next two decades. Coaches such as Dean Smith, Lefty Driesell, Norm Sloan, and Terry Holland fueled the fire of fans and generated unsurpassed media attention. Outstanding players—Jordan, Bias, Thompson, Sampson—filled the rosters, and championships became as frequent as beautiful Southern sunsets. National titles in 1974, 1982, and 1983, National Players of the Year (10 awards), and national rankings that routinely included five or six conference teams—more than half the league's membership—were celebrated fervently.

The 1980s and 1990s brought leaders such as Mike Krzyzewski, Jim Valvano, Bobby Cremins, and Gary Williams, as well as more great players—Laettner, Price, and two of my personal favorites, Childress and Duncan. Over a 19-year span, eight more national championship banners were hung in ACC arenas.

In no other sport in any other conference has the media been more woven into the fiber of history than with ACC basketball. Through the written word and stirring broadcasts long into the night, journalists and colorful commentators have always been part of ACC lore. Fans revel in the play-by-play calls and can't wait until the next day to read their favorite columnist's analysis of action on the court and the locker-room aftermath. Television, of course, has played a key role in the popularity of ACC basketball, first on the regional level, then throughout the country, helping to make the ACC truly America's conference.

Few, if any, reporters have covered ACC basketball longer or more capably than Dan Collins. He came on the scene as an undergraduate student in the days of the peerless David Thompson and witnessed arguably the greatest game ever played in the league when N.C. State defeated Maryland in the 1974 ACC championship game. Dan joined the *Winston-Salem Journal* staff in 1978 and has continued to follow closely every aspect of the ACC through portions of five decades.

In *The ACC Basketball Book of Fame*, Dan shares his unique perceptions from a lifetime of covering the country's premier college basketball conference. To diehard ACC fans, this volume will prove a treasure chest of the names and games that have made ACC basketball truly the lifeblood of college sports for more than half a century.

Dave Odom

No. 84 Ronnie Shavlik, N.C. State's center from 1953–56

Michael Jordan
and Dean Smith
Courtesy of Robert Crawford

Phil Ford and Dean Smith
UNC Athletic Communications

Sam Perkins, Roy Williams and Michael Jordan

Everett Case (*left*), and N.C. State's
No. 84 Ronnie Shavlik
N.C. STATE ATHLETICS

INTRODUCTION

In the late summer and early fall of 2002, on the impending grand occasion of the ACC's 50th anniversary, a "blue-ribbon committee" selected the 50 greatest players in the league's illustrious basketball history. The committee had 120 members, and I was one.

Thinking back, I never got my blue ribbon to show for it.

Regardless, it was a great honor, of which I wrote for the *Winston-Salem Journal* edition of September 27, 2002. An even greater honor was bestowed when the ACC reprinted the article on the first page of the conference's 2002–3 media guide. Of my millions of words as a sportswriter since joining the staff of the *Chapel Hill Newspaper* in the fall of 1972, these, given the subject and how they were used, may be my favorites:

We grew up together, my generation and the Atlantic Coast Conference. This is not ancient history, although my kids might beg to differ.

The league will turn 50 in May. I turned 50 last month. My freshman year in college was 1970, which means that of the 49 years of the ACC's existence, I was involved in 32 of them.

And I am not alone. As a member of the Baby Boomer Generation, I seldom am. The ACC yesterday released the long-awaited list of its 50 greatest basketball players, selected by a panel of which I was a member. I saw 40 of them play in college, and if you're 60, and were lucky enough to have lived close to an ACC school, you might well have seen them all. No wonder it means so much to so many. It's a part of who we are and who we have always been.

Who, among us, could imagine a cold, hard winter without ACC hoops? I can't.

Or at least I would prefer not.

ACC basketball has been called a religion, but the truth is that many religions don't command as much devotion or as many devotees. Unlike most of the other major college conferences, the ACC built much of its reputation on basketball. And for that we have coaches such as Everett Case, Frank McGuire, Vic Bubas and Dean Smith to thank, as well as the 50 players on the league's all-time team and all the others who have ever suited up for an ACC game.

1

And while we're at it, we might as well include you, the fans, and me, the media.

For we've all been in it together, some of us from the very start.

And that, to me, is what makes it worth celebrating.

Looking back at the handiwork of our BRC (blue-ribbon committee), I can say without much reservation that we did a pretty good job. As a longtime fan of Bill James, I'm convinced we could have done much worse. From reading James's scathing indictment, *Whatever Happened to the Hall of Fame? Baseball, Cooperstown and the Politics of Glory*, it's apparent that we humans, in all our earthbound, bumbling mortality, are simply not capable of judging immortals. Time gets in the way, as do pride and all the prejudices that contaminate even the purest efforts. Memories fade, and having faded, distort. Some heroes profit from those distortions, while others are relegated to obscurity. It's unavoidable; subjectivity allows for nothing else.

And speaking of the subject of subjectivity . . .

We wouldn't have been human, we members of the BRC, if we hadn't at least bobbled, if not dribbled off our feet and out of bounds, our honest attempt at selecting the ACC's 50th-anniversary team.

To illustrate four instances that, upon research and reflection, cause me at least a twinge of regret, I'll employ a method favored by James. I'll analyze the qualifications of four anonymous players: Player A, Player B, Player C, and Player D.

Player A was a consensus second-team All-American as a junior and a consensus first-team All-American as a senior. He made first-team All-ACC all three years he was eligible, and received every vote cast as a senior. He got the fifth-most votes as a sophomore and the third-most as a junior. Though he was never ACC Player of the Year, he finished only four votes back of the winner his senior season. He made first-team All-Tournament as a sophomore and senior, and his teams, during his three years, had a record of 64–18 and won an ACC title.

Player B was a consensus second-team All-American as a senior, the one season he made first-team All-ACC. He was fourth in the order of voting for All-ACC that season. He made second-team All-ACC as a junior, getting the sixth-most votes overall. And he made second-team All-Tournament as a junior. His teams, during the three years he was eligible, had a record of 73–19 and won an ACC championship.

Player C was a consensus second-team All-American twice, as a junior and senior. Eligible all four seasons, he made second-team All-ACC as a sophomore and first-team as a junior and senior, collecting more votes than anyone over a two-year span. He actually received every vote as a senior as a unanimous selection. He tied for ninth in the voting as a sophomore. He was the ACC Player of the Year as a junior and finished second in the voting as a senior, taking 33 votes to the winner's 86. He made first-team All-Tournament as a senior, the only season his team advanced past its first game. His teams had a record of 72–41 and played for the ACC title one season, but lost.

Player D was ACC Rookie of the Year. He made second-team All-ACC as a sophomore and junior, receiving the eighth-most votes as a sophomore and the sixth-most (just missing first team) as a junior. He was second-team All-Tournament as a sophomore and first-team as a junior. His teams, during the three seasons he played before leaving for the NBA after his junior year, were 64–28 and lost the ACC championship by one point his sophomore and junior seasons.

I can't say I knew Player B, Bobby Jones, well. We were at the same school, North Carolina, at the same time, and I always enjoyed dealing with him. I enjoyed watching him play even more, in that he excelled in the often unheralded aspects of the game. And he was clutch.

Player D, Buck Williams, was one of my favorites of his time. He was the consummate center and teammate—solid, hardworking, reliable, willing to do whatever it took for his team to win. I loved how his coach, Lefty Driesell, referred to him simply as "Buck." And Buck could play the game, as he subsequently proved for almost two decades with the Nets, Trailblazers, and Knicks.

But as good as they were, neither was as good as Player A, Bob Verga, or Player C, Rod Griffin. And as you can see by their credentials, neither accomplished anywhere close to as much as Verga did at Duke or Griffin did a decade later at Wake Forest.

So, as you've probably surmised from the way this argument is going, the BRC included Jones and Williams on our 50th-anniversary team and left off Verga and Griffin. The omission of Verga was particularly glaring, in that a compelling argument can be made that he was one of the 25 best to ever play in the ACC.

All of which proves how going on reflections and remembrances—no matter how honest, well meaning, and capable those doing the reflecting and remembering may be—is not the way to choose an all-anniversary team. Nor is it a suitable method of selecting a Hall of Fame.

So what is the best way? That's a question I started bouncing around in my head awhile back. And the more Bill James I read, the clearer the answer became.

First off, objectivity beats subjectivity. If I could establish a methodology, a formula, an "Awards Points" system, that would enable me to plug in variables and let the chips rest where they fell. That would have to be better than relying on statistics, reputations, or memories growing fainter by the day.

Second, contemporaneous judgments beat any made the next day, next week, next year, next decade. They're never perfect, but straining them through the hippocampus doesn't make them any better.

Third, players should be judged against who they played. Basketball has changed, and changed again, again, and again since James Naismith got around to cutting the bottom out of the peach basket. Many of those changes have come since the ACC began. The players have changed. The rules have changed. Everything has changed, making it useless to compare the 19.5 rebounds Ronnie Shavlik averaged in 1955–56 to the 8.3 Jared Dudley averaged in 2006–7. But it is instructive to know that Dudley, like Shavlik, pulled down more rebounds than anyone else in the conference in those particular seasons.

My basis for selecting who might belong in an ACC Basketball Hall of Fame crystallized when, while perusing an ACC basketball media guide, I remembered something I had known and forgotten. The conference office, to its everlasting credit, has kept not just a record of first-team, second-team, and (since 1990) third-team All-ACC performers, but the actual votes earned by everyone on the teams as well. And that's going all the way back to the beginning.

From those records, I could see that, whereas David Thompson and Gary Melchionni were both first-team All-ACC in 1973, Thompson was considered by those who saw him play to be a much, much better player. Thompson received every vote, as he did all three years he was eligible. Melchionni was the fifth-leading vote-getter by a long shot, collecting 176 votes to the 212 received by Tom McMillen, who finished fourth in the voting.

The more I studied the tool, the more convinced I became that it held the key to my efforts. The judgments of all the players named (or not named, as the case may be) All-ACC had already been made. And they were made by people who saw the players play. So why take into account the statistics of players when those statistics had already been factored into the original voting?

Buzz Wilkinson scored 30.1 points a game for Virginia in 1953–54, and Barry Parkhill scored 21.6 points for the Wahoos in 1971–72. But I know that Parkhill was considered a better player by those who saw him because he received every vote cast for All-ACC that season, whereas Wilkinson finished a distant fifth in the voting in his season.

Were mistakes made in the original voting? Of course. Anyone who might dispute that has forgotten—or was never aware of—the season David Thompson led N.C. State to the national championship as a consensus first-team All-American, yet didn't receive every vote for ACC Player of the Year.

Two voters opted for Jones, and one voted for Thompson's five-seven teammate, Monte Towe.

The yardstick is far from perfect, but I submit that, given those were contemporaneous calls by people who were on the scene, it's the best yardstick available to measure how good the players were and what they meant to their teams and the conference at large.

Assign values to each spot in the voting, give extra credit for everything else deemed too important to disregard, add all the points, and decide where the cutoff should be. Accumulate the requisite total and you're in. Come up short and you're not. No arguing, no lobbying, no persuading, just tabulating.

The heavy lifting, obviously, is deciding what accomplishments should be considered and what value to give them. The core standard should be the vote totals for All-ACC. Anything else might even be considered extraneous, or perhaps redundant.

For instance, if a player received the most votes for All-ACC and won Player of the Year, should one feat receive as much weight as the other? One way to avoid excessive overlap is to establish a core standard and then award bonus points for such honors as ACC Player of the Year, ACC Rookie of the Year, the Everett Case Award for ACC Tournament Most Valuable Player, first- and second-team All-Tournament, National Player of the Year, consensus first- or second-team All-American, and Final Four MVP.

For about two years, I wrestled with these questions, establishing one set of criteria after another and tearing them all up to start over. What drove me was knowing that if I could actually come up with an objective framework for Hall of Fame standards, my work would be done.

And then the brouhaha could begin.

THE FORMULA

Baseline

425 points—Unanimous first-team All-ACC
400 points—Most votes, first-team All-ACC
375 points—Second-most votes, first-team All-ACC
350 points—Third-most votes, first-team All-ACC
325 points—Fourth-most votes, first-team All-ACC
300 points—Fifth-most votes, first-team All-ACC
275 points—Sixth-most votes, second-team All-ACC
250 points—Seventh-most votes, second-team All-ACC
225 points—Eight-most votes, second-team All-ACC

200 points—Ninth-most votes, second-team All-ACC
175 points—Tenth-most votes, second-team All-ACC
150 points—Eleventh-most votes, third-team All-ACC
125 points—Twelfth-most votes, third-team All-ACC
100 points—Thirteenth-most votes, third-team All-ACC
75 points—Fourteenth-most votes, third-team All-ACC
50 points—Fifteenth-most votes, third-team All-ACC

Bonusphere

250 points—Consensus National Player of the Year
250 points—Unanimous ACC Player of the Year
200 points—Consensus first-team All-American
200 points—Runaway ACC Player of the Year
175 points—Contested ACC Player of the Year
150 points—Heavily contested ACC Player of the Year
150 points—Consensus second-team All-American
150 points—Final Four MVP
100 points—Everett Case Award (ACC Tournament MVP)
100 points—ACC Rookie of the Year
125 points—Runner-up for ACC Player of the Year in a heavily contested
     vote (within one-third of vote total of POY)
100 points—Runner-up for ACC Player of the Year in contested vote (within
     one-half of vote total of POY)
75 points—First-team All–ACC Tournament
50 points—Second-team All–ACC Tournament

Having stayed as far from a physics lab as possible during my undergrad days at North Carolina, all I know of Albert Einstein is what I've gleaned through popular culture. Awhile back while watching a documentary on Uncle Albert, I picked up a factoid I found fascinating—how his theory of relativity is so precise, and so interrelated, that if one variable can be disproved, then the whole kit and caboodle will fall apart.

Talk about pressure.

Bob Latford wasn't quite so ambitious. Latford was the man who devised the points system NASCAR used to determine its championship. He laid it out to a couple of Big Bill France's lieutenants on a cocktail napkin at an infamous Daytona Beach surfer and lifeguard establishment called the Boot Hill Saloon. Latford's handiwork, like that of Einstein, was the result of some deep thinking. But instead of convincing the world's entire scientific community of its validity, Latford knew he had to win over only leadfoots (or leadfeet) like Richard Petty, Cale Yarborough, and Richard Childress to have his system adopted.

He did, and it was, serving as the official method of crowning the series champion from 1975 through 2010. As controversial as it remained through the 35 years NASCAR relied on Latford's formula, it effectively solved a problem for a sport that had gone through five points systems in the previous nine years.

Not surprisingly, my own methods of calculation tend to mirror Latford's more than Einstein's. Latford, I imagine, arrived at his conclusion through tinkering with numbers, eyeballing the results, asking the opinions of others, tinkering some more, eyeballing some more, and finally coming up with something that made the most sense while avoiding the most obvious pitfalls. And that, in short, is how I arrived at the Awards Points system used to determine which worthies are worthy enough to deserve enshrinement in the ACC Basketball Hall of Fame.

A vignette concerning Casey Stengel came to mind as I concocted one formula after another in an effort to get it as right as I could. I'm rather sheepish to admit it came from *Dynasty: The New York Yankees, 1949–1964* by Peter Golenbock, considering that Golenbock also wrote the largely discredited hit job *Personal Fouls: The Broken Promises and Shattered Dreams of Big Money Basketball at Jim Valvano's North Carolina State.*

The story told was of Yankees owner Del Webb dropping by Stengel's hotel room the morning of the first game of the 1949 playoffs against Boston. It was 9:30, and Stengel, red-eyed from a sleepless night, was still in his pajamas. Wadded balls of paper littered the room.

"What are those?" Webb asked.

"Lineups," Stengel responded.

I can't say I lost any sleep arriving at my points system, but I did go through about a dozen legal pads.

If this thing was going to fly, then the formula, the framework, the Awards Points system had to be credible. Not universally accepted as genius, because there are always critics who have in their DNA a need to insist they know a better way. But the bar had to be set at least at *credible.*

All the subjectivity in this project would come while establishing the formula for admission. From that point on, all that would be required to determine who was in and who wasn't would be an ACC basketball media guide, a sharp pencil, and a pad of paper.

So if the formula was fatally flawed, then so would be the Hall of Fame.

The true greats like Thompson, Len Chappell, Art Heyman, and Tyler Hansbrough were going to qualify no matter what the standards. If they didn't, I should have spent all that time playing Solitaire. I recognized that the battles would be waged on the border, as my forebears, the fightin' Scots-Irish, invariably found to be the case.

None of this should imply that I spent 40 days and 40 nights on Mount Sinai and brought the Awards Points system down on stone tablets. I hope I haven't given the impression of taking myself that seriously. It's my intention that this will not be seen as the last word on who should be in the ACC Basketball Hall of Fame, but rather the first. And I do not aim to ignore the mistakes and oversights of the original voting and deny how they flaw the finished product. Throughout this work, I endeavor to shine as much light as possible on those injustices.

"It has been said that democracy is the worst form of government except for all the others that have been tried," Winston Churchill observed.

To wit, the formula I've come up with is the worst way of determining membership in the Hall of Fame.

Except for all the others that have been tried.

Since beginning this project, I can no longer see a freshman play for an ACC team without wondering if he'll one day join the ranks of the immortals in *The ACC Basketball Book of Fame*. Never again will I allow a modest pedigree to dissuade me from the possibility that a player may one day fool us all. If the likes of Everett Case, Dean Smith, and Bobby Cremins can be fooled, no one is immune from misguided basketball judgment. All either passed on, or had to be talked into taking, players honored in this book.

What I learned during this labor of love is that a player's greatness cannot be assessed by what he can or cannot do with a basketball. The great ones are great because they have to be. Whether it was sweating away 10 pounds in a hothouse gym during July or climbing out of bed at 5:30 on a frigid February morning to get in 45 minutes of shooting before school, the players in this book did what was necessary to achieve excellence. They did it because they couldn't bear the thought that somewhere someone was working harder than they were.

That's how a five-nine high-school benchwarmer could show up at N.C. State and turn out to be Lou Pucillo. That's how a left-handed guard with no spring in his legs or jump shot could turn out to be John Lucas. That's how a poker-faced unknown from the Virgin Islands could turn out to be Tim Duncan. And yes, that's how the player Cremins was convinced wasn't quick or athletic enough to get off the bench in the ACC could turn out to be Matt Harpring.

As you read this, there are current ACC players who have it in them to be great. And there are players in junior high and even youth leagues who burn to play basketball in the ACC, whether for an original school or one of the expansion additions that have come along since.

The conference once enjoyed what today would be considered unattainable stability. The same eight teams—North Carolina, Duke, N.C. State, Wake Forest, Virginia, Clemson, Maryland, and South Carolina—competed for the same spoils for the first 18 years until South Carolina opted for independent status after the 1970–71 season.

One way of looking at the ACC of the early days is as a town—a small town at that, with a small town's rivalries and shared experiences forging a deep sense of identity. Like small-town families, the schools fought like crazy for superiority and harbored slights and injustices, perceived or real.

Eventually, the ACC became a city as the schools, the basketball programs, and the arenas expanded. But even then, the conference retained its identity. The teams' greatest battles were among themselves.

Today, following the addition of Virginia Tech, Miami, and Boston College and the pending arrival of Syracuse, Pittsburgh, Notre Dame, and Louisville, the conference has grown into a metropolis. As in any metropolis, it's hard to know where the boundaries lie—especially considering that Virginia Tech, Miami, Boston College, Syracuse, Pittsburgh, and Notre Dame have all fought their own battles as members of the Big East. When Maryland, which announced its departure in the fall of 2012, is playing in the Big Ten and Louisville is in the ACC, it is indeed a new day.

Which doesn't suggest the new day has to be a dark day.

The ACC has lost part of its identity, to be sure. I'm still having trouble getting my head around the fact that North Carolina and Wake Forest don't play each other home and away every season.

But with change come new and enticing possibilities. The prospect of Duke playing Syracuse or North Carolina playing Louisville in Madison Square Garden for the conference title doesn't sound half bad even to someone as gray in the beard and steeped in ACC tradition as yours truly.

Maybe the next Hall of Famer will play for Jim Boeheim at Syracuse, Rick Pitino at Louisville, Jamie Dixon at Pittsburgh, or Mike Brey at Notre Dame.

Or maybe, just maybe, he'll play for Clemson. After 60 seasons, it would be about time.

Tyler Zeller
Courtesy of Robert Crawford

TYLER ZELLER

7-0 Center | North Carolina | 2008–12 | No. 44

2011	Second-team All-ACC, sixth-most votes	275
	First-team All-Tournament	75
2012	First-team All-ACC, unanimous	425
	ACC POY	200
	First-team All-Tournament	75
	Second-team All-American	150
Awards Points		**1,200**

Nothing Tyler Zeller accomplished his senior season at North Carolina was above and beyond what one might expect from the middle son of one of the first families of basketball-crazy Indiana.

Players with his pedigree are expected to have games like he had at Virginia, where he spiked a 20-point performance with the game-winning bucket over Mike Scott, or his final home game against Maryland, when he drained a school-record 23 free throws on the way to a 30-point explosion.

"He does have tremendous savvy," Coach Roy Williams said of Zeller after the 88–64 victory over the Terps. "He can turn to either shoulder and be able to score. And then he's got a little of that Ichabod Crane clumsiness to him. He gets his arms and legs and head going in every direction. I suppose defensive players have a lot of things that they can foul."

Given that Zeller's older brother, Luke, played at Notre Dame and his younger brother, Cody, was the 2012 Big Ten Freshman of the Year at Indiana, he probably had to make room on the family mantel for the ACC Player of the Year award he wrested from Scott down the stretch.

No, the only surprise from all he did during his marvelous senior season was how long it was in coming. Blame it on injuries, blame it on the stacked North Carolina roster, blame it on whatever, but if Zeller wasn't a bust through his sophomore season—by which time he was averaging only 7.1 points and 3.7 rebounds a game—then he was close enough to be mistaken for one.

The Zeller brothers were about as big as one could get at Washington

High School, where as many as 11,500 fans shoehorned their way into the school's 7,090-seat gymnasium to watch the Hachets (now, that's a name for a basketball team) hack out another victory. All three won state titles. Tyler scored 43 points in a championship-clinching victory over Fort Wayne Harding. But his little brother did him one better; Cody's teams won titles back to back. All three were named Mr. Basketball in Indiana—making the Zellers the first family to accumulate three trophies—and all three were McDonald's All-Americans.

Mother Lorri was secretary of the high school's athletics department, so she had the keys to the gym. But six-four Steve Zeller was the taskmaster known for pushing his sons around with the blocking pads most often associated with football.

So overbearing was Steve Zeller that he had to back off. He learned that lesson when Luke was in the sixth grade, when he railed at his son every mile of a four-hour drive home from an AAU tournament. When Luke asked, "Was there anything I did right?" Steve was brought up short. Going forward, he stuck with positive criticism, and only when asked.

The Zellers were driving through the Midwest shopping for scholarships for Tyler when they stopped by Missouri. They had an in; Tyler's mother was the sister of Al Eberhard, a one-time Tigers star who played four years for the Detroit Pistons.

It was bad enough that Mike Anderson, then the coach at Missouri, wasn't sufficiently impressed to offer a ride. What was worse was that the family heard the word not through Anderson but through Eberhard.

And despite Tyler's recognition as a McDonald's All-American, Anderson's assessment appeared spot-on early in Zeller's career at North Carolina. He did make a splash with 18 points in his debut against Penn while filling in for star Tyler Hansbrough, who was sidelined with shin splints. But Zeller, saddled with a broken wrist, spent most of his first season watching Hansbrough, Ty Lawson, and the rest of his teammates bring home the school's fifth national championship.

"Coach talks to us a lot about [Zeller] and what he's turned out to do," James Michael McAdoo, a freshman when Zeller was a senior, told Caulton Tudor of the Raleigh News & Observer. "I remember one time Coach asked us if we knew what Tyler's stats were his first year. I think it was maybe two points and one rebound a game.

"That's what makes Tyler a role model for all of us—his work ethic."

Even so, Zeller didn't set the ACC on fire as a sophomore, when he missed more time with a broken foot and failed to crack the regular starting lineup for a team that lost 17 games and finished 5–11 in ACC play. But when teammates Larry Drew II and the Wear twins, Travis and David, bolted for what they perceived to be the greener pastures of UCLA, Zeller stuck it out.

"There were some rough periods, but nothing a lot of other people haven't been through," he said. "I'm a person of faith. I knew God had a reason for everything. I didn't doubt that at all. I knew I had to stay on track to get well, and then get better."

Zeller managed to do both his junior year, when he increased his scoring from 9.3 points a game to 15.8 and his rebounding yield from 4.6 to 7.2.

Success came more quickly in the classroom, where he excelled. He twice made Academic All-American and in 2012 became the school's first Academic All-American of the Year. His grade point average was 3.62 in business administration.

Those are the kinds of accomplishments that warm the cockles of a coach's heart, which remained well above room temperature during Zeller's four seasons with the Tar Heels.

"You're talking about a guy who's perfect," Williams said. "And I'll never say that in front of him. But even when he screws it up, I tell him. Whether it's very viciously when I'm telling him or just matter-of-factly, he just says 'Yeah, you're right.'

"There's not been one time that I've ever been mad at Tyler Zeller."

NOLAN SMITH

6-2 Guard | Duke | 2007–11 | No. 2

2010	Second-team All-ACC , seventh-most votes	250
	First-team All-Tournament	75
2011	First-team All-ACC, unanimous	425
	ACC POY	200
	Everett Case Award	100
	First-team All-American (with Jimmer Fredette of Brigham Young, JaJuan Johnson of Purdue, Jared Sullinger of Ohio State, and Kemba Walker of Connecticut)	200
Awards Points		1,250

Nolan Smith, as everyone knows, played for Duke. And Smith, as everyone knows as well, played there for Mike Krzyzewski. And like every player who ever picked up a basketball, Smith also played, in one sense, for himself.

But what made Smith's college career so compelling was that besides playing for his school, his coach, and his own self-interest, he played for his father.

Or, more accurately, he played for the memory of his father.

Derek Smith, a manly guard whose physical and mental strength helped will Louisville to the 1980 national title in Indianapolis, died of a heart attack in 1996. He was 34, his son Nolan eight.

The family was on the Atlantic cruise sponsored each year by the Washington Bullets, for whom Derek Smith was coaching as an assistant. A noted family man, he had taken along wife Monica, daughter Sydney, and Nolan.

Out on the waves, Nolan was going one-on-one on the ship's basketball court against a 14-year-old boy. When Nolan lost, he tossed the basketball overboard into the drink. Derek Smith, looking on, chastised his son for his fit of pique, telling him no one would want to play with a teammate who couldn't lose any better than that.

The concept of losing took on a far deeper meaning later that day, when Nolan and his sister, hanging out in the children's play area, heard the ship's public-address system summon Monica to the upper deck. Brother and sister ran but arrived too late.

A defibrillator had sent currents through Derek Smith, but no heartbeat was to be found. Monica remembers that, in her hour of deepest shock and grief, her son sat beside her, put his arm around her, and said, "I'm the man of the house now."

But he wasn't so much a man that his mother didn't object a few years later when Nolan announced he wanted a tattoo. Once he explained what he wanted inscribed on his body, she agreed.

"But just one," she said.

On Smith's right bicep are a likeness of his father, "Forever Watching," four *RIP*s, and "Derek Smith, 1961–1996."

"He told me to play every game like it was my last," he explained.

Smith was also not so much of a man that he didn't need a friend to help him through his adjustment to life without a father. He found one in Michael Beasley, who he got to know as a teammate on the AAU team D.C. Assault, founded by Nolan's stepfather, Curtis Malone. The two actually became such fast friends that, by the time he reached the eighth grade, Beasley moved in with the Malone family. For years, he spent his vacations at the Malone home, where he had his own room.

Smith, like many budding college stars, played his high-school basketball at Oak Hill Academy for Steve Smith, who was so impressed that, for the first

Nolan Smith
COURTESY OF ROBERT CRAWFORD

time ever, he named a junior—guess who?—team captain.

Smith was afforded the honor again as a senior—the year he was also class president, resident assistant of his dormitory, and a member of the National Honor Society.

The college basketball world did not come calling, since pretty much everyone assumed Smith would play for Louisville. That was, after all, where his father had become a legend and where his mother and sister both earned their degrees. Nolan was born in Louisville, and his grandparents lived in the city.

But Johnny Dawkins, then an assistant at Duke, had become close friends with Derek Smith when the two played for the Philadelphia 76ers. One day, Dawkins called to check in on Monica Malone for several reasons—one being that his own wife, Tracy, was her best friend.

Dawkins grew excited when Malone mentioned her son might not be the lock for Louisville everyone assumed. Dawkins's next call was to Krzyzewski. One thing led to another, and Smith ending up wearing blue instead of red.

Smith's relationship with Dawkins—so longstanding he grew up calling Dawkins "Uncle Johnny"—helped him through the difficult transition to ACC basketball. It also prompted whispers that Smith might transfer to Stanford after Dawkins was named head coach there after Smith's freshman year.

But he stuck it out at Duke, blossoming as a junior following an intense off-season regimen conducted three hours daily by a personal trainer.

That was the season Krzyzewski relieved Smith of his duties as primary ball handler by installing Jon Scheyer as the point guard. But Smith continued to check the other team's point guard. Krzyzewski, as he has said time and again, has never been one to overdefine the role of any of his players.

"Jon is a leader on the court, and I'm off the ball," Smith said. "It kind of simplifies the game for me. I catch and I'm already in a playmaking mode. That definitely makes it a lot easier."

College basketball is first and foremost a guard's game, and few, if any, teams in 2009–10 had a more formidable backcourt than Duke. Kyle Singler, a sharp-shooting junior wing forward, made first-team All-ACC along with Scheyer, and Krzyzewski cobbled together a front court from retread parts Lance Thomas and Brian Zoubek.

But it was the one-two perimeter punch of Scheyer and Smith—who between them averaged 37 points and 9.5 assists—that led the Blue Devils all the way to Indianapolis for the Final Four.

Smith was well aware that Indianapolis was the site of his father's triumph. Hours before Nolan scored a career-high 29 points against Baylor in the regional final, ESPN reared its *Outside the Lines* segment on Derek Smith's untimely death.

After the Blue Devils outlasted Butler 61–59 for the school's fourth national title, Nolan visited his father's grave site. There, he told Derek Smith he also had a national championship ring, and that he would do all he could to see that Duke won another the next season.

True to his word, Smith did all he could, emerging as the ACC's best player and the undisputed leader on one of college basketball's finest teams. But the quest for a second-straight title ended before it could pick up any real momentum, as the Blue Devils lost to Arizona 93–77 in the regional semifinal.

Smith was drafted as the 19th pick in the first round by the Portland Trailblazers.

KYLE SINGLER

6-8 Forward | Duke | 2007–11 | No. 12

2008	ACC ROY	100
	Third-team All-ACC, 11th-most votes	150
2009	Second-team All-ACC, ninth-most votes	200
	First-team All-Tournament	75
2010	First-team All-ACC, fifth-most votes	300
	Everett Case Award	100
	Final Four MVP	150
2011	First-team All-ACC, fourth-most votes	325
	First-team All-Tournament	75
Awards Points		**1,475**

Given his lineage, Kyle Singler was born to be a special athlete.

The only questions were what sport he would play, and where.

His father, Ed Singler, played quarterback at Oregon State. His mother, Kris, played basketball there. Ed's brother, Bill, played wide receiver at Stanford. Two of Kris's brothers, Greg and John Brosterhous, played football at Oregon. Another, B. G. Brosterhous, played basketball at Texas. Yet another brother, Rick Brosterhous, played basketball at Oregon.

So Kyle exhibited what might be construed as a rebellious streak in his early days, at least until his family moved from Salem to Medford (both in Oregon) when he was in the second grade.

"When I was younger I played hockey and nothing else," Singler told Al Featherston of GoDuke.com. "That's when I lived in Salem. When I moved to Medford, there really wasn't much of a hockey program, so I picked up football and basketball and a little baseball.

"I was just a kid who just loved to play something. I decided later to just take up football and basketball."

His football coach growing up was his uncle Bill, his basketball coach his father. He was good enough in football to attract scholarship offers from several West Coast colleges as a quarterback or wide receiver. He was good

Kyle Singler
COURTESY OF ROBERT CRAWFORD

enough in basketball to bring the ball upcourt, even though he was the tallest player.

Ed Singler saw to it that he did.

"Being the tallest person on the court, it's so easy to put that person in the post, where they can't really utilize their skills to the fullest," Kyle told Featherston. "So basically it was the coaching that helped me develop different skills and be the basketball player I am."

He needed all the versatility his game could attain to stand up against high-school rival Kevin Love, the beefy center who starred at Lake Oswego High, a school from the suburbs of Portland.

Singler's athletic career reached a crossroads when his South Medford High team lost to Love and Lake Oswego in the 2006 6-A state championship. After Love put up 24 points and nine rebounds—to Singler's 15 points, six rebounds, and five assists—Singler took two steps to improve his game. First, he decided to give up football to concentrate on basketball. Then, starting the morning after the title game loss, he began working daily on his ball handling and his shooting touch.

The regimen produced results. South Medford met Lake Oswego in an invitational tournament early the next season. This time, with Singler guarding Love, South Medford prevailed 71–63. The next night, South Medford rallied furiously against powerhouse Oak Hill Academy, only to come up short 99–90. Coach Steve Smith of Oak Hill, whose own Nolan Smith scored 30 points in the game, called Singler as good a high-school player as he had ever seen.

Though folks in Oregon hoped to keep their homegrown star home, Singler pared his list of suitors to Arizona, Kansas, and Duke before heading east to play in the ACC.

"It still is a weird factor to it," Singler told Steve Wiseman of the *Durham Herald-Sun* during his senior season at Duke. "I was so used to having my family around supporting me. I know they are always with me. We play on TV a lot. That helps."

Oregon did receive a consolation prize. E. J. Singler, Kyle's younger brother, signed with the University of Oregon Ducks, saying it was important to him to represent his home state.

For all their countless games of one-on-one on the family court, the brothers played their first organized game against each other in 2011 when Mike Krzyzewski took Duke across the country to play the Ducks in the Rose Garden in Portland, home of the NBA's Trailblazers. Big brother's team prevailed as Kyle, a senior with a Final Four Most Valuable Player award under his belt, scored 30 points to carry the Blue Devils to a 98–71 romp. Little brother, an understandably nervous sophomore, failed to score in the first half before coming alive to contribute 14 in the final 20 minutes.

Big brother wasn't really that big early in his career, and it showed in the mano a mano world underneath the basket. Recognizing that he wore down late in his freshman season—which ended with West Virginia outrebounding the Blue Devils by 20 in a 73–67 victory in the second round of the NCAA Tournament—Singler spent the summer packing 20 pounds of muscle on his 215-pound frame.

"Kyle plays as hard as anybody," Krzyzewski commented. "But because we didn't have any depth inside, he had to play more minutes than he should have guarding people who were bigger."

Like most coaches, especially the good ones, Krzyzewski has always been alert to the slings and arrows aimed at his players. When reporter Joe Drews of the school paper, the *Duke Chronicle*, suggested in 2010 that Singler should be benched for his own good and that of the team after a 2-for-13 shooting performance against Georgia Tech, Krzyzewski couldn't let it pass without comment. Singler provided his own response by returning from winter break to contribute double-figure points and rebounds in a 79–59 home victory over Boston College. Afterward, Krzyzewski gave his.

"It's our first day back and we read the student newspaper and it's about benching our guy," Krzyzewski said, trying in vain to keep it lighthearted. " 'Welcome back,' I guess. Unbelievable. But for those people who are really in support of Kyle, they should be happy that he had a hell of a game. He had a double-double. Without going to the bench."

Some in the media suggested Singler would have been better off leaving Duke for the NBA after being named Most Valuable Player of the 2010 Final Four. Perhaps they were right, in that Singler slipped to the second round before being selected by Detroit with the 33rd pick.

Singler's mother said her son just couldn't pry himself away.

"It was really important for him to graduate and be the captain of his team and be there for his senior speech and senior banquet," Kris Singler told the *Durham Herald-Sun*. "Kyle, not only has he given his all on the court, he's loyal almost to a fault. If he had left, he would have felt like he let his team down, let Nolan [Smith] down. They came in together and are going out together."

Krzyzewski is fiercely protective of Kyle's legacy at Duke: "He'll be one of the top four or five players to ever play here as far as the credentials. When you win a national championship during your four years, you've already set yourself apart. He's one of the best defenders we've had here. He's been amazing. In my 31 years, he's one of the really great players that we've had here."

MALCOLM DELANEY

6-3 Guard | Virginia Tech | 2007–11 | No. 23

2009	Third-team All-ACC, 11th-most votes	125
	Second-team All-Tournament	50
2010	First-team All-ACC, unanimous	425
2011	First-team All-ACC, third-most votes	350
	Second-team All-Tournament	50
Awards Points		**1,000**

Say what you want about Dino Gaudio and his three-year stint as Wake Forest's head coach, but he got at least a couple of important things right. One, he recognized the necessity of building a defensive mind-set into the fabric of a successful program. And two, he saw right off that a coach can't reach too deep into the ranks of college basketball programs—down where the VMIs and N.C. Centrals and Longwoods and USC Upstates dwell—and come up with any victory that will impress those charged with setting the NCAA Tournament field come March.

Seth Greenberg's Virginia Tech teams played the kind of defense it takes to win ACC games. They played it most nights with an admirable passion and intensity—and often had to in order to overcome a deficiency in overall talent. But they never won quite enough games to be invited to the NCAA Tournament in the four years Malcolm Delaney played. To me, that was a crying shame.

Even harder to take, though, was the crying Greenberg did every March about how his team had been wronged by the NCAA Tournament Selection Committee. And every time I saw him do his bit, which became a standing joke by Delaney's senior season, I thought back to a conversation I had with Gaudio after Wake Forest was not invited to the NIT in 2008 despite finishing 17–13.

You get no credit for beating anybody ranked in the bottom 100 of the RPI, he explained. If anything, just playing those teams is held against you.

Malcolm Delaney
Courtesy of Virginia Tech

So Gaudio scraped most of the dregs off his schedule and replaced them with teams ranked between 100 and 225—teams Wake Forest should by all rights have beaten anyway. In February during Gaudio's final two seasons, there was never really a question whether or not the Deacons would make the NCAA Tournament field.

But no matter how many times the selection committee sent Greenberg the memo, he never got it. Or if he did, he didn't read it.

In at least three of Delaney's four seasons at Virginia Tech, the Hokies were as good as, if not better than, a number of the teams picked for at-large berths. His junior season, they actually tied for third in the ACC at 10–6 and finished 25–9 overall.

Much of what reporters wrote during Delaney's senior season dealt with the one accomplishment he felt he needed to cap his college career.

"The NCAA Tournament is my biggest goal," Delaney told Don Markus of the *Baltimore Sun*. "And if we don't make the tournament this year, I'll be very disappointed in all the hard work I've put in for four years."

He was indeed disappointed. The Hokies were 9–7 in conference play and 22–12 overall, but their body of work was devalued by victories over Campbell (number 279 in the RPI), North Carolina–Greensboro (298), USC Upstate (312), Mount St. Mary's (230), and the ubiquitous Longwood (318). And for a fourth-straight March, Malcolm Delaney's season ended in the NIT.

Truth is, Greenberg's blind spot in scheduling obscured the fact that he was in fact a good basketball coach at Virginia Tech. Blacksburg is not an easy place to win, and Greenberg's Hokies, playing with a boulder-sized chip on their shoulders, relished taking on the Dukes and North Carolinas of the college basketball world.

Which is why Delaney might be considered the quintessential Virginia Tech player.

He was good enough as a senior at Towson Catholic High School in Baltimore to be named Metro Player of the Year by the *Baltimore Sun*. He had come along playing AAU basketball with best friend Donte Greene, a star at Syracuse now in the NBA. Early in Delaney's high-school career, there was talk that he and Green would sign with Maryland as a package deal, until Green decided his future lay with the Orange.

That prompted Coach Gary Williams of the Terps to begin looking at backcourt prospects Greivis Vasquez, Eric Hayes, Adrian Bowie, and Cliff Tucker. Delaney told Don Markus that Maryland never really pulled its scholarship offer from the table. But it doesn't sound as if the Terps were calling at all hours of the night.

"I could have gone to Maryland, but they just weren't steady," Delaney said.

His character and work ethic were never in question. His father, Vincent (who played basketball at Voorhees College), and mother, Patricia, made sure his homework was done before he was set free to play. An older brother, Vincent Jr., played football at Stonehill College. And the friends like Green he hung around with were goal-oriented enough to dub themselves "the Circle of Success."

But as he watched area players including Bowie and Austin Freeman and Chris Wright sign with power programs such as Maryland and Georgetown, Delaney couldn't help wondering why he wasn't getting more attention. It may have been that college coaches weren't sure if he was better suited for the point or the wing. But Delaney himself concluded that the street agents and runners he turned his back on during his recruitment had reciprocated by spreading damaging rumors.

So he showed up at Virginia Tech bound and determined to prove to the power programs what they had missed. He also showed up to win, brandishing a will so strong that after a pummeling by North Carolina, the cheeky freshman said the Hokies "just gave up."

"Malcolm's his own worst critic and he's hard on himself. He takes a lot of things personally," Greenberg told Mark Giannotto of the *Washington Post*. "That's what makes Malcolm Malcolm. I'm not sure if it's good or bad sometimes, but who am I to judge someone for taking things too personally? That's kind of what makes him pretty good. That drives him."

As for where Delaney should play, he answered that question by developing into one of the conference's best combination guards. As a freshman, after Nigel Munson transferred and fellow freshman Hank Thorns couldn't lock down the position, Delaney took over the point. As a senior, after Dorenzo Hudson went down with an injury and Erick Green proved capable of running the show, Delaney moved off the ball.

He flirted with leaving after his junior season and making himself available for the NBA draft. But he didn't hire an agent and decided to return to Blacksburg for one last run at that elusive NCAA Tournament berth.

Delaney did achieve some accomplishments no one can take away. Not many people, for instance, can bait the banshees of Maryland's Comcast Center and get away with it. Delaney not only got away with it as a senior, he put the banshees in their place. Two days after blasting the Maryland faithful as "the worst fans ever," he spiked a 19-point performance by taunting the fans down the stretch of a resounding 74–57 victory.

Along the way, the Virginia Tech class of Delaney, Jeff Allen, and Terrell Bell won 87 games, tying the school record set by the 1986–87 senior class anchored by Dell Curry. It's just a shame that none of those games were in the NCAA Tournament.

In June 2011, Delaney signed to play with Elan Chalon, a professional team in France, and declared he would honor the contract if he went undrafted later that month.

He honored the contract.

GREIVIS VASQUEZ

6-6 Guard | Maryland | 2006–10 | No. 21

2008	Second-team All-ACC, sixth-most votes	275
2009	Second-team All-ACC, tenth-most votes	175
	Second-team All-Tournament	50
2010	First-team All-ACC, unanimous	425
	ACC POY	200
	Second-team All-American	150
Awards Points		**1,275**

Before the 2006–7 season, Gary Williams was busy planning his first practice, scheduled for later that day, when he heard a knock at his office door.

He looked up to see the hyperactive freshman from Caracas, Venezuela, Greivis Vasquez, standing at attention. When Vasquez saluted sharply and announced, "Reporting for duty, sir!" Williams knew he had a pistol on his hands.

That pistol blasted gaping holes in the comfort zones of pretty much everyone, friend and foe alike, he came into contact with over his four-year career. At times, he went off half-cocked. Other times, he couldn't miss the bull's-eye even if he tried.

He was an equal-opportunity provocateur, once infamously bringing the wrath of his director of athletics, his coach, the local and national media, and the fans at the Comcast Center down on his head for his reaction to getting booed by the home crowd.

Vasquez and his teammates were stinking up the court against Georgia Tech in the ACC opener of the 2008–9 season when the notoriously intemperate Terp fans let their star junior guard have it. It wasn't until Maryland rallied on the way to a 68–61 victory that Vasquez responded by putting his index finger to his lips and mouthing, "Shut the fuck up."

And he wasn't done. Reporters flocked to him afterward to hear Vasquez go off on the paying customers.

"We're 12 and three," Vasquez railed. "We were nine and five last year

Greivis Vasquez

Courtesy of Greg Fiume / Maryland Athletics

about this time. What the hell are they thinking? If they don't want to believe in us, get the hell out. We don't need them here. We need people who are going to support and be with us. I want to say thank you to the people who were supporting us and believing in us. If you don't want to support us, get out."

In the firestorm that followed, Vasquez had a sit-down with Athletics Director Debbie Yow, was chastised by Williams, and apologized to the public at large through Peter Schmuck of the *Baltimore Sun.*

"I'm definitely not like that," Vasquez told Schmuck in a classic example of irony.

Vasquez was indeed like that, and he became that way long before showing up at College Park to play for a coach who had that same fire in the belly.

"I'm a demonstrative person on the sideline," Williams told Steve Yanda of the *Washington Post.* "And Greivis kind of plays like that, and he receives some criticism for that.

"But you know, it's much easier to calm somebody down a little bit than to try to get him up all the time. Plus, on your team you need different people, different personalities. . . . Greivis is the guy that kind of gets things stirred up."

Gregorio Vasquez was a baseball fan who favored the New York Yankees, but America's pastime was too boring for his wide-open son. Greivis turned to basketball at age nine and made Venezuela's junior national team by 16. By then, he was known in the barrios of Caracas as "Callejero"—or "Street-baller"—for his flashy, hell-bent style of play.

Still, he might never have escaped that scene if not for the sharp eye of Robert Gonzalez, the director of a nonprofit sports organization. Gonzalez had some contacts in the United States, one of whom was Tommy Lloyd, an assistant coach at Gonzaga, who in turn knew Stu Vetter. The man responsible for grooming Randolph Childress for ACC stardom, Vetter saw enough in Vasquez to invite him to Maryland's Montrose Christian School, where he played alongside a developing big man named Kevin Durant.

Vasquez played well enough for Vetter to be signed by Maryland as the fourth South American and second Venezuelan in ACC basketball. He was preceded by Diego Romero of Argentina (Florida State, 2004–6), Pablo Machado of Venezuela (Georgia Tech, 1996–98), and Fabio Nass of Brazil (Miami, 2006–8).

Sorry, but Mike Eikenberry, who played for Virginia during the 1967–68 season, doesn't count. He hailed from Peru—Peru, Indiana, that is.

Four years after enrolling at Maryland, Vasquez would own twin distinctions as the first ACC player to amass 2,000 points, 750 assists, and 600 rebounds and as the first Venezuelan to be drafted by the NBA. The Memphis Grizzlies plucked him with the 28th pick of the 2010 draft.

Veteran announcer Johnny Holliday of the Maryland radio network called Vasquez—who as a senior won the Bob Cousy Award for best point guard in the nation—possibly the most versatile player to ever wear the Maryland uniform. He'll never be described as the most forgettable.

No one in the Comcast Center on February 21, 2009, is likely to forget Maryland's 88–85 home upset over third-ranked North Carolina, when Vasquez erupted for 35 points, 11 rebounds, and 10 assists for the school's first triple-double since Derrick Lewis notched two in 1987.

And few who were in Raleigh on March 1, 2009—two games later—want to remember the way Vasquez sparked the Terps' 71–60 victory over N.C. State. After jawing with the Wolfpack fans in the final seconds, Vasquez brought the boos cascading down around him by taking—and making—a three-pointer at the buzzer.

Vasquez apologized afterward, but not before impressing the Wolfpack's coach.

"He's cocky," Sidney Lowe said. "And you know what? I like players like that. I like players who have a lot of confidence in their game and themselves and won't be denied."

Vasquez's jersey hangs in the rafters of the Comcast Center, above the student section that once booed him.

"I know sometimes they hated me," Vasquez said of his time at Maryland. "But inside, I think they really loved me."

TYLER HANSBROUGH

6-9 Center | North Carolina | 2005–9 | No. 50

2006	ACC ROY	100
	First-team All-ACC, unanimous	425
	First-team All-Tournament	75
	Second-team All-American	150
2007	First-team All-ACC, third-most votes	350
	First-team All-American (with Kevin Durant of Texas, Alando Tucker of Wisconsin, Acie Law IV of Texas A&M, and Arron Afflalo of UCLA)	200
2008	First-team All-ACC, unanimous	425
	ACC POY, unanimous	250
	Everett Case Award	100
	National POY (with fellow first-team All-Americans Chris Douglas-Roberts of Memphis, D. J. Augustin of Texas, Kevin Love of UCLA, and Michael Beasley of Kansas State)	250
2009	First-team All-ACC, unanimous	425
	First-team All-Tournament	75
	First-team All-American (with DeJuan Blair of Pittsburgh, Stephen Curry of Davidson, Blake Griffin of Oklahoma, and James Harden of Arizona State)	200
Awards Points		3,025

To my mind, nothing could be more appropriate than the way Tyler Hansbrough passed Phil Ford to become the most prolific scorer in North Carolina history, two months before J. J. Redick's ACC mark fell as well.

Hansbrough got the ball on the right block. He turned over his right shoulder, elevated, took a jarring blow from the Evansville Purple Ace defending, righted his sights, and let fly with a shot soft enough to bank off the backboard and cleanly through the net at the Smith Center.

There was nothing pretty about it. With Hansbrough, there seldom, if ever, was. He didn't pound his chest or point a finger toward the heavens. In fact, he spent the duration of the brief ceremony that resulted looking like he wanted nothing more than for the game to resume.

What made it so appropriate was that, in the 142 games Hansbrough played for North Carolina, I saw him make dozens and dozens of baskets in that very fashion. I never stopped marveling at what an exquisitely tuned inner gyroscope he had to have to be able to absorb that much contact—at times enough to send his 250-pound body flying—and still get a shot up softly enough to have a better-than-even chance of putting it through the net.

For four years, opponents pounded Hansbrough. And for four years, he proved he could take whatever anyone was able to dish out.

"I've never coached anybody who's had to face as much on the court as he's had to face," Roy Williams said. "To do the things he's done with two and three guys hanging off him, and as physical as he's played . . . I find it hard to believe."

What many others in the ACC found hard to believe was that Hansbrough, to their way of looking at things, got away with beating the shit out of those he played. Over those same four years, a heated debate raged as to who was mainly responsible for all the contact that left both Hansbrough and whoever was unlucky enough to guard him so bruised and battered.

And hearing the media fawn over Hansbrough's drive and intensity made opposing fans even less inclined to give him a break. So moved was Bill Raftery that during a timeout, and with ESPN cameras focusing on the North Carolina huddle, he blurted the immortal line, "Watching Tyler Hansbrough listen is special."

That said, Hansbrough never made any effort to cultivate such adoration and never acted as though he cared what people said about him one way or the other. He just played basketball as hard as he could and let everybody else worry about where the chips fell.

Hansbrough was no thoroughbred. He was a workhorse whose job wasn't done until the last charge or block was called.

He wasn't particularly fast, he wasn't particularly quick, and he didn't jump particularly high. But he burned with a wild-eyed intensity that earned him the nickname "Psycho T," and he showed up every game ready to throw his body into the fray, which ultimately won him the respect of even his most ardent adversaries.

Tyler Hansbrough
COURTESY OF GRANT HALVERSON

"He's one of the best that has played not just here but in the ACC," Duke's Mike Krzyzewski said. "When you think of Tyler, you're going to think of a warrior. You would never say that there was a possession that he did not play. . . .

"[That] puts him in a really elite class in the history of this conference. So he deserves all that he gets. He's earned it."

Call Hansbrough courageous and he would shrug. If you want to see real courage, he'd tell you, check out my brother.

He wasn't talking about his younger brother, Ben, who was a good enough basketball player to wear a jersey at Mississippi State and Notre Dame. No, it was the eldest of the three Hansbrough boys born and raised in Poplar Bluff, Missouri, who provided Tyler his inspiration. He wore number 50 at North Carolina because that was the high-school number of his big brother, Greg.

Greg Hansbrough showed promise as an athlete until the age of seven, when doctors found a tumor the size of a baseball in his brain. He survived the most delicate of surgeries, but the ordeal left him without full control of the left side of his body. When doctors said his athletic endeavors were over, Greg proved them wrong. He made the basketball team but found more success as a distance runner, building up his endurance until he was able to complete multiple marathons and half-marathons.

Tyler and Greg loved each other like brothers, but that never stopped them from going at each other tooth and nail. In one infamous Hansbrough family fray, the two broke a chair against each other's legs.

So a surreptitious forearm to his ribs or a not-so-surreptitious Gerald Henderson elbow to the nose was never enough to stop Tyler Hansbrough.

Hansbrough was widely considered too ponderous and unathletic to flourish in the NBA, but Larry Bird of the Indiana Pacers saw something he liked. What Bird saw was a bit of himself. The Pacers invested the 13th pick of the 2009 draft in Hansbrough and have been rewarded with a career more productive than most people were willing to predict.

JARED DUDLEY

6-7 Forward | Boston College | 2005–7 | No. 3

2006	Second-team All-ACC, ninth-most votes	200
	First-team All-Tournament	75
2007	First-team All-ACC, unanimous	425
	ACC POY, heavily contested	150
	Second-team All-American	150
Awards Points		1,000

Although Coach Al Skinner will forever be credited for seeing in Jared Dudley what others did not, he owes an assist to Dan Coleman for landing the best big man in school history. Coleman was a recruit who headed home to Minnesota before ever playing a game for the Eagles, leaving a spot on the roster for the largely unknown Dudley from, of all places, San Diego.

A classic late-bloomer, Dudley appeared prep-school-bound before Coleman left Beantown. Dudley had led the Horizon High School Panthers to two state championships and had also held his own in AAU circles but still wasn't receiving any real attention from name programs. He visited St. Mary's and Creighton, and the local school, San Diego State, showed some interest. But Dudley felt he could play higher. When Coleman left and Skinner needed another big body, Dudley made a cross-country recruiting trip to Boston. He asked the Eagles basketball staff for a copy of the roster and some game video to see where he might fit in. Convinced he could be of help early in his career, he committed.

It didn't take him long to prove he was right. Dudley averaged 11.9 points and 6.6 rebounds as a freshman.

"If you looked at him in high school, you would have never imagined that he could have risen to this level," Skinner said. "But no one could measure the size of his heart and his desire, along with his intelligence."

Dudley said he never could have risen to said heights without the love and support of his mother, Melinda Schall, who hired personal trainers for her son and spent countless hours chauffeuring him through Southern California traffic to practices, clinics, and games. The extra miles mother and son traveled brought out a cerebral side in Dudley's game that compensated for what he lacked in quickness. From the way he bolted out of bed at six on summer mornings to shoot baskets, Melinda Schall could see her son burned to be good.

His diligence paid off at BC, where he was known for never coming out of a game still in doubt. In the final six games of his junior season, Dudley sat out a total of 27 seconds.

A gregarious personality, Dudley spread good energy around the locker room on a team known for its strong camaraderie. But when the rest of the team members shaved off their hair before the 2006 NCAA Tournament—showing solidarity with Sean Williams, who had botched his haircut so badly he had little choice—Dudley was having nothing to do with it.

"I had had my braids for three years and I didn't want to cut them off," Dudley explained later. "They are part of my identity."

Much of the fun he had in Chestnut Hill came from his appearances on "The BC"—an Internet parody of the Fox TV show *The OC*—in which students, professors, and members of the administration played roles. A favorite

Jared Dudley

episode was the one in which Dudley, cast as himself, slipped Tim Russert tickets to the Duke game. All he asked in return was to sit in for Russert as host of *Meet the Press*. And though he remained a Southern Californian at heart, Dudley discovered advantages to living in Boston for four years. One was eating Italian food in the North End.

The Big East took a hit in 2005 when BC bolted for the ACC, but at least conference coaches could console themselves with knowing they no longer had to regularly figure out how to control Dudley.

"He's so great around the basket and great off the dribble," Coach Jay Wright of Villanova explained to Andy Katz of ESPN.com. "He's so quick and long. He's a tough match-up."

Dudley nearly led the ACC in both scoring and rebounding as a senior. He ranked first with 8.3 rebounds a game, but his 19 points per contest came up shy of the 19.7 averaged by Al Thornton.

When Dudley beat out Thornton for ACC Player of the Year, he told Michael Vega of the *Boston Globe* how much the honor meant.

"Something like this is bigger in the ACC than in any other conference," Dudley allowed. "Living in San Diego, I didn't grow up watching the Pac-10. I grew up watching the ACC. I had huge ties in North Carolina. My father was born and raised in Wilmington, and his brother went to high school with Michael Jordan. Every game I played in North Carolina, I had at least eight or 10 people go.

"So to come to BC and play in the Big East, and then go to the ACC and win the Player of the Year in the ACC, with all these schools like Duke and Carolina, man, it's like a dream come true."

Drafted in the first round by the Charlotte Bobcats with the 22nd overall pick, Dudley had played six NBA campaigns with the Bobcats and Phoenix Suns through the 2011–12 season, averaging 8.5 points and 3.8 rebounds.

As for Dan Coleman, he was good enough to make honorable mention All–Big 10 twice at Minnesota. That paled, however, when compared to the contribution he made to Al Skinner and Boston College.

SHELDEN WILLIAMS

6-9 Center | Duke | 2002–6 | No. 23

2004	Second-team All-ACC, 10th-most votes	175
	First-team All-Tournament	75
2005	First-team All-ACC, third-most votes	350
	First-team All-Tournament	75
2006	First-team All-ACC, unanimous	425
	First-team All-Tournament	75
	First-team All-American (with J. J. Redick of Duke, Adam Morrison of Gonzaga, Randy Foye of Villanova, and Brandon Roy of Washington)	200
Awards Points		**1,375**

If futures were traded on which newborns would someday grow up to be world-class athletes, then Lailaa Williams would have been a coveted pick the day she was born, May 13, 2009.

Her father is Shelden Williams, an All-American at Duke who has spent his days since leaving Cameron Indoor Stadium making serious cash playing professional basketball. Her mother is Candace Parker, an All-American at Tennessee who has played for less, yet still considerable, cash in the WNBA and Russia.

How Lailaa's parents met is a story worth retelling. Candace Parker was visiting Duke on a recruiting trip in 2003 when she was introduced to Shelden Williams. She remembered the occasion well enough to reconnect with Williams when Tennessee played at Duke during Williams's senior season. The two were married in November 2008, when Williams was playing for the Sacramento Kings.

Except for some faith and trust shown by those who knew him best, Williams never would have been at Duke to become an All-American and meet his future bride. He was accused of rape before he arrived on campus, while his team from back home in Oklahoma was playing in a tournament in Ohio.

It was heavy stuff—heavy enough that he was kicked off his Midwest City High School team and eliminated from consideration for the McDonald's All-American team.

Sexual abuse is an egregious breach of privacy that robs victims of what they believe and who they are. And when it's performed by the powerful and strong on the weak and helpless, it's cowardly beyond words.

That said, in my career as a sportswriter, I've also seen the damage false accusations can do. An ensuing rush to judgment without ascertaining the facts can ruin a life.

When Williams said he was innocent, his parents, Bob and Jeannette Williams, believed him. They based that belief on who Shelden Williams was and how he was raised.

Bob, a teacher and coach, and Jeannette, a member of the state insurance board who sang in the church choir, instilled in Shelden a strong faith. They allowed him to shop for CDs only at Walmart, where no X-rated rap selections were sold. They held his feet to the fire on chores and wouldn't let him out of the house on summer days until he had read both the Bible and a text from school.

Williams's preacher, the Reverend Kenneth West, believed him. He had taken special interest in the bright, devout young man, who from time to time slept over in the West family home. West had also heard Williams sing in the church choir. He'd watched him feed the homeless. He knew his grades were good enough to make the National Honor Society. He recognized the work

Williams had done as a member in good standing of the Fellowship of Christian Athletes.

Mike Krzyzewski also believed Williams.

Krzyzewski encountered Williams early on, when Williams, heading into his freshman season of high school, piled up 42 points and 10 blocked shots in a national AAU game. Krzyzewski got to know him well enough during the recruitment process to learn who Williams was and what he was all about.

So when the accusation was leveled, Williams himself called to tell Krzyzewski.

The criticism Krzyzewski got for not pulling his scholarship offer was probably inevitable. It was also, as it turned out, sadly misguided. For if Krzyzewski and the Duke administration hadn't done their own investigation, if they hadn't talked with Williams's people and the authorities to ascertain what had really happened, then a great wrong would have been done.

Ultimately, the authorities agreed with Williams's parents, preacher, and coach to be. He was not indicted on the charges.

Williams spent pretty much every day of his time at Duke proving he wasn't the kind of person to do what he was accused of doing in a motel room in Ohio.

If anything, the episode stunted Williams's development as a player. He admits to putting up a wall. Teammates and coaches complained that they couldn't drag a word out of him. Krzyzewski and Steve Wojciechowski, the assistant coach charged with developing Duke's big men, stayed on Williams constantly about communicating more frequently and forcefully on defense. It wasn't until Williams's junior season that he began barking orders from the lane, finally getting both Krzyzewski and Wojo off his back.

Williams, from what I've picked up, was a hard person to know at Duke. That was especially the case in his early years, when he received the business, and then some, while playing road games in front of hostile, brutally irreverent fans.

Those he did let in, most notably teammates Lee Melchionni and J. J. Redick, were struck by how straight an arrow Williams was. Freewheeling enough in high school to wear an Afro and scribble "Land" on one sock and "Lord" on the other, Williams was so fastidious by the time he arrived at Duke that his habits became the stuff of legend. He made his bed every day, stored his CDs and DVDs in alphabetical order, lined the drawers of his dresser with linen, cooked chicken and macaroni and cheese for entertainment, and insisted on locking his locker, no matter how many times he was told it wasn't necessary.

And he always made it a point to pray before, during, and after the completion of the national anthem.

Shelden Williams
COURTESY OF ROBERT CRAWFORD

For Williams to attend a party, it had to be a very, very special occasion. Even then, he sipped sodas and mostly kept to himself.

In a wonderfully exhaustive piece for *ESPN: The Magazine*, Tom Friend recounted the time Krzyzewski got into Williams after an uninspired effort against Georgetown. Krzyzewski's message, stripped of all its profanity, was that if Williams really wanted to win, he should show it. Williams, after praying on what his coach told him, called the team together to apologize for his lackadaisical deportment.

Along the way, Williams became more trusting of his coaches and teammates and even allowed them to see facets of his personality—his love for music and his offbeat sense of humor—he had previously kept so tightly under wraps.

On the court, Williams generally confined his shot selection to the ones he could make. Meanwhile, he controlled the middle of the Blue Devils' defense with length, court sense, and fundamentally sound technique. Only the third ACC player (after Ralph Sampson and Tim Duncan) to accumulate

1,500 points, 1,000 rebounds, and 350 blocks, he was named Defensive Player of the Year in 2005 and 2006.

The fifth pick of the 2006 draft by Atlanta, Williams through the 2011–12 season had played six NBA campaigns with the Hawks, Sacramento Kings, Minnesota Timberwolves, Boston Celtics, Denver Nuggets, New York Knicks, and New Jersey Nets.

J. J. REDICK

6-4 Guard | Duke | 2002–6 | No. 4

2003	Third-team All-ACC, 11th-most votes	150
	Second-team All-Tournament	50
2004	Second-team All-ACC, sixth-most votes	275
2005	First-team All-ACC, unanimous	425
	Everett Case Award	100
	ACC POY, contested	175
	First-team All-American (with Andrew Bogut of Utah, Wayne Simien of Kansas, Hakim Warrick of Syracuse, Chris Paul of Wake Forest, and Dee Brown of Illinois)	200
2006	First-team All-ACC, unanimous	425
	Everett Case Award	100
	ACC POY	200
	National POY (with fellow first-team All-Americans Adam Morrison of Gonzaga, Brandon Roy of Washington, Randy Foye of Villanova, and Shelden Williams of Duke)	250
Awards Points		**2,350**

Whatever might be considered a typical upbringing for a young man destined to play basketball among upper-crust scions of wealth and privilege at Duke, the one J. J. Redick experienced down a gravel road outside Roanoke, Virginia, wasn't it.

Redick's father, Ken, wasn't an investment banker. He coordinated employee substance-abuse programs. His mother, Jeanie, was not a high-powered corporate attorney and society-ball regular. She was a nutritionist who raised

J. J. Redick
DUKE SPORTS INFORMATION
©JON GARDINER/
DUKE PHOTOGRAPHY

her five younguns on what vegetables the good earth produced, washed down with organic milk.

Maybe Ken and Jeanie weren't hippies. But when they were living among other counter-culture types outside Cookeville, Tennessee—where Ken cranked a wheel to churn out pottery and, along with Jeanie, sold local crafts and artifacts—they were probably the closest to be found east of Haight-Ashbury.

To fire-bake his love for pottery into the family tree, Ken named his third-born child Jonathan Clay. Only Jonathan Clay didn't like clay—at least not the cold squishiness of it between his fingers. Instead, he gravitated toward sports, in particular baseball and basketball. He was a good enough pitcher at age 12 to star for a local AAU team that really went places, including a two-week national tournament in Salt Lake City. And he was a determined enough competitor to shrug off a broken left thumb and fly back east through the night to strike out 15 batters in an extra-inning game of the state AAU championship.

The center of Ken Redick's son's universe was the basketball court outside the weathered country home on a hill overlooking three acres of family property. As basketball courts go, it wasn't much. The gravel surface made dribbling difficult, so Redick concentrated on fine-tuning a shooting stroke that would become the envy of aspiring sharpshooters everywhere. Shooting from the left side took a little extra arc to clear the protruding tree branch. Day after day, night after night, rain or shine, Ken and Jeanie Redick looked out and saw their son launching jumpers.

At age seven, when he was still being home-schooled by his mother, Redick decided he would play basketball at Duke. He made that decision because that's where Christian Laettner played. Laettner had captured the young boy's imagination by hitting the most celebrated shot in college basketball history, against Kentucky.

Redick got letters from a lot of schools, but if they didn't come from Duke, he didn't bother opening them. He was going to Duke.

As it turned out, Coach Mike Krzyzewski agreed after watching Redick, playing with a throbbing heel injury, score 43 points to lead Cave Spring High School to the state title. What Krzyzewski saw was a fierce competitor who not only survived but thrived under the most intense pressure that could be brought to bear.

The J. J. Redick who showed up at Duke as a freshman in the fall of 2002 was full of himself, as he admitted. He talked a little trash when he hit a shot and was known to bob his head as he ran back down the court. He got a couple of tattoos, though they weren't visible when he was in uniform. One on his stomach is inscribed Isaiah 40:31 ("But they that wait upon the Lord shall renew their strength; they shall mount up with wings as eagles; they shall run, and not be weary; and they shall walk, and not faint"). The other, on his chest, combines the Japanese word for courage with another Bible verse, Joshua 1:9 ("Be strong and of good courage; do not be afraid, nor be dismayed, for the Lord your God is with you wherever you go").

He was also known to be a tad high-strung and quick to bellyache at officials and taunt opponents. Sitting courtside, I once saw him so upset with Chris Paul that he reached out and squeezed Paul's jaw. It all happened in a flash, and no whistle was blown. But I saw it.

None of that adequately explains just how deeply he managed to bore under the skin of opposing fans across the land, and how those fans responded by heaping upon him industrial-strength volumes of abuse. The perpetually unhinged legions at Maryland's Comcast Center outdid themselves during Duke's 66–60 victory there in 2004, when ESPN microphones picked up the chant, "Fuck you, J. J." The cameras tried not to show the T-shirts bearing equally profane sentiments.

The powers that be at Maryland realized they had, as Barney Fife used to say, a situation on their hands. After seeking counsel from a state assistant attorney, the school adopted voluntary behavior guidelines that strongly discouraged the kind of vulgarity that had rained down on a white shooting guard from Duke.

Redick's mother wondered why everyone wouldn't just leave her child alone. So did Coach Leonard Hamilton of Florida State, who couldn't help noticing that the more vicious the scorn, the more J. J. Redick scored.

"All it does is motivate him and cause him to be even more focused, and that's a dangerous thing to deal with," Hamilton said.

The preoccupation with making Redick's life miserable took on a 21st-century twist when fans from other schools made it their ambition to call his cell-phone number deep into the night. Redick had to change numbers almost as often as he changed socks, to the point that for a while even his brother didn't have it.

But to Redick's credit, he tried as hard as humanly possible not to take it personally. He disagreed with those who speculated that his race might have somehow mobilized the moronic masses. Instead, he chalked it up as the price to be paid for playing where he did.

"I think if I played for another school, and still played the way I play, I wouldn't get it as bad," Redick told the *Washington Post*. "I get it from fans because it says Duke on my jersey. I'm not really sure why it's white guys.

"I know people didn't really like Chris Duhon and Dahntay Jones. They got it bad on the road, and they're not white."

Nobody hates a scrub. The real reason the vitriol was so pervasive and raw was that Redick was so damn good. And he was not just damn good but historically great his final two years at Duke, after working through some personal issues of the sort many young people face when on their own for the first time.

Redick took the loss to Connecticut in the national semifinal his sophomore season hard—so hard he gave up fast food, returned to the healthy diet espoused by his vegetarian parents, lost 15 pounds, and turned what was left into rock-hard muscle.

He got right with himself and his family, fell in love, read *The Purpose Driven Life*, and kept pouring in three-pointers until he buried more (457) than had ever been scored by any player in college basketball history. He left Duke as the conference's all-time leading scorer, though his record of 2,769 points was broken just three years later by Tyler Hansbrough. Redick is also the greatest free-throw shooter in conference history, hitting 91.2 percent of his attempts.

"I regained my passion for basketball," Redick told *Sports Illustrated*. "My relationships with my family members were as good as they've ever been—and my first two years, those were sometimes rocky.

"I met my girlfriend during that year and regained my spirituality."

He also feathered his nest for a productive NBA career. Plucked by Orlando with the 11th overall pick of the 2006 draft, Redick has been nailing three-pointers for the Magic and Milwaukee Bucks ever since.

JULIUS HODGE

6-6 Guard | N.C. State | 2001–5 | No. 24

2002	Second-team All-Tournament	50
2003	First-team All-ACC, second-most votes	375
	First-team All-Tournament	75
2004	First-team All-ACC, second-most votes	375
	Second-team All-Tournament	50
	ACC POY, contested	175
	Second-team All-American	150
2005	Second-team All-ACC, seventh-most votes	250
	Second-team All-Tournament	50
Awards Points		**1,550**

To hear him tell it, he was "Da Jules of Harlem on His Way 2 Stardom."

To everybody he came into contact with during his four years at N.C. State, he was quite a piece of work.

High-strung, funny, and forever full of himself, Julius Hodge got away with what others could not because his coaches and teammates saw that, in the end, he was more than willing to do what it took to be great.

He was that way from an early age, learning the value of a strong work ethic from his mother, Mary.

Hodge decided as a five-year-old that he was going to be a basketball star, the day his dad took him to Madison Square Garden to see the Knicks play the Lakers. As family lore has it, Magic Johnson of the visitors gave young Hodge one of his big, famous smiles.

Julius Hodge
N.C. State Athletics

His father split soon afterward, leaving the fate of the family in the hands of Mary Hodge, who worked multiple jobs to feed her three children. Hodge's strongest male role model was big brother Steve Hodge, who played basketball at Sullivan Community College in Manhattan and later at Division II Long Island University–South Hampton. It was Steve Hodge who named his younger brother Julius, after NBA great Julius Erving.

Hodge grew up across the Harlem River from Yankee Stadium but got the break of his young life when he received a scholarship to St. Raymond High School. He'd caught the right eyes when he twice attended basketball camp at the private school in the Bronx.

There was one hitch. To get to school an hour early, and thus be on hand to talk a janitor or teacher into letting him into the gym to shoot, he had to rise between 5:00 and 5:30 in the morning, catch the train to the Bronx, and walk seven blocks to St. Raymond.

Driven to succeed, Hodge hung around after practice to work on his game until he was finally driven out of the gym at nine or 10 o'clock. Coaches told of watching him walk across the street to clear the courts at Jackie Robinson Park of leaves or snow so he could shoot baskets another hour or two.

A college recruiter once showed up late for an appointment, after Hodge had already left the school. Oliver Antiqua, an assistant coach at St. Raymond, directed him across the street, where he found Hodge shooting baskets in the rain.

National powers from across the college basketball landscape beat a path to the Bronx while Hodge was leading St. Raymond to Federation A city and state championships and receiving such accolades as first-team *Parade* All-American, New York's Mr. Basketball, and *New York Daily News* Player of the Year.

Coach Herb Sendek of N.C. State pulled off quite a coup by signing Hodge, who on his recruiting trip was enchanted by Raleigh and the slow pace down south. It didn't hurt N.C. State's prospects that his mother had grown up down the road in Wilson, and that Hodge, by the time he was ready for college, saw the perils of remaining near home.

"It's easy to get distracted where I am from," Hodge told Tim Peeler in *Legends of N.C. State Basketball*. "People think there are three ways you can get out of there: play sports, go to school or sell drugs."

Hodge immediately outworked everyone on the N.C. State roster, honing his game for up to six hours a day during the summer. Then, once the season started, he became known for climbing off the bus after road trips and hitting the gym to shoot 1,500 jumpers.

During his time at N.C. State, Hodge was one of those stars who said what he had to say, regardless of where the chips fell. The Wolfpack faithful adored him; the opposition hated his guts. They indeed found something to hate when Hodge, as a freshman, hit Steve Blake of Maryland in the back of the head and was suspended by the ACC for a game. He was on the receiving end of an equally infamous blow three years later, when Chris Paul of Wake Forest popped him in the private parts during the regular-season finale in Raleigh— an act that earned Paul a first-game suspension during the ACC Tournament.

Hodge always claimed to feed off the energy of the crowd, which he wasn't adverse to provoking. His comment on playing at Duke in front of the notorious Cameron Crazies was classic Da Jules of Harlem on His Way 2 Stardom: "I am not going to let a kid with a 4.5 GPA, acne, and bad breath determine how I play."

His prediction of NBA stardom never came true. He was selected in the first round of the 2005 draft by Denver as the 20th overall pick but played only 23 NBA games with the Nuggets and Milwaukee Bucks.

In April during his rookie season with the Nuggets, Hodge left a night-club and was driving on Highway 76 in North Denver at two in the morning when a car pulled alongside and the passengers inside opened fire. Hit three times in the leg, Hodge was later told he came within five minutes of bleeding to death.

The case has never been solved.

Hodge knocked around Italy, Australia, and Vietnam before returning to Raleigh to open a skills camp for developing players.

JOSH HOWARD

6-6 Forward | Wake Forest | 1999–2003 | No. 5

2001	Second-team All-ACC, ninth-most votes	200
2002	Third-team All-ACC, 11th-most votes	150
2003	First-team All-ACC, unanimous	425
	Second-team All-Tournament	50
	ACC POY, unanimous	250
	First-team All-American (with David West of Xavier, T. J. Ford of Texas, Nick Collison of Kansas, and Dwyane Wade of Marquette)	200
Awards Points		**1,275**

A proud, complex, easily offended firebrand who could infuriate even his most ardent admirers, Josh Howard tangled with opponents, officials, administrators, tutors, teammates, and coaches from the time he showed up at Wake Forest until he left.

His mother, Nancy Henderson, understood him when others tried but failed.

"He's the kind of child who you cannot just constantly push him," she said. "He has to gradually let it come on his own. If you constantly nag him, he will rebel. You can tell him, and you think he's not listening. But he's listening."

His iron will may have been forged in his first painful and frustrating months of life. Howard was born with legs so curved they had to be broken,

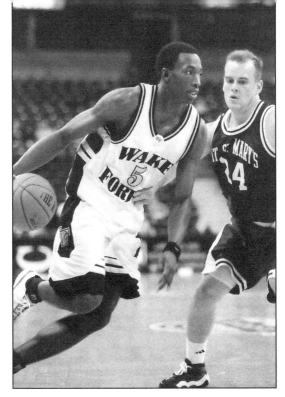

Josh Howard

straightened, and put in casts. His grandmother Helen Hunt, who along with Henderson and other family members raised Howard, remembers having to take baby Josh back time and again to have the casts reset.

To say he was bowlegged would be an understatement.

"That was worse than bow. I don't know what you call that," Hunt said. "That was the summer it was very, very hot. We had to carry him back, and they would take the casts off and look at his legs and do something, and put them right back on. It took two or three months. It was so hot."

He didn't know his father, at least not until he was 11, when Kevin Robinson gave Henderson a call.

"My mom put me on the phone, and the person said, 'This is your dad,' " Howard recalled. "I was like, 'Okay.' I didn't have a clue about him. I was always just around my mom and my grandmother."

Howard came to learn that Robinson was something of a hard-court legend around Winston-Salem.

"I got a chance to meet him," Howard said. "I finally started getting the story on him and why he left. But I've kind of distanced myself away from him. I'll speak to him whenever he comes around or whenever I see him, but other than that I don't call him."

Though largely overlooked by major colleges during his career at Glenn High School in Winston-Salem, Howard signed with Wake Forest after a season at Hargrave Military Academy to improve his academic standing. He made enough of an immediate impact at Wake to average 9.2 points and 4.7 rebounds as a freshman, by which time he was already calling out his older teammates for their lack of drive and effort.

Howard was never easy, as anyone who dealt with him could attest. He locked horns with academic adviser Jane Caldwell until both had enough. He stormed out of a session, vowing to leave Wake Forest, only to be calmed down and talked into returning by a graduate student named Ericka Harrison. Meanwhile, on the court, he was gaining a well-deserved reputation for unacceptable behavior.

Herman Eure, a black professor who chaired the Wake Forest biology department, was chagrined to see Howard draw another technical by lashing out at an opponent during a game at Joel Coliseum.

"It incensed the hell out of me," Eure said. "I went the next week to find him. I ran into him, and I told him who I was. I said, 'Now, you don't know me from Adam, and you can tell me to go to hell once I leave, and everything's fine. But the behavior you exhibited the other night was embarrassing to me as a black man. You do not have to respond that way.' He stood there, and he listened, and he acknowledged it.

"After that point, he and I talked a great deal, and I invited him to my house. He's a good young man. I could tell that."

Howard reached loggerheads with Coach Dave Odom long before the 79–63 meltdown against Butler in the first-round of the 2001 NCAA Tournament, infamous for the Deacons' 43–10 halftime deficit.

Odom left a month later for South Carolina. One of the first orders of business for new coach Skip Prosser was to connect with his best player. Prosser jumped in a car with Howard one day and asked for a tour of Howard's hometown.

"He showed me where he grew up, and where he went to school, and things like that," Prosser said. "I could tell in that car ride that this was a young man with intense pride—proud of where he was from and what he had been able to accomplish to that point."

It took awhile, but Prosser finally got through to Howard by his senior season, which Prosser spent lavishing praise on his star. Putting together a season that was indeed praiseworthy, Howard hoisted on his back freshmen Justin Gray and Eric Williams and sophomores Taron Downey, Vytas Danelius, and Jamaal Levy and carried them to a first-place regular-season finish at 13–3.

Those voting for postseason honors were dutifully impressed, bestowing on Howard the honor of being just the second player (after David Thompson) to be named unanimous ACC Player of the Year. (Tyler Hansbrough would become the third five seasons later.)

"Courage is contagious," Prosser proclaimed. "And it's like that old adage, you'd rather face an army of lions led by a lamb than an army of lambs led by a lion.

"He's a lion for us. And in times where maybe our guys—in their relative youth—were reduced to sheepishness, he's been Richard the Lionhearted. And I think that's one of the reasons we've done as well as we've done."

Affected strongly by the events of 9/11, Howard changed his major from sociology to religion and grew close to Charles Kimball, the highly regarded chairman of Wake Forest's religion department.

As the Wake Forest beat reporter for the *Winston-Salem Journal*, I somehow managed to get along well with Howard. The attribute I most appreciated was his honesty.

"Joshua will tell you the truth if it hurts," his grandmother Helen Hunt said.

Howard's professional career proved as turbulent as his days at Wake Forest. He enjoyed the success of the Dallas Mavericks' rise to NBA prominence, but not the attention that comes to those unafraid to speak their mind. He was lambasted after admitting in an interview that he smoked marijuana, and again after being caught on a YouTube video saying that, because he was black, he didn't stand for the national anthem.

The last time I saw Howard, he didn't have much to say. I'm media, and he was obviously done with my kind.

But I'll never be done with the kind of player who can do what Josh Howard did for Wake Forest his senior season.

JASON WILLIAMS

6-2 Guard | Duke | 1999–2002 | No. 22

Jason Williams became the ACC's most recognizable "player to be named later" after he was picked by the Chicago Bulls in the 2002 NBA draft and began calling himself Jay.

2000	Third-team All-ACC, 11th-most votes	150
2001	First-team All-ACC, unanimous	425
	First-team All-Tournament	75
	First-team All-American (with Shane Battier of Duke, Casey Jacobsen of Stanford, Joseph Forte of North Carolina, and Troy Murphy of Notre Dame)	200
2002	First-team All-ACC, unanimous	425
	First-team All-Tournament	75
	ACC POY, close runner-up	125
	National POY (with fellow first-team All-Americans Dan Dickau of Gonzaga, Drew Gooden of Kansas, Juan Dixon of Maryland, and Steve Logan of Cincinnati)	250
Awards Points		**1,725**

But he will always be remembered in College Park as "the Miracle Minute Man." Maryland fans still stew over his eight points in the final 54 seconds of regulation to help overcome the Terps' 10-point lead on January 27, 2001, during Williams's sophomore season.

Williams had already committed 10 turnovers, and Duke was out of time-outs, when he scored a layup that cut the deficit to eight. He then stole the ball from Drew Nicholas and drained a three-pointer from the corner before finishing with a three-pointer from the top of the key.

Given a reprieve, Duke rallied for a 98–96 overtime victory on the way to a 35–4 record and its third national championship.

"The great ones, even when they're playing badly, can still find a way to win games for their team," Coach Gary Williams of Maryland said. "Most guards are looking to get the ball inside to their big guys. But he looks to get the ball to the rim. He can dunk over six-seven guys, and he can step back and make the three."

Exceptionally well rounded, Williams was captain of his high-school chess team in Plainfield, New Jersey, an altar boy at church, and the winner of a poetry contest. But he wasn't the nation's most highly sought recruit as a junior and in fact was not invited to the ABCD Camp, held at Fairleigh Dickinson University, near his hometown.

So he paid his own way to the Nike Camp in Indianapolis.

"I asked myself, 'What can I do to get noticed?' " Williams told Don Markus of the *Baltimore Sun*. "Everybody there could score, so I went there with the idea of trying to pass. I averaged something like 17 assists for the nine

Jason Williams

or 10 games I played. That kind of put me on the map."

Williams told ACC historian Al Featherston he had his heart set on playing at North Carolina, but that Coach Bill Guthridge—not sure Williams was big enough to play the wing or adept enough with the ball for the point—was not forthcoming with a scholarship offer. So he told Coach Kevin Bannon of Rutgers to save him a jersey, after confiding in friends that he was staying close to home to help restore the Scarlet Knights to relevance. But then his mother, Althea, convinced him to make an unofficial visit to Duke.

Four years later, he returned to Cameron Indoor Stadium during his rookie season with the Bulls to see his jersey retired.

Williams explained his change of plans to John Roth and Ned Hinshaw in *The Encyclopedia of Duke Basketball*: "When I first walked into that gym, the first thing that I did when I came here on my unofficial visit, I looked up at the rafters. I saw Johnny Dawkins. I saw Dick Groat. I saw Christian Laettner, Grant Hill, all these great names. And I just sat there and stared at them. The light was kind of gleaming on them in a different way and I was like, 'This is what this is about.'

"I saw pictures of Coach [Mike Krzyzewski] and his guys hugging and then winning national championships and going through the hard times, growing up together, and I was like, 'I want to be part of that. I want to be part of something bigger than myself.' And that's what it is. It's not just me getting my jersey retired. I'm becoming part of something that is bigger than myself, becoming part of a family."

Williams started all 108 games he played at Duke and set the school's single-season record with 841 points, breaking the mark of 831 Groat had held since 1951. During his three seasons, the Blue Devils went 41–7 against ACC teams, 9–0 in the ACC Tournament, and 10–2 in the NCAA Tournament.

Not everything came easily. Williams's freshman season ended in ugly fashion. He made only six of 20 field-goal attempts and missed eight of nine three-pointers in an 87–78 loss to Florida in the NCAA regional semifinal. A week later, while watching Michigan State beat the Gators for the national title, he wrote in his journal that playing for it all was where he wanted to be.

So he lost 10 pounds, rededicated himself to greatness, and came back stronger and quicker.

"I would worry about stuff last year," Williams told Markus of the *Sun*. "I didn't let on, but there were times I didn't play the way I was capable of playing because of it. This year I'm much more mentally stronger than I was last year. I've improved dramatically not only on the court but off the court."

A quirk of age is that what happened 30 years ago may come to mind quicker than what happened just a dozen or so years ago. I confess I had forgotten until reading accounts of the Blue Devils' 2001 title run that Carlos Boozer injured his foot on Senior Day, prompting Krzyzewski to move Williams off the ball and insert freshman Chris Duhon into the lineup as point guard.

If his mother had prevailed, Duhon wouldn't have even been at Duke. Valerie Harper was concerned that her son would spend his first three seasons riding the bench behind Williams. It was Williams himself who convinced Duhon there was room for both not just to play but to flourish. And flourish they did, winning six straight NCAA Tournament games by at least 10 points.

Williams scored 31 in the second round against Missouri and 34 in the regional semifinal against UCLA. He averaged 25.7 points and 5.2 assists in the tournament while shooting 46 percent from the floor. And it's easy to see why Krzyzewski couldn't bring himself to take Duhon out of the lineup, even after Boozer returned. In 203 minutes of tournament play, Duhon committed only 10 turnovers.

In a testament to how tough the ACC was his junior season, Williams was named National Player of the Year despite finishing runner-up to Maryland's Juan Dixon for the conference honor. Dixon, whose Terps won the 2002 national championship, received 41 votes for the ACC honor to Williams's 38. Williams had teammate Mike Dunleavy—named POY on four ballots—partly to blame for splitting the vote.

Williams was quick and could really fill up the basket when he found his range. He was also incredibly powerful off the dribble. All in all, he had a skill set well suited for the NBA. Sadly, before he could establish himself in the league, he crashed his motorcycle and landed in the hospital, never to play another NBA game. The damage—a severed main nerve, a fractured pelvis, and three torn knee ligaments—was too much to overcome.

Always loquacious, he found his niche as a basketball analyst for CBS Sports and ESPN.

JOSEPH FORTE

6-4 Guard | North Carolina | 1999–2001 | No. 40

2000	ACC ROY	100
	Second-team All-ACC, 10th-most votes	175
2001	First-team All-ACC, unanimous	425
	ACC POY, heavily contested	150
	First-team All-Tournament	75
	First-team All-American (with Shane Battier and Jason Williams of Duke, Casey Jacobsen of Stanford, and Troy Murphy of Notre Dame)	200
Awards Points		**1,125**

North Carolina has always promoted the family atmosphere of its basketball program, often for good reason. It's compelling to see how many former players return to Chapel Hill and not only remain involved in the program but maintain an almost fanatical loyalty to Dean Smith and, somewhat by extension, Bill Guthridge and Roy Williams.

But not all families are the Brady Bunch, and not all heads of families command the respect given to Smith.

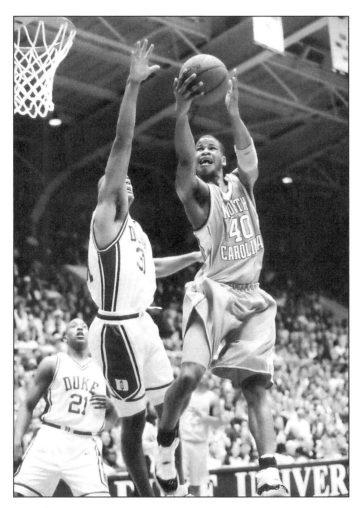

Joseph Forte

Joe Forte happened along during a dysfunctional period of the North Carolina program and as a consequence endured the indignity of having a ball bounced off his forehead by first-year coach Matt Doherty. According to various reports, the Tar Heels were practicing, and that was Doherty's way of making a point.

Forte didn't go to North Carolina to play for Doherty. He picked the Tar Heels so he could play for Guthridge, who in many ways reminded him of his high-school coach, Morgan Wootten of DeMatha.

"My whole life, I had people looking out for me," Forte told Eli Saslow of the *Washington Post.* "At DeMatha I had Coach Wootten, and at North Carolina I had Coach Guthridge.

"Those guys took me under their watch, man. They made sure I did everything right."

Forte was so heralded as an eighth-grader in Atlanta that Campbell High—where he was expected to spend his freshman year—received 95 applications for its vacant position of head basketball coach.

But Wanda Hightower, Forte's mother, didn't want her son to get above his raising. Hightower, who had been abandoned by Forte's father, packed the family off to Rockville, Maryland, where she worked three jobs while Forte played for the venerable Wootten. The move paid off, as Forte blossomed into one of the most coveted recruits in the nation.

"Morgan made Joseph what he is today," Hightower said during Forte's career at North Carolina.

"I love him," Forte said. "He taught me that life is won inch by inch."

Soft-spoken and at times too sensitive for his own good, Forte flourished as a freshman under Guthridge, who took pains to deflect the heavy mantle of leadership to more experienced players on the team, such as Ed Cota and Brendan Haywood. Nor did it hurt Forte's development that Phil Ford, an assistant on Guthridge's staff, was on hand to help guide him through the travails of early college stardom.

"Forte is an unbelievable player," Coach Pete Gillen of Virginia said. "He's one of the best two-guards I've seen in a long time."

Upon succeeding Guthridge, Doherty alienated many in the Carolina family by not retaining Ford. But he did make a celebrated outreach to his star when, three days into his tenure as the Tar Heels' head coach, he trekked to Rockville to assuage Forte of any doubts he might have about the coaching change.

The era of good feelings was short-lived. By the time the Tar Heels played an exhibition game leading into the 2000–2001 season, Doherty jumped Forte's case for making a sloppy pass.

"He told me to save it for the NBA," Forte revealed. "He told me if I did it again, I'd burn on the bench."

Instead of buying in, Forte tuned his coach out. When Doherty decreed midway through the season there would be no more scrimmages during practice, Forte skipped practice that day and played pickup games in the university rec center wearing his UNC shorts.

Suffice it to say "Kumbaya" wasn't the theme song of the final frustrating weeks of Forte's college career.

Now the focus of every opponent's game plan, Forte found it more and more difficult to get his shots. He also found it increasingly difficult inside the locker room, where teammates, most consistently Jason Capel, were known to grouse about him and his shot selection.

More bad energy helped short-circuit Forte's final days in Chapel Hill when the Raleigh *News & Observer* launched an investigation into the circumstances surrounding Wanda Hightower's employment as an accountant with the sports agency Octagon—which ultimately represented Forte in his NBA negotiations. The story raised the question of whether or not officials at North Carolina had helped her land the position.

The school's athletics department conducted an investigation and proclaimed itself satisfied that no NCAA rules were broken and that North Carolina had been "abundantly cautious" in making sure the hiring was according to Hoyle—not Doherty, Guthridge, or Smith. But it does bear noting that in June, just days before the draft, Hightower was terminated from the position. Though no reason was disclosed, it was reported she was in legal difficulty stemming mostly from her failure to return rental cars on time.

The aggressiveness of the paper 30 miles to the east didn't sit well in Chapel Hill, as Art Chansky chronicled in *Blue Blood*. The Tar Heel coaches, as hypersensitive as they were hypercompetitive, bellyached among themselves how the *News & Observer* failed to look into what was going on at Duke, where the parents of stars Carlos Boozer and Chris Duhon had secured employment in the Durham area working for friends of Mike Krzyzewski and the Duke program.

Despite all the rancor surrounding Forte's final days at North Carolina, Smith still took it upon himself to call friends in professional basketball to inquire about Forte's prospects. Hearing what he did, Smith advised Forte to return for his junior year.

But Forte had apparently endured enough. He made himself available for the draft, then slipped all the way to the 21st pick before being selected by the Boston Celtics.

The day he signed his three-year deal for $3.2 million was probably the best of his professional career. He had few good ones to choose from. Over two tumultuous NBA seasons, during which he played in 25 total games and scored 1.2 points per contest, Forte sat the bench in Boston before getting traded to Seattle—where he enraged his teammates first by wearing a Michael Jordan T-shirt into the locker room and then by singing in the shower after a loss in such a carefree fashion that he was attacked by seven-one center Jerome James. Forte had to know what the organization thought of him when he was suspended for a game and fined $11,000, whereas James, the instigator, went unpunished. Nor did his standing with Seattle improve when he was pulled over doing 95 in a 65-miles-per-hour zone. With him in his car were a .22 pistol and an illegal green, leafy substance.

By 2005, he was riding a bus and playing for the Asheville Altitude of the NBA Development League for $15,000 a season. Eli Saslow tracked him down and wrote for the *Washington Post* a long and painful but utterly cautionary tale of the precipitous fall of a young man who, a scant four years earlier, had been considered one of the best five players in college basketball.

"It's a little embarrassing to be here," Forte told Saslow. "I mean, All-Americans aren't supposed to end up in this league.

"I vowed so many times that I wouldn't play here. It's funny, man, because I really promised that to myself. I thought it was under me. But the truth is, this is the only way to get everything back. I want to redeem myself. I want back in the NBA. This is the place where that all has to start."

It's impossible to project where Forte's path would have led if Bill Guthridge hadn't retired after the 1999–2000 season, to be succeeded by Doherty.

Doherty moved on to head-coaching jobs at Florida Atlantic and SMU—where, as fate would have it, he was replaced after six forgettable seasons by another North Carolina alum, Larry Brown.

Back in 2003, three weeks after he was fired at North Carolina, Doherty acknowledged making mistakes.

"If I had it to do over, I'd slow the process of change," he said.

The lesson learned didn't come fast enough for Forte.

"He demeans people," Forte told Leonard Laye of the *Charlotte Observer*. "He belittles them in front of teammates, classmates, and people watching practice. He tried to embarrass me as a person.

"It's the demeaning people that's the problem. He's not a bad person. He needs to learn how to talk to people."

There must be, after all, a way to make a point without bouncing a basketball off someone's head.

JUAN DIXON

6-3 Guard | Maryland | 1998–2002 | No. 3

Juan Dixon was the little kid dribbling down the street looking to be somebody nobody gave him much of a chance of being.

During his younger days, Dixon most often dribbled to Cecil-Kirk Recreation Center, a cinder-block structure near East 25th Street in Baltimore,

Juan Dixon
COURTESY OF
ROBERT CRAWFORD

2000	First-team All-ACC, third-most votes	350
	First-team All-Tournament	75
2001	First-team All-ACC, fourth-most votes	325
	First-team All-Tournament	75
2002	First-team All-ACC, unanimous	425
	ACC POY, heavily contested	150
	Final Four MVP	150
	First-team All-American (with Dan Dickau of Gonzaga, Drew Gooden of Kansas, Steve Logan of Cincinnati, and Jason Williams of Duke)	200
Awards Points		**1,750**

where he came of age under the stern but loving guidance of director Anthony Lewis.

"He started coming here when he was about in the fifth grade and he never stopped," Lewis told Todd Richissen of the *Baltimore Sun* in 2001. "What we do here is try to strengthen their values and get them to think about their morals and hope they become productive citizens. Juan took to it."

Other city rec centers were closer to Dixon's home in northeast Baltimore, but Lewis and the high-caliber brand of basketball at Cecil-Kirk prompted Dixon to go the extra mile—or, in this case, extra miles.

Much was later made during Dixon's Maryland career of the fate that befell his parents, Juanita and Phil. Both were drug addicts who died of AIDS just months apart when Juan was a sophomore at Calvert Hall College High School.

But as Dixon was always quick to point out, he didn't lack for love. He was raised from age four by his maternal grandparents, Roberta and Warnick Graves. Roberta cleaned houses, and Warnick worked on a sanitation crew. Others taking a special interest in young Juan were his paternal grandmother, Winona Dixon, an older cousin named Sherrice Driver, and Aunts Victoria Rose, Janice Dixon, and Sheila Dixon.

"Everybody wants to talk about his mother, how my daughter died of AIDS," Roberta Graves told the *Sun*. "They need to know Juan always had a place to stay and people to watch him and love him."

Nobody played a bigger role in the Juan Dixon story than his brother Phil, a terror on the court himself during his days at Baltimore's St. Frances High School who, partly because he was only five-nine and partly because he didn't play in the highly regarded summer leagues, wasn't recruited by major colleges. He ended up at Shenandoah College in Winchester, Virginia, where he became a first-team Division III All-American and set the school record with 2,297 points.

Phil Dixon became a police officer in Baltimore.

After wearing number 5 as a freshman, Juan Dixon switched to number 3 as a sophomore. That was Phil Dixon's number at Shenandoah.

"He would bust my butt," Juan told Duff Durkin of theACC.com. "He made me cry, he beat me up. He is one reason why I'm tougher mentally, I got that from him, being strong."

The tattoo on Dixon's left arm says, "Only the Strong Survive."

"He plays with his heart," teammate Lonny Baxter said.

It was that heart that sold Gary Williams of Maryland, who watched Dixon giving all he had with his AAU team down by 25 in a scalding gym in Georgia in the middle of summer. Williams out-recruited Providence, Clemson, and Virginia to keep Dixon near home.

"The only doubt I had about Juan was the same everyone else had," Williams told Gary Lambrecht of the *Baltimore Sun*. "He certainly was quick enough to play and score in the ACC, but would he be strong enough?"

He proved strong enough, both of body and will, to torment Duke two years in a row in Cameron Indoor Stadium. As a sophomore, he drained 14 of

19 field-goal attempts for 31 points to lift Maryland to a 98–87 victory. As a junior, he went off for 11 field goals on 20 attempts to score 28 in a 91–80 win.

Tired, perhaps, of hearing Maryland fans rename their home arena Dixon Indoor Stadium, the Blue Devils exacted their revenge in 2002 by holding him to two field goals on nine attempts for 10 hard-earned points. Having neutralized its nemesis, Duke rolled 99–78.

Patrick Stevens, the longtime Maryland beat reporter for the *Washington Times*, proclaimed Dixon to be the best player of the Gary Williams era—better even than the more dominant Joe Smith. Who am I to argue with Stevens, a good buddy who knows a far cry more about Maryland basketball than I?

Stevens based his opinion (which I'm happy to say corresponds to my own rankings for this book) on what Dixon did when it mattered most—during the Terps' remarkable run to the school's first national title, during Dixon's senior season.

Frustrated by Maryland's 86–82 loss to N.C. State in the semifinals of the 2002 ACC Tournament, played in Charlotte, Dixon told Stevens it was time he took charge.

"In a situation like this, I have to be more of a leader and let guys know we need to be ready to play," Dixon said. "We need to grow up some. I'm definitely going to have some words to say."

The best leaders lead by example, and Dixon did just that by going on a scoring spree that carried him past Len Bias to become Maryland's all-time leader in career points. He scored 155 of those 2,269 points in the six games of the NCAA Tournament.

His 33 points carried the Terps past Kansas 97–88 in the semifinals, putting them in a Monday-night championship showdown against Indiana. And in the climactic game of his career—and for the Maryland basketball program as a whole—Dixon made six of nine shots from the field, scored 18 points, pulled down five rebounds, and dished out three assists in the 64–52 victory for the national championship. He was named Most Valuable Player of the Final Four.

"I grew up a lot in college," Dixon told Paul McMullen of the *Baltimore Sun*. "I grew so much. A lot of people back home counted me out. I went there and got better each year, led my team to the national championship. It's a great feeling, man. I'm speechless. I really don't know what to say.

"I'm going to talk forever."

Drafted 17th overall in the first round by Washington, Dixon played seven NBA seasons for the Wizards, Portland Trailblazers, Toronto Raptors, and Detroit Pistons.

SHANE BATTIER

6-8 Forward │ Duke │ 1997–2001 │ No. 31

1999	Third-team All-ACC, 11th-most votes	150
	Second-team All-Tournament	50
2000	First-team All-ACC, second-most votes	375
	First-team All-Tournament	75
	Second-team All-American	150
2001	First-team All-ACC, unanimous	425
	ACC POY, heavily contested	150
	Everett Case Award	100
	Final Four MVP	150
	National POY (with fellow first-team All-Americans	250
	Casey Jacobsen of Stanford, Jason Williams of Duke,	
	Joseph Forte of North Carolina, and Troy Murphy of	
	Notre Dame)	
Awards Points		**1,875**

I've never come across an ACC player remotely comparable to Shane Battier in my 40 years of covering the league. Bobby Jones of North Carolina did many of the same things, but Jones was never in the running for Player of the Year in the ACC, much less the nation.

Unless you dislike Duke on general principles, or perhaps harbor an aversion to players who, in the course of drawing a charge, flop to the floor upon minimal contact, it was hard not to like Shane Battier.

For me, it was impossible.

Battier did all the things needed to win games. And the bigger the game, the more he could be counted on to do them. He was a peerless passer for a big man, he had a smooth, sure handle, he blocked shots, and he could shut down the other team's best scorer—as national writers recognized by naming him the National Defensive Player of the Year in three of his four seasons.

His scoring was almost an afterthought. Battier seldom stepped outside the team's offense to seek his points.

Shane Battier
DUKE SPORTS INFORMATION

"Shane is the most complete player I've ever coached," Mike Krzyzewski said. "He may not be the most talented we've ever had here at Duke, but he's the most complete. You hear so many good things about Shane, and you think nobody could be like that. But he is. He's the real deal."

And after doing all the marvelous things he did, Battier would stand in front of his locker, look you in the eye, and offer wonderful insights on what just transpired and why. He took a vow at Duke never to use one cliché all season.

If he did, I didn't hear it.

"One of Shane's great joys in life is shattering stereotypes," former Duke player and assistant coach Quin Snyder told Tim Crothers of *Sports Illustrated*. "He loves to answer the tough questions, and you can almost hear him snickering to himself when he shocks some unsuspecting reporter."

Two exhaustive pieces—one called "The No-Stats All-Star" that Michael Lewis wrote for the *New York Times* and the other Crothers's "Players' Player" for *SI*—tell a great deal about what makes Shane Battier tick.

He grew up in Birmingham, Michigan, the son of a black father who managed a small trucking company and a white mother who was a corporate secretary. The day a three-year-old Shane asked his mother if she thought he would make a good president, Ed and Sandee got a hint of what they were in for.

By age 12, Battier played the trumpet so well he was first chair in Birmingham's annual youth concert orchestra. It was a big youth orchestra, needing 106 chairs for the trumpets alone.

He wanted to attend Detroit Country Day in the seventh grade and was accepted with a near-perfect entrance-exam score. What school wouldn't want a student who, a couple years later, would begin spending his New Year's Eves listing on index cards the 10 goals he wanted to accomplish over the next year?

Some ACC players have had to be slipped past the admissions board, but Battier wasn't one. That became apparent during his interview at Duke, when Battier famously answered questions from admissions director Christoph Guttentag in German.

Dan Wetzel of *Basketball Times* spent five months hanging out in Birmingham during Battier's recruitment and was amazed by his maturity and intellect. Wetzel chronicled how Battier took ownership of the recruiting process, first narrowing the field to Kentucky, Kansas, North Carolina, Duke, Michigan, and Michigan State, then establishing a weekly 15-minute time period for a coach from each school to call. Rick Pitino broke the agreement by attempting to give Battier a ring outside his allotted time—and just like that, Battier's list was down to five. Kentucky had been crossed off.

Battier has never shied from discussing his biracial background and how it shaped him not only as a person but as a basketball player. As the only nonwhite student in his class at Detroit Country Day, he was handed a pick on Picture Day. All his classmates were given combs.

He followed Chris Webber, the national high-school player of the year, at Detroit Country Day. But Battier's game was, shall I say, a bit more intellectual than that of the flashy phenom.

"I remember trying to add some flair to his game," high-school coach Kurt Keener told Michael Lewis. "But it was like teaching a classical dancer to do hip-hop. I came to the conclusion he didn't have the ego for it."

But as Battier proudly recounted, his more refined dance steps took him just as far.

"Chris Webber won three straight state championships, the Mr. Basketball Award and the Naismith Award," Battier told Lewis. "I won three state championships, Mr. Basketball and the Naismith Award."

What Battier didn't mention was that his teams won three ACC championships to go with a national title, and Webber's Michigan team never cut down the nets in the Big Ten or the NCAA Tournament.

And to update the comparison, Webber played 15 seasons in the NBA. Through 2011–12, Battier had played only 11.

But it was during his 11th season that Battier played his 832nd NBA game. Webber retired in 2008, having played 831.

Given his ultimate aspiration, Battier might as well play in the NBA until the 2016 election season. He was born September 9, 1978, and according to the laws of our country, a citizen can't be president until he's 35 anyway.

CHRIS CARRAWELL

6-6 Forward | Duke | 1996–2000 | No. 23

1998	Second-team All-Tournament	50
1999	Third-team All-ACC, 11th-most votes	150
2000	First-team All-ACC, unanimous	425
	First-team All-Tournament	75
	ACC POY	200
	First-team All-American (with Marcus Fizer of Iowa State, A. J. Guyton of Indiana, Kenyon Martin of Cincinnati, Chris Mihm of Texas, and Troy Murphy of Notre Dame)	200
Awards Points		1,100

Good things, I've been told, happen to good people. Chris Carrawell didn't hurt his cause by being one of the best guys ever to play ACC basketball.

The interview Carrawell gave to dukebasketballreport.com after his college playing days were over should be required reading for any freshman. It's my experience that when a player or coach shows the media regard, the sentiment is returned tenfold.

"The media is the media," Carrawell explained. "They have a job to do. When I was in school, when somebody wanted to talk to me I was like, shit, let's do it. Just naturally, I'll talk to anybody. Then I had some people who really want to talk and listen to what I have to say and I'll be honest, I thought it was cool. I enjoyed it.

Chris Carrawell
DUKE SPORTS INFORMATION

"I didn't worry whether or not I was going to say something that was going to get taken out of context. I just spoke from the heart. Of course I watched what I said, but at the same time, if I said something that was on my mind, something I believed, I would say it, and I really didn't worry about what was going to happen."

But to suggest Carrawell made ACC Player of the Year in 2000 because I and others of my profession liked dropping by his locker for postgame chats would be selling his accomplishments as a player woefully short. He was the mainspring on a vintage Blue Devils team that finished first in the regular-season race by a whopping four games and rolled unimpeded through the ACC Tournament to a second-straight title.

If nothing else, he was special for his versatility, which allowed him to defend almost any opponent. Coach Mike Krzyzewski, having seen enough of 6-10 Duke senior Greg Newton, even lined the freshman Carrawell up against

Tim Duncan. Although Duncan was his usual dominant self on the way to 26 points and nine rebounds, Carrawell and the Blue Devils made off with a 73–68 victory over the second-ranked Deacons.

To appreciate how far Carrawell had come by then, one had to know where he'd been. Jalen Rose of Michigan could not have been talking of Carrawell when he made his infamous charge, "I hated Duke. They only recruited black players who were Uncle Toms."

Raised in inner-city North St. Louis, Carrawell honed his game on mean asphalt courts with chain nets. He later told Tim Crothers of *Sports Illustrated* that seven of the 10 players he competed against in those days were either dead or in jail.

"The image of Duke guys is of white picket fences, not barbed-wire fences, but I can bring a piece of the playground here, getting guys thinking that when a guy busts you, you've got to bust him back," he told Crothers.

He played with Jahidi White (Georgetown) and Loren Woods (Wake Forest, Arizona) at Cardinal Ritter High School—and rooted, ironically enough, for Michigan, along with Syracuse, Nevada–Las Vegas, and North Carolina. He attracted Krzyzewski's eye at Five-Star Camp before his junior season and was offered a scholarship.

"Coach K gets you in the back room and sits you down, it's kind of hard to tell that guy 'No,' " Carrawell explained to dukebasketballreport.com. "And I didn't. That's why I came."

As a recruit, he was ranked lower than Duke classmates Mike Chappell and Nate James. But he became the class when Chappell transferred to Michigan State and James had to sit out as a freshman while recovering from knee surgery.

Carrawell was set back three times early in his career by shoulder operations. Through his first three seasons, he averaged 8.6 points and four rebounds, though his game did display dramatic improvement when his assist total exploded from 35 as a sophomore to 130 as a junior.

Setting the stage for Carrawell's senior season was the exodus of Elton Brand, William Avery, and Corey Maggette to the NBA. Carrawell remembered when he, James, and Shane Battier made a visit to Krzyzewski's house while Coach K was recovering from hip surgery.

"We talked to him about how the year was going to go, and to see if he was on board," Carrawell told dukebasketballreport.com. "And if he was on board and was ready to coach us, we were ready to lead a young team that had a Carlos Boozer, a Jason Williams and a Mike Dunleavy, along with Nick Horvath and Casey Sanders.

"We were going to lead that team to be a good team. We didn't know if it could be a great team because I was a role player, so to speak. Shane was a role player. Nate was a role player. Now you're asking us to take all the leadership responsibilities and also lead a young team and also become stars.

"I said, 'Coach, if you're ready to coach us, we're going to have a great year.' He said he was ready and he felt that we were going to have a great year."

Krzyzewski's feeling proved prophetic. The Blue Devils dominated the ACC regular season at 15–1, rolled to the conference tournament title, and advanced to the semifinals of the East Regional before losing 87–78 to Florida. Their final record was 29–5.

At halftime of the game against N.C. State on January 30, Krzyzewski pulled Carrawell aside.

"Where you go, we go," Krzyzewski said.

It was a lot to ask of a player who had already endured three operations on his shoulders. But it apparently wasn't too much. Recognizing the need to assume a more aggressive role, Carrawell increased his production from 9.9 points and 4.8 rebounds as a junior to 16.9 points and 6.1 rebounds as a senior. And game after game, he took on the challenge of guarding the other team's best perimeter threat.

Impressed, Krzyzewski detoured from his scouting report before the Senior Day game against North Carolina in Cameron Indoor Stadium. He had a more important matter to address with his team.

"Forget about North Carolina, seedings, and all that stuff," Krzyzewski said, as related in John Roth and Ned Hinshaw's *Encyclopedia of Duke Basketball*. "The most important thing about this game is that we owe it to Chris to win. He's already leaving here a winner. He deserves to win his last game, and we owe it to him to win it for him."

The Blue Devils did just that, rolling to a 90–76 victory.

"There'll never be another Chris," Battier said afterward. "He's one of a kind, just the best."

Though drafted in the second round by the San Antonio Spurs, Carrawell never latched on in the NBA. But he did get his degree in sociology and see the world while playing professionally in Lithuania, Germany, Australia, the Philippines, and Holland.

I always thought that, given his savvy and engaging personality, he would make a great coach. Here's hoping he gets a chance to prove me right as an assistant with the Springfield Armor of the NBA Development League.

ANTAWN JAMISON

6-9 Forward | North Carolina | 1995–98 | No. 33

1996	First-team All-ACC, fifth-most votes	300
1997	First-team All-ACC, second-most votes	375
	First-team All-Tournament	75
	Second-team All-American	150
1998	First-team All-ACC, unanimous	425
	Everett Case Award	100
	ACC POY	200
	National POY (with fellow first-team All-Americans	250
	Mike Bibby of Arizona, Miles Simon of Arizona, and Paul Pierce	
	and Raef LaFrentz of Kansas)	
Awards Points		1,875

If the age-old saying is correct, then up ACC way, Hurricane Hugo was no ill wind.

For all the damage it wreaked, Hugo also did two conference basketball programs a great deal of good.

Much has been made about Tim Duncan, the Wake Forest great who turned from swimming to basketball after Hurricane Hugo whipped through his native Virgin Islands and destroyed the club pool. Well, Hugo was at least partly responsible for Antawn Jamison's ending up at North Carolina as well.

Alfred Jamison was a carpenter in Shreveport, Louisiana. Seeing there was work to be had in Charlotte cleaning up after Hugo, he began commuting there until finally moving his family a year and a half later.

Antawn Jamison was 12 when his family migrated north to North Carolina. Four years later, when recruiters came calling, his closeness to his family convinced him the only two schools he would consider attending were North Carolina and South Carolina.

"If the hurricane hadn't come through, I probably wouldn't be in a Carolina uniform," Jamison told Alexander Wolff of *Sports Illustrated*.

And North Carolina wouldn't have had maybe the quickest six-nine forward ever to play ACC basketball. He was never brawny and didn't have a

Antawn Jamison
COURTESY OF
ROBERT CRAWFORD

reliable jumper beyond 16 feet—which might have resulted from the mistake his father made by putting the family goal 12 feet off the ground on a telephone pole, instead of the regulation 10.

Jamison said that by the time he reached junior high, he could jump and grab the rim.

"I used to try to tear it down," he told Steve Wise of the *Washington Post*. "But it wouldn't fall for nothing in the world."

Jamison was a defender's nightmare—even a defender the caliber of Duke's Shane Battier.

"Once you think you have him defensively, he'll move, find a new spot and catch the ball," Battier told *SI*. "Before you can say, 'Where did he go?' he'll score."

Battier's coach, Mike Krzyzewski, said another of Jamison's attributes was his ability to shoot from odd angles.

"You hear about his quick release," Krzyzewski told *SI*. "But where's that release from?"

Dean Smith thought he had a good one when he recruited Jamison in a class that included Vince Carter and Ademola Okulaja. He didn't know how good until practice began.

"He just came out of the blue in practice," Smith said. "We were pleasantly surprised with Antawn Jamison and Ademola Okulaja. It's rare on a top-10 team to see freshmen carrying the load."

Upon succeeding Smith in 1998, after Smith's 36 years and 879 victories, Bill Guthridge was lucky he had Jamison. The Tar Heels won a second-straight ACC title, advanced to the Final Four, and set what was then a school record with 34 victories.

Those closest to Jamison said he had two sides during his days at North Carolina—the polite, unassuming kid of good cheer who sang in his church choir, and the fierce competitor on the court.

His competitive streak flared as a sophomore when the Tar Heels lost their first three ACC games. He blew off the press after his team botched a 22-point second-half lead to Maryland, only to lose 85–75 at home. And he called home despondent after the Tar Heels lost 75–63 the next time out, at Virginia, telling his father he didn't want to be part of the worst North Carolina team in 30 years.

As it turned out, he wasn't. The Tar Heels won 16 straight and finished 28–7. One of the sweetest victories during the run was a 93–81 cuffing of Maryland in sold-out and rocking Cole Field House. Jamison's 29 points and 10 rebounds led the way.

"You have to talk about Antawn Jamison's overall play," Smith said afterward. "He was so determined. All he could think about was the game at Chapel Hill."

What I remember about Jamison during his college days, besides what a blur he was on the court, was how friendly and upbeat he usually was in the locker room after games—that is, until anyone mistakenly pronounced his name An-tawn.

His mother once explained that the family had every intention of naming him Antoine. But when an employee at the hospital screwed up and wrote Antawn on the birth certificate, the family members took a look and decided to go with that spelling and their own pronunciation.

It's too bad all families don't look after each other as well as did the Jamisons. Besides the work Hurricane Hugo provided, another reason Alfred Jamison moved his family out of Louisiana was that the convenience store where his wife, Kathy, worked had been robbed at gunpoint.

"My father made me the man that I am, the person I am," Jamison told Mary Schmitt Boyer of the *Cleveland Plain Dealer* years later. "He was always smiling and he taught me to be who I am.

"He's pretty much the perfect father, always smiling. I love him to death."

Jamison was selected by Toronto as the fourth pick of the 1998 draft but was traded to Golden State for the rights to college teammate Vince Carter. As of the 2012–13 season, he had played 15 seasons for five NBA teams.

After reaping NBA riches, Jamison moved his family into an $850,000 home in the tony Providence Country Club area of Charlotte. Finally, after four years, he talked his father into leaving his job as a forklift driver for Lance's snack products.

Contrary to what I'd read about Jamison's two sides growing up, coaches and teammates have seen only one. It's one they love to witness every chance they get.

Eric Musselman, who coached Jamison with the Golden State Warriors, raved about the player's ability to foster positive energy and harmony in the team's oft-rancorous locker room.

"I thought he had a unique ability to get along with the highest-maintenance and the lowest-maintenance guy on the team," Musselman told the *Plain Dealer*. "He had a special gift to bridge that gap, and he can go back and forth in the locker room, communicating with the toughest guys you have and the easiest guys you have.

"There's not a lot of guys who can walk that fence between the two ends of the spectrum in your locker room."

TRAJAN LANGDON

6-3 Guard | Duke | 1994–99 | No. 21

1997	First-team All-ACC, fourth-most votes	325
1998	First-team All-ACC, fourth-most votes	325
	First-team All-Tournament	75
1999	First-team All-ACC, second-most votes	375
	Second-team All-American	150
Awards Points		**1,250**

His parents met at a Black Panthers rally. His father, Steve Langdon, was a professor of anthropology at the University of Alaska–Anchorage. His lab part-

Trajan Langdon
DUKE SPORTS INFORMATION

ner in the eighth grade in Anchorage was a girl named Jewel Kilcher, whose claims to fame are the two top-10 hits she sang under the stage name Jewel. When a sprained foot sidelined him from the ACC Tournament as a senior, he received a healing salve made from a spiritual herb called "devil's club" from a village elder in Tlingit, Alaska.

And did I mention he was signed by the San Diego Padres after a scout looked out his hotel window one day to see him playing catch with his father?

Trajan Langdon should be included in this book for his life story alone.

Steve Langdon moved from Portland to Anchorage at age nine when his psychiatrist father was hired to develop mental-health programs in Alaska.

He named his own son Trajan in honor of the Roman emperor from the second century who built bridges and aqueducts, distributed food to the poor, and ended the persecution of Christians.

Trajan's middle name is Shaka, in honor of the South African chieftain who organized his people into a nation. He paid his own way to Duke, and could afford to after signing a $325,000 contract as a sixth-round pick of the Padres. He played two summers with the organization.

"I don't know if I've ever been around an 18-year-old with so much poise," Padres scout Kevin Towers told Al Featherston of the *Durham Herald-Sun* upon signing Langdon. "We're rolling the dice on a great athlete."

From his son's birth, Steve Langdon was not about to let the family's remote home scuttle Trajan's opportunities at stardom. The lengths he went to in developing a world-class athlete were prodigious. He discovered in his anthropological pursuits that basketball had a long and surprisingly strong tradition in Alaska, having been introduced to the Tlingit and Haida Indians as early as 1910. Not only did Steve Langdon fish with the Tlingits and Haidas, he played on their basketball teams that traveled from community to community. Growing up, Trajan was steeped in the tales of great native hoopsters, many of whom earned their fame while playing in the Gold Medal Tournament, held in Juneau every year since 1947. When at the age of eight he decided to take up the sport, he was lucky enough to have a father who knew how to teach him the right way to play it.

Trajan was the boy to beat in his age group at the Elks Hoops Shoot free-throw shooting contest, winning every year from ages 10 through 13 and once finishing third nationally. He developed his body through a rigorous regimen, rising early in the bone-chilling Alaska mornings to lift weights 90 minutes three days a week before school. By the time he entered East Anchorage High School, he was rising even earlier to shoehorn in an hour of shooting jumpers.

Even with all that, father and son realized Trajan wasn't facing the same level of competition as high-school players in New York, Chicago, Los Angeles, or, for that matter, Durham. So Steve Langdon arranged for Trajan to hone his game against Muff Butler, a playground legend back in the Bronx who enjoyed a standout career at the University of New Orleans.

Steve Langdon, who received his Ph.D. in cultural anthropology from Stanford, also took pains to see that his son's intellectual growth was never neglected. He took Trajan along from a young age on research trips to isolated native villages, exposing him to the awesome wilderness wonderland he called home.

By his junior year at East Anchorage, Trajan was beefing up his transcript with college calculus and engineering classes at the University of

Alaska–Anchorage. If he could attract an offer to play basketball in college, grades would not be a problem.

Speaking of college, it was Steve who in 1992 sent a letter to Tommy Amaker, then an assistant coach at Duke. He no doubt mentioned how Trajan was a bona fide star at East Anchorage, a local phenom who could draw 5,000 spectators to see his team play cross-town rival West Anchorage.

Instead of sending Amaker, Mike Krzyzewski himself made the long trip to check out Langdon.

After Krzyzewski took Trajan to dinner, the two were standing in the driveway of the Langdon home when the otherworldly spectacle of the northern lights appeared in the sky. Langdon, his childhood in Anchorage notwithstanding, had seen them only once.

"Trajan," Krzyzewski said, "this is a sign that you've got to come to Duke." Langdon had his own interpretation.

"I thought they might be a sign," he told *USA Today* years later. "But deep down, I already knew I was going to Duke."

The knocks on Langdon's game were that he wasn't especially quick and didn't have a great handle—which may explain why he made most of his money playing not in the NBA but for teams in various European countries. At Duke, he had 250 assists and 210 turnovers.

But he was strong and smart and fearless and could shoot the eyes out of any basket. His forte was his range. He shot at least 40 percent from three-point distance for three of his four college seasons—and you can make it all four if you round up the 39.5 percent he shot as a junior. His career percentage of .426 ranks seventh all-time in the ACC, and his 342 total three-pointers rank fourth, behind J. J. Redick, Curtis Staples, and Dennis Scott.

And at the line, he was all but automatic. His free-throw percentage of .862 ranks fifth all-time in the ACC. Only Redick, Jack McClinton, Charlie Davis, and Roger Mason were more deadly on the unguarded 15-footer.

Early in his career, Langdon survived the 13–18 meltdown of 1994–95 and major surgery that sidelined him for the 1995–96 season. And the last memories of Langdon at Duke were ones to forget. In the final six seconds of the 1999 national championship against Connecticut in St. Petersburg, Langdon, hounded by the Huskies' Ricky Moore, first traveled, then fell to the court and lost the ball as time expired in a 77–75 loss.

Afterward, Krzyzewski adamantly defended his decision not to call timeout with the ball in the hands of Langdon, who led the Blue Devils with 25 points.

"Absolutely," Krzyzewski said. "Positively. Absolutely. I want Trajan Langdon to take that shot. Win or lose with Trajan Langdon. I will walk down any road with Trajan Langdon, and I'm proud of Trajan Langdon."

Teammate Shane Battier was of the same mind.

"If we're in that situation 100 times, I want Trajan to take that shot 100 times," he said.

After graduating with a double major in mathematics and history, Langdon was the first-round pick (11th overall) of the Cavaliers and became the first Alaskan to play in the NBA. After three seasons in Cleveland, he spent the next 10 with various professional teams in Italy, Turkey, and Russia.

MATT HARPRING

6-7 Forward | Georgia Tech | 1994–98 | No. 15

1996	First-team All-ACC, fourth-most votes	325
	First-team All-Tournament	75
1997	First-team All-ACC, fifth-most votes	300
1998	First-team All-ACC, second-most votes	375
Awards Points		**1,075**

Matt Harpring's last name, it should go without saying, was Harpring.

The coach he wanted to play for called him Matt Hopping.

Matt Harpring thought he could play ACC basketball.

The coach he wanted to play for didn't.

Matt Harpring wanted nothing more than a chance to prove he was right.

The coach he wanted to play for thought Harpring would be wasting everyone's time.

So convinced was Bobby Cremins that Harpring couldn't help Georgia Tech that he suggested the player lower his sights. Cremins had friends at schools including Davidson and Furman and was willing to put in a good word.

"I was devastated," Harpring recalled.

Harpring played with Cremins's son, Bobby Jr., at Marist High School in Atlanta, and Yellow Jackets assistant coach Kevin Cantwell liked his game. But no one could convince Cremins that Harpring had the quickness and athleticism to match up in the ACC hoops wars.

In Cremins's defense, Harpring as a high-school junior bore little resemblance to the six-seven wing forward who became one of the best players in

Matt Harpring
GEORGIA TECH ATHLETICS

Yellow Jackets history. He was actually a six-three point guard until he grew two inches over the summer to move inside to forward. Considered a much better bet as a football quarterback, he was good enough in that role to draw offers from Wake Forest and Northwestern.

It wasn't until other college basketball coaches—most notably Hugh Durham of Georgia and Dave Odom of Wake Forest—offered Harpring scholarships that Cremins decided he better cover his rear end. Harpring was, after all, the state player of the year, and Marist went 32–0 his senior season.

Even then, Cremins warned Harpring he would be on the bench as the 10th or 11th man as a freshman. Harpring accepted the challenge. Practice wasn't a week old before Cremins found himself singing a new tune.

"He said, 'Hey, why don't you guys play like Harping? He's kicking everyone's ass,' " Harpring told author Jack Wilkinson. "Bobby became my biggest supporter. He's the biggest reason why I had such success at Georgia Tech."

Harpring won over Cremins like he did everyone else—with his will, drive, and confidence.

He came by his athletic attributes naturally. His grandfather Norb Harpring played football at Army, his father, Jack, at Michigan (where he was a tackle on the same line as Dan Dierdorf), his uncle Chip at Notre Dame, his brother John at Akron, and his brother Brian at Northwestern. And he wasn't the only one in his family to play basketball at Georgia Tech. His sister Megan competed for the Yellow Jacket women, starting 30 games over a four-year career from 2002 through 2006.

So he knew how to compete, as teammates soon found out.

"He played with this . . . well, I don't want to say arrogance, but this confidence," point guard Drew Barry told Wilkinson.

Barry saw that during a pickup game the summer before Harpring's freshman year. Harpring, leading a three-on-one fast break, pulled up for a 16-footer. Barry admonished the rookie, telling him he was open for a layup.

"I was open for a jumper," Harpring replied.

Harpring was never one to be outworked, whether in the classroom or on the court. As a student, he twice made Academic All-American and graduated on time with a degree in management. As an athlete, he scored 2,225 points (just seven fewer than the Georgia Tech record, held by Rich Yunkus), pulled down 997 rebounds (third in school history), piled up 176 steals (sixth in school history), and played 4,472 minutes (third in school history).

He considered not coming back for his senior year, since his junior campaign had been such a drag. The Yellow Jackets, bottoming out after their run to the conference championship game, slipped to 9–18 and finished dead last in the regular season at 3–13. Harpring discussed the matter with Wake Forest's Tim Duncan, whom he had gotten to know well enough to really like. The two weighed the pros and cons of leaving college early.

"I told [Cremins] that if I was going to come back here next year, he was going to have to get some players," Harpring explained.

Cremins complied, bringing in Dion Glover, Alvin Jones, and T. J. Vines. The Yellow Jackets weren't world-beaters, but they were more competitive, finishing 19–14 overall and 6–10 in ACC play.

Cremins once openly fantasized about what he could do with a team of Matt Harprings. The sports media relations staff at Georgia Tech subsequently released a poster of Cremins and nine players—all of them Harpring.

His jersey was retired before his final home game, making him the sixth Georgia Tech basketball player so honored.

But a more spontaneous and more rewarding tribute came during Harpring's final ACC game. He was walking off the court toward the end of an 83–65 loss to Maryland in the quarterfinals of the 1998 ACC Tournament when the Georgia Tech fans rose to give him an ovation. Then, one by one, fans in all corners of the Greensboro Coliseum rose as well to honor the player who had only wanted a shot at showing what he could do.

Harpring, prompted by his coaches and teammates, stood to acknowledge the ovation. Chill bumps spread down the Georgia Tech bench, along press row, and around the coliseum as everyone shared the special moment.

"Unbelievable," Cremins said. "I've been in this league a long time, and it's one of the nicest gestures and best compliments I've seen."

Drafted by Orlando with the 15th pick in 1998, Harpring averaged 11.5 points and 5.1 rebounds over 11 NBA seasons with the Magic, Cleveland Cavaliers, Philadelphia 76ers, and Utah Jazz.

TIM DUNCAN

6-10 Center | Wake Forest | 1993–97 | No. 21

1995	First-team All-ACC, fourth-most votes	325
	First-team All-Tournament	75
1996	First-team All-ACC, unanimous	425
	Everett Case Award	100
	ACC POY	200
	First-team All-American (with Ray Allen of Connecticut, Marcus Camby of Massachusetts, Allen Iverson of Georgetown, Tony Delk of Kentucky, and Kerry Kittles of Villanova)	200
1997	First-team All-ACC, unanimous	425
	First-team All-Tournament	75
	ACC POY	200
	National POY (with fellow first-team All-Americans Danny Fortson of Cincinnati, Keith Van Horn of Utah, Raef LaFrentz of Kansas, and Ron Mercer of Kentucky)	250
Awards Points		**2,275**

Tim Duncan

Having the honor to cover Tim Duncan every game of his college career—from the time he was thrust in the starting lineup by default and failed to score in a loss to Division II Alaska-Anchorage to the coronation of his senior season—was one of the great pleasures of my sportswriting career. I found Duncan to be a valiant warrior, a peerless athlete, and an infinitely interesting individual.

That was when I could find him at all.

As deeply as I appreciate his sublimely anachronistic attitude in our look-at-me culture, there were times Duncan could be as hard on those trying to cover him as he was on opposing centers. While others craved and even demanded attention, Duncan deflected it like a soft layup in the lane while he rolled along, scoring 20 points a game, pulling down 11 rebounds, winning NBA championships (three) and Most Valuable Player awards (two), and talking so infrequently that the media and the outside world finally learned to leave him alone.

The wall he built posed problems for my endeavors as the Wake Forest beat reporter for the local paper. But it was even more a challenge for the school's media relations department, which had to deal with many more requests than mine.

Those who worked there learned to stand at the back door of the athletics building on days Duncan had an interview scheduled. If the session was set for 2:00 P.M., they'd intercept Duncan at 1:45, heading for parts unknown.

What made it all the more maddening was knowing that when Duncan was available, he could be fascinating. He might stand around looking down at his shoe tops when among those he didn't know, but he was a sharp guy with an undeniable intellectual curiosity that came out when he allowed it.

And his sense of humor, when he deigned to show it, could be delightfully droll.

Remember the time Greg Newton, Duke's yeoman center who averaged 7.6 points and 5.1 rebounds, said Duncan wasn't all he was cracked up to be, and even mentioned the words *soft* and *babyish*?

And remember Duncan's reaction when we sportswriters flocked breathlessly to his locker to ask him about Newton?

"He's the greatest player I've ever seen," Duncan said.

My easiest times talking with Duncan were early in his career, when he was a largely overlooked recruit from an exotic locale, the United States Virgin Islands. I did a series of stories that mentioned how his sister Tricia was a swimmer at Swarthmore who had represented the Virgin Islands in the 1988 Olympics, and how Duncan was a budding star in the pool as well, before Hurricane Hugo blew that pool away. Bored with training in the ocean breakers, he drifted away from swimming and found basketball.

As fate would have it, his brother-in-law, Ricky Lowery, had played college basketball at Capital University, a Division III school in Columbus, Ohio. He wasn't a particularly accomplished player, but his contribution to the game proved lasting. Lowery taught his brother-in-law the game as he knew it—and what he knew best was how to play not as a center but as a guard.

Duncan attributed his advanced skill set to that early training.

"I know Coach [Dave] Odom doesn't want to hear this, but I was a guard," Duncan said. "Seriously, I was practicing to be a guard. I didn't expect to be 6-10. I expected to be six-five or six-six or somewhere along there, where I would have some mobility.

"I remember [Lowery] telling me, 'College coaches just love six-six and six-seven guards.' So I'm out there practicing to be a guard, and I grow up to be 6-10."

As much credit as Hurricane Hugo received for driving Duncan from the pool to the basketball court, there was more to the story. On April 24, 1990, the day before Duncan's 14th birthday, his mother died of cancer. Ione Duncan had been the gale force behind her son's dream to be a great swimmer, the one who got him out of the house and into the pool. From the day she died, Tim Duncan never swam competitively again.

"He didn't want anything to do with swimming," Lowery said. "When she left, he lost it all."

Though never an extrovert, Duncan retreated ever deeper inward. He became a closed book—even, at times, to those who knew how to read people as well as Odom did.

Chris King, who played at Wake Forest during Odom's first three seasons as head coach, happened to mention he'd just been in the Virgin Islands. When Odom asked if he'd seen anybody who could play, King told him about a young beanpole who had stood up against Alonzo Mourning.

Finding Tim Duncan wasn't easy, but talking with him proved even harder. When Odom began his recruiting pitch in Duncan's living room, he became disconcerted because Duncan wouldn't turn to look at him. Duncan was intent on playing a video game on the television.

Tired of talking to the side of Duncan's head, Odom got up and sat beside the television. That way, Duncan would at least be looking in his general direction.

The explanation always given around Wake Forest during Duncan's time there was, "Tim is going to do what Tim is going to do."

In maybe the most revealing moment I shared with Duncan, he traced his abiding streak of independence and his steadfast determination not to be pushed out of his comfort zone to the day before his 14th birthday.

"I think my mom dying is what did that to me," Duncan said. "I love my dad, but after my mom died, I never listened to anybody, pretty much.

"It wasn't that I was a pain or a problem child or anything. I just got my own views, and I went with them. It's something that, from that point on, it was clear to me I had to do what I wanted to do."

Odom can be excused for not knowing exactly what to expect from Duncan. The Deacons had two other frontcourt recruits in that class, Makhtar Ndiaye and Ricardo Peral, who were much more highly regarded. And besides, it was obvious that the competition Duncan had faced in high school wasn't elite.

But once Ndiaye and Peral were declared ineligible for the 1993–94 season, Odom didn't have anyone else to play center except the skinny 6-10 kid from the Virgin Islands.

I'm talking about the same skinny 6-10 kid from the Virgin Islands who, upon meeting teammate Randolph Childress, asked where Childress was from.

"D.C.," Childress replied.

"Where's that?" asked Duncan.

"It's just the nation's capital," Childress explained. "It's just where the president lives."

To land the best player ever at Wake Forest, Odom had to out-recruit Providence, Boston College, and Hartford. Dennis Felton, who later became an assistant coach at Clemson, was the lead recruiter for Providence.

"Now that I'm in the ACC, that's one of the toughest things I've had to deal with—seeing him on the court," Felton said. "My heart breaks every time I see him play. I think he will be a Hall of Fame player."

Odom was asked once what made Duncan special on the court.

"His strength is his demeanor, his personality, his attitude, his court presence, his fearlessness," Odom said. "He has a lot of attributes, but the basis of him being as good as he is is his persona. And that has grown, even right before your eyes.

"He's not overcome by the awesomeness of the moment. He's not afraid of the consequences. He's not overcome by disappointment, and he's not afraid of the moment. And I think that's the biggest asset that he has.

"Beyond that, he has tremendous hand-to-eye coordination. His hands are a good size. He's stronger than he looks. Physically, probably the best thing he has is footwork. His footwork is extraordinary. His feet get him in the right place all the time."

Duncan was also intelligent enough to take full advantage of his educational opportunity, earning a degree in psychology. Wake Forest was more than a way station on Tim Duncan's road to the NBA.

"He has incredible discipline," Deborah Best, Duncan's adviser and chairman of the psychology department, said. "He's right there at the eight o'clock lab, which most students hate. He said he has to get up to jog anyway, so he might as well come to class.

"We're probably as impressed with him as any athlete we've had."

In what I have to think will prove the last sit-down interview I'll have with Tim Duncan, before he left Wake Forest for NBA stardom, I broached the subject of his recalcitrant relationship with the media.

"You don't like doing this," I said. "But when you do, you're good."

"I'm not good at it, I'm just used to it," he replied.

I begged to differ, telling him he was one of the most honest people I'd ever known.

"If honesty is what makes me good at it . . . ," Duncan said. "I would never lie to you. I won't tell you anything just because you want to hear it. I'm going to tell you what I think. That's just how it goes. That's how I've been taught."

JOE SMITH

6-10 Center | Maryland | 1993–95 | No. 32

1994	ACC ROY	100
	First-team All-ACC, fifth-most votes	300
1995	First-team All-ACC, most votes	400
	Second-team All-Tournament	50
	ACC POY	200
	National POY (with fellow first-team All-Americans Damon Stoudamire of Arizona, Ed O'Bannon of UCLA, Jerry Stackhouse of North Carolina, and Shawn Respert of Michigan State)	250
Awards Points		**1,300**

Few coaches had a sharper eye for untapped talent than Gary Williams of Maryland. But even Williams outdid himself when he landed Joe Smith.

Smith was well known enough to be recruited by Wake Forest, N.C. State, Florida State, and Virginia, but North Carolina, Duke, and Clemson showed no interest. The Tar Heels had their eyes on Jerry Stackhouse and Rasheed Wallace, Duke preferred Greg Newton and Joey Beard, and Clemson was hard on the heels of Sharone Wright.

The quintessential late bloomer, Smith was six-five and 170 pounds as a high-school sophomore and six-seven and 180 pounds as a junior. He didn't attend any camps before his senior season.

He had already told Jack Baker, his coach at Maury High in Norfolk, Virginia, that he hoped someday to play college ball at a school like Coastal Carolina.

"Joe has never thought of himself as special," his mother, Letha Smith, told Don Markus of the *Baltimore Sun*. "That's the way he's always been."

Assistant Art Perry of Maryland, who knew Norfolk well from his experience as an assistant at Old Dominion, came across Smith while scouting Ed Geth, a big man who ended up riding the bench at North Carolina. When Williams saw Smith for the first time, he was intrigued.

Joe Smith

"His quickness and timing were there for two years," Williams told Barry Jacobs in the *Fan's Guide to ACC Basketball*. "I saw him play in the summer league after his sophomore year, and he was only 6-6 and a half, 6-7 maybe, and real thin, but he still could get the ball.

"He'd get pushed around, but could time his jump. A lot of guys can't do that."

Smith played on the same Boo Williams AAU team as Allen Iverson, so it wasn't like he was unknown. Bob Gibbons ranked him the eighth-best freshman entering the ACC in 1993–94, but Dick Vitale overlooked him in his top 35 newcomers.

Smith needed one game to make Vitale regret the snub. Debuting against

D.C.-area rival Georgetown, Smith set a school record for most points in a first game by contributing 26 in the Terps' 84–83 victory.

By January, Mike Brey, then an assistant at Duke, was commiserating with Markus of the *Sun* over just how bad Perry and fellow Maryland assistant Billy Hahn had made ACC recruiters look by landing Smith from under everyone's noses.

"When I went up to the Boston Shootout last spring, I knew the rest of us were in trouble," Brey told Markus. "He was on the same team as Joey Beard, and you had no trouble telling who the better player was.

"But he wasn't just better than Joey. He was better than everybody else."

Smith averaged 19.4 points his first season, the most ever by an ACC freshman other than Mark Price (20.6) and Kenny Anderson (20.3). He also was the first freshman to lead the ACC in rebounding, posting 10.7 a game.

"When he doesn't get the ball, he goes and gets it," Coach Mike Krzyzewski of Duke told Jacobs. "I've never seen a kid come into the league and have so many rebounds. He's top drawer."

A banner unfurled at College Park during Smith's sophomore season read, "On the eighth day, God created Joe Smith."

That was the season he warmed up with 33 points and 10 rebounds against Utah in the Maui Invitational and then . . .

. . . made eight of eight shots from the floor in a 56–51 victory at Clemson . . .

. . . blocked a 10-foot jumper by Erik Meek to seal a 74–72 victory over Duke . . .

. . . amassed 29 points and 21 rebounds in a 71–62 victory over Virginia . . .

. . . contributed 14 points and 16 rebounds in an 86–73 win over number-one North Carolina . . .

. . . scorched Clemson again with 33 points in an 84–68 victory during his final game at Cole Field House . . .

. . . capped a 40-point performance at Duke with a game-winning tip that carried the Terps to a 94–92 victory and their first share of an ACC regular-season title since 1980 . . .

. . . and delivered 21 points and seven blocks in an 82–68 victory over Texas in the second round of the NCAA Tournament.

Smith bruised his hip midway through the first half of the regional semi-final but still finished with 22 points and 14 rebounds in a 99–89 loss to Connecticut. He closed his career by becoming the first sophomore since Ralph Sampson in 1981 to be named the consensus National Player of the Year.

After Smith smoked Florida State with 23 points and 20 rebounds as a freshman, Coach Pat Kennedy of the Seminoles cracked, "He's a pro. I wish he would turn. Soon."

Kennedy didn't have to wait terribly long.

On April 14, 1995, Smith announced he would forgo his final two years to make himself available for the NBA draft. He was the first player chosen, by the Golden State Warriors.

RANDOLPH CHILDRESS

6-2 Guard | Wake Forest | 1990–95 | No. 22

1993	Second-team All-ACC, seventh-most votes	250
1994	First-team All-ACC, second-most votes	375
	First-team All-Tournament	75
1995	First-team All-ACC, third-most votes	350
	Everett Case Award	100
	Second-team All-American	150
Awards Points		**1,300**

In its darkest hour, Wake Forest reached out to one of the brightest stars in the school's sports firmament to help light the path back to at least respectability, if not glory.

The Deacons looked to Randolph Childress to show them the way, as he had once before.

Childress today serves as an assistant coach, but when he was hired in August 2011 it was as assistant to the director of athletics, Ron Wellman. That's assistant *to* the director of athletics, not assistant director of athletics. Childress replaced nobody. The position was created once Childress returned from Italy, where he had played professionally for 11 seasons.

The basketball team, in its first season with Jeff Bzdelik at the helm, had staggered down the stretch, losing 20 of its last 22 games to finish an abysmal 8–24. The fan base was revolting. The Deacons had become a punch line to a bad joke.

If Wellman was desperate to turn around his program's fortunes, he was no more so than Dave Odom had been when he recruited Childress out of

Randolph Childress

Clinton, Maryland, as part of the foundation class of 1990 that included two Hall of Famers (Childress and Rodney Rogers) and two other solid starters (Trelonnie Owens and Marc Blucas).

Wake Forest finished 3–11 in the ACC in Odom's first season—the season before the cavalry arrived. The Deacons improved to 8–6 when Childress and Rogers were freshmen, before slipping back to 7–9 in 1991–92, when Childress sat out the season while recovering from knee surgery.

He was back in the lineup the next three seasons, over which the Deacons were 33–15 in ACC play, beat Duke eight straight times (the streak would stretch to nine before being snapped in 1996), played in the NCAA Tournament all three years, and made off with the school's first ACC title since the days of Bones McKinney, Len Chappell, and Billy Packer in the early 1960s.

"He had what we needed at the time that he came here," Odom recalled.

"We needed confidence. Because, if you think back, Wake was a talented team that couldn't finish it. We'd get right to the door and couldn't open it. And he was one of those who didn't ask why. He asked why not. His attitude just permeated the whole team, and really the whole campus."

Odom didn't need long to realize what a cynosure he had in Childress, who had played his senior season for Stu Vetter at Flint Hill School in Oakton, Virginia. In the third game of his career, as the legend goes, with the Deacons playing on the road at number-six Alabama, Childress launched two airballs in a row. Passing the visitors' bench on the way back downcourt, he implored Odom, "Don't take me out now, I'm getting hot."

"I just looked over to my staff, shook my head, and said, 'What are you going to do with a guy like that?'" Odom recalled.

The Deacons' 96–95 overtime loss couldn't be laid on Childress, who made seven of 12 from the floor to score 22 points.

Many times, I've recalled in print the night in Nashville's Memorial Coliseum when Wake Forest played Vanderbilt in Childress's junior season. He missed 10 straight shots down the stretch—which didn't impede him from taking the last shot of regulation. He drilled it while falling into the Commodores' bench to send the game into overtime. Again, the Deacons lost, this time 91–83 in two overtimes. I couldn't wait to ask Childress how anyone who had missed 10 straight shots found the sand to take another with the game on the line.

His answer was one that those who aspire to be the best at anything should never forget.

"I don't care if I make 10 shots in a row or miss 10 shots in a row," Childress said. "The next shot I take is the only one that counts."

Opposing fans loathed him, none with greater passion than the bedlamites of Duke's Cameron Indoor Stadium. Of course, none had a better reason.

Two seasons in a row, Childress stuck it to the Blue Devils in Cameron. The first game was in January 1994, when he stepped back behind the three-point line and shot the jumper over Grant Hill that beat Duke 69–68. The second was in February 1995, when he answered a late go-ahead dunk by the Blue Devils' Erik Meek by draining a game-winning 12-footer with six seconds remaining.

Longtime *Winston-Salem Journal* compadre Lenox Rawlings and I were the last ones in the media room afterward. We were tapping out our stories when Pete Gaudet stuck his head through the door. Gaudet was a good man, a sympathetic character for the way he took over that season for an ailing Mike Krzyzewski and ended up catching the flak for the Blue Devils' 2–14 tank job in the ACC.

As we chatted, Gaudet mentioned how ecstatic Meek had been when his dunk put the Blue Devils ahead. But he later confided to Gaudet that his euphoria had immediately given way to one anxiety-producing thought.

"Childress," Gaudet related.

One reason Lenox and I were so long at our stories was that we wanted to recount what happened not just in the game but afterward as well. Incensed that the officials stopped play during Wake's final possession to wipe moisture off the floor—forcing the Deacons to execute another inbounds play to get the ball back in his hands—Childress took out his gum and whipped it into the stands. Then, as he waited on the court for his postgame televised interview, he happened to pick up the ball, rear back, and heave it toward the far backboard. Only it sailed over the board and right into the face of a fan still in his seat.

Tim Duncan, standing alongside, wryly critiqued Childress's form as the Crazies pelted the two with cups and other debris.

"Decent arm," Duncan observed. "Nice follow-through."

Duke wasn't as amused. Childress was compelled to issue an apology to the fan and the school.

If any ACC player has ever been more sure of himself, I haven't met him.

"I can't imagine anybody having more confidence in me than I have in myself," Childress told me once. "And if I could, that wouldn't say very much for me."

Which ACC player had the best game ever, or the best season, is a matter for debate. But nobody among the 23,000 fans who flocked to the Greensboro Coliseum in March 1995 could doubt who had the best ACC Tournament.

The top-seed Deacons immediately fell behind ninth-seed Duke by 18. Yet Childress, playing with a bum shoulder and a dislocated pinkie on his right hand, wasn't about to make an early exit.

Odom called time, but it was Childress who did the talking.

"You're embarrassing me," Childress said. "We will not lose this game."

He was right. The Deacons didn't lose, not with Childress pouring in 10 straight shots over one stretch to finish with 40 points to spark an 87–70 victory.

After scoring what was for him a quiet 30 in a 77–68 semifinal victory over the Wahoos, Childress delivered his signature game when it mattered most, against North Carolina in the championship. Famously breaking Jeff McInnis's ankles with a crossover, then motioning for McInnis to rise while he sank yet another three-pointer, Childress drilled 12 of 22 shots from the floor and nine of 17 from three-point range on the way to 37 points. His 10-foot runner with four seconds left in overtime simultaneously clinched the title and broke Lennie Rosenbluth's record for most points in the ACC Tournament, which had stood since 1957.

"There's never been a more fitting way to end a career in the Atlantic Coast Conference Tournament," Odom proclaimed. "Never. He truly is special."

Odom was thankful. His counterpart, Dean Smith, was glad he would never have to see it again.

"I congratulate him," Smith said. "I'm glad he's gone."

Childress's current job at Wake Forest, besides helping to mollify a disaffected fan base, is to help the Deacon players learn how to win. For that, Ron Wellman got the right man.

GRANT HILL

6-8 Forward | Duke | 1990–94 | No. 33

1991	Second-team All-Tournament	50
1992	Second-team All-ACC, eighth-most votes	225
	Second-team All-Tournament	50
1993	First-team All-ACC, fifth-most votes	300
	Second-team All-American	150
1994	First-team All-ACC, most votes	400
	Second-team All-Tournament	50
	ACC POY	200
	First-team All-American (with Jason Kidd of California, Donyell Marshall of Connecticut, Glenn Robinson of Purdue, and Clifford Rozier of Louisville)	200
Awards Points		**1,625**

Grant Hill, as polished a person as I've ever seen come through the conference, was a true joy to watch play and to be around.

He grew up in affluence in Reston, Virginia, the son of a Yale graduate father who was a star running back in the NFL and an attorney mother who was a suite mate of Hillary Rodham's at Wellesley College. A Porsche and a Mercedes were parked in the driveway, though when Hill was picked up at school he preferred his father to be driving the family's less-conspicuous Volkswagen.

"I've always wanted to blend in and be like everybody else," Hill told the *Sporting News*. "I didn't want anybody, especially my friends, thinking I was better than them.

"I just wanted to be a down-to-earth guy and have my own identity."

As such, he was slow to warm up to sports, preferring during his early childhood to concentrate on music. His chosen instruments were the piano, trumpet, and bass. Hill didn't aspire to become a basketball star until he was 13, after he acquitted himself in impressive fashion in AAU competition against some of the best players in the country. Even then, he remained ambivalent.

So why, Barry Jacobs asked him, did he start playing basketball?

"Because I was tall," Hill said in Jacobs's *Three Paths to Glory*. "If you're tall and you're black, people assume that you're either playing basketball or you're supposed to be playing basketball."

Bill Brill noted another dynamic that made young Grant Hill the person he would become.

"Not only am I an only child," Hill said in *A Season Is a Lifetime*, the book Brill wrote with Mike Krzyzewski. "But I don't have any cousins, or aunts or uncles, either."

What he did have was a father who, because of his day job as a running back with the Dallas Cowboys, Washington Redskins, and Cleveland Browns, wasn't always home as much as either child or father would have preferred. When he was around, Calvin Hill made up for his absences by studiously critiquing his son's performances on the battlefields of athletic competition.

Grant Hill called the sessions PGA—postgame analysis.

"Sometimes it was for fifteen minutes, sometimes it was an hour," he told Brill. "We discussed what Grant did wrong. I never listened and he knew I didn't listen.

"I'm just happy to say PGA has ended."

Though he grew up a fan of North Carolina and Georgetown basketball, his reason for picking Duke was simple.

"It was just that when I got on campus, I fit," Hill told Brill.

Krzyzewski left no doubt how happy he was to land Hill, starting him from the first college game he played.

"I think Grant will emerge as one of the truly outstanding players," Krzyzewski said in Jacobs's *Three Paths to Glory*. "Especially early, I want him to try things and make mistakes. Of commission, not omission.

"I don't want to hold back Grant."

Hill, throughout his time at Duke, remained an extremely hard person to dislike. Teammates marveled at his ability and personal charm.

After watching Hill hit 12 of 13 shots for 28 points against Canisius—and

Grant Hill

rebounding the one miss and putting it back in—teammate Kenny Blakeney had seen enough.

"It's scary," Blakeney told Jacobs in *Three Paths to Glory*. "He can do whatever he wants whenever he wants. It's disgusting. I hate him."

It was a testament to Hill's all-around game that the recognition for his ability transcended his relatively modest career statistics of 14.9 points, six rebounds, and 3.6 assists per game. He thus became just the third honoree to be named ACC Player of the Year despite not ranking in the top five in the conference in scoring or rebounding. The first was Lou Pucillo in 1959, the second Steve Vacendak in 1966. As a senior, Hill averaged 17.4 points, 6.9 rebounds, and 5.2 assists. Travis Best ranked fifth in the ACC with 18.3 points a game, while teammate Cherokee Parks and Todd Fuller of N.C. State tied for fifth in rebounding with 8.4 a game.

All of which makes one wonder what Hill would have become if he hadn't mangled his ankle in the final week of the NBA's 1999–2000 regular season.

Chosen with the third pick of the NBA draft by the Detroit Pistons, Hill had already established himself as one of the league's stars, sharing co–Rookie of the Year honors with Jason Kidd in 1995, playing for the gold-medal Olympic team in 1996, and making first-team All-NBA in 1997 and second-team in 1996, 1998, 1999, and 2000.

His comeback began in rocky fashion. After his ankle was refractured and aligned with his leg bone in March 2003, Hill contracted a frightening infection that caused his temperature to soar to 104.5 degrees. He was confined to a hospital for a week and took antibiotics for six months.

He never regained all his athletic ability but remained good enough to be a valued contributor with the Orlando Magic, Phoenix Suns, and Los Angeles Clippers.

RODNEY ROGERS

6-7 Forward | Wake Forest | 1990–93 | No. 54

1991	ACC ROY	100
	Second-team All-ACC, eighth-most votes	225
1992	First-team All-ACC, fourth-most votes	325
	Second-team All-Tournament	50
1993	First-team All-ACC, unanimous	425
	ACC POY, heavily contested	150
	Second-team All-American	150
Awards Points		1.425

Rodney Rogers spent his formative years on the meanest streets of North Carolina, on McDougald Terrace in Durham.

Barring a miracle, he will spend the rest of his days in a wheelchair after breaking his back in a 2008 wreck on a dirt bike.

During the 15 years in between, Rogers combined an uncommon blend of strength and speed to become one of the most powerful athletes the game has ever seen.

"To me, power is best described as a combination of speed and strength," Coach Dave Odom of Wake Forest said. "That's him. He can play inside against anybody his own size or smaller—and some bigger—because he has the strength, speed, quickness, and power to do all those things. But against

Rodney Rogers
<small>COURTESY OF BILL SETLIFF</small>

people who are taller than he is or bigger than he is, he can take them to the outside and let his speed and quickness go to work on them."

His father, Willie Wadsworth, died when Rogers was eight. One brother, Stacy, was deaf. Another, Stanley, was sentenced to 20 years for armed robbery. When his mother, Estelle Spencer, barely survived a horrendous car crash, she made the painful decision to allow Rogers to spend his final two years at Durham's Hillside High School in the care of a family that had taken him in.

"She lost one son to the streets, and that's one of the roughest areas in the city," said Chet Mebane, Rogers's basketball coach at Hillside High. "She was determined not to lose Rodney."

Nathaniel Brooks, a masonry contractor, and his wife, Barbara, treated Rogers like their own two sons, Daryl and Nathaniel Jr.

"That was understood," Brooks said. "He looked to me as a father image. If he has any questions or problems, he knows he can discuss them with me and my wife."

Though an honor student at Hillside High, Rogers had to take the Scholastic Aptitude Test four times to get the score he needed for Wake Forest. He attended his graduation banquet but was in bed by the time the prom, held later that night, was cranking up. He explained to Caulton Tudor of Raleigh's *News & Observer* that his next shot at the SAT was the following morning.

"This is what it's come down to," Rogers said. "So far, not getting that score is about the biggest disappointment of my life. I'm not going to feel good about myself until I prove I can get it.

"There will be other parties. I can go to dances later."

Rogers turned out to be a breakthrough recruit for Odom's effort to rebuild Wake Forest's basketball fortunes. Randolph Childress met Rogers at the Nike Basketball Camp, where Rogers was a teammate of Childress's close friend, future Wake Forest teammate Charlie Harrison.

"I remember watching him and seeing how he just stood out physically more than anybody," Childress said. "You're usually looking at kids and you're thinking how skinny they are. And you never had that opinion about Rodney. He was always built like a man among boys as an athlete.

"And when Rodney committed to Wake, it was instrumental to my decision to come to Wake. They were on my radar, but believe me, he had a lot to do with it. We were bad and had struggled before, but I knew when he committed that I had something to come here with—that there were going to be some players here to work with."

If Rogers had come along several years later—after Kevin Garnett in 1995 opened the floodgates for high-schoolers good enough to go pro—Odom might never have had the pleasure of coaching him at Wake Forest. Mebane, Rogers's high-school coach, said NBA coaches were already salivating.

"This is one time that the player's as good as his billing," Mebane said. "It's no overstatement when I say Rodney has extraordinary ability. I've been told by some good coaches—and I fully believe—he could make an NBA roster right now. He wouldn't play, but he's good enough to make it as a 12th man on somebody's NBA roster."

At Wake Forest, Rogers was a big man on campus in more ways than one. He came out of high school known as "the Durham Bull" but was elevated to one-name status.

"To Wake Forest, Rodney was Rodney Rogers," Odom said. "You don't have to complete it. Rodney was Rodney Rogers."

Rogers had retired from professional basketball and was by all accounts well set financially when he went to work for the public works department in Durham. His explanation? He liked to drive big trucks.

He also liked to ride off-road vehicles, which was what he was doing that fateful day in late fall 2008 when his dirt bike hit a hole and he went flying. He broke a vertebra in his back and woke up paralyzed from the neck down. He was given at best a 5 percent chance of ever walking again.

But his college coach refused to rule out the possibility.

"As I look at him as an athlete and a person, God has endowed him with great strength and a powerful body," Odom said. "And those are important elements when you're fighting the battle that is ahead of him. You've got to have a strong body, and he's got one."

In all my years of covering ACC basketball, I've never seen one stronger.

BOBBY HURLEY

6-0 Guard | Duke | 1989–93 | No. 11

1991	Third-team All-ACC, 13th-most votes	100
1992	Second-team All-ACC, seventh-most votes	250
	First-team All-Tournament	75
	Final Four MVP	150
1993	First-team All-ACC, second-most votes	375
	ACC POY, close runner-up	125
	First-team All-American (with Calbert Cheaney of Indiana, Anfernee Hardaway of Memphis State, Jamal Mashburn of Kentucky, and Chris Webber of Michigan)	200
Awards Points		**1,275**

Being a guy who despised losing worse than anything in the world, Bobby Hurley certainly chose the right school. In his four years at Duke, three of which ended at the Final Four, and two of those with the Blue Devils cutting down the nets, Hurley's teams won 121 games and lost but 24.

Even that, though, was tough to take after Hurley's high-school career. Playing for his fabled father, Bob Hurley, at St. Anthony's High School in Jersey City, Hurley experienced only three losses in his three and a half seasons on the varsity and graduated with the Friars on a 50-game winning streak.

"I always hated to lose, even in pickup games," Hurley said. "When you lose then, you wait 45 minutes on the playground before you can play again.

Bobby Hurley
COURTESY OF ROBERT CRAWFORD

"I'll do anything it takes."

Hurley grew up a North Carolina fan and dreamed of playing for the Tar Heels until Coach Dean Smith told him he would not quit recruiting Kenny Anderson even in the event he landed Hurley. Coach Mike Krzyzewski made Hurley his number-one target and was richly rewarded by a player whose jersey would be retired by the school.

"He and Kenny Anderson were the two best guards in the country, and they came out the same year from high schools about 10 miles apart," Krzyzewski told Rick Telander of *Sports Illustrated*. "A lot of schools were recruiting both. We didn't.

"We told Bobby, 'You're the one.' "

The quintessential gym rat, Hurley became a great player because, in his heart, that's what he had to be. Little came easy for him, especially during his maiden voyage through a college basketball season. He chafed under the constant criticism of teammate Christian Laettner, once asking Krzyzewski to tell the unfailingly caustic Laettner to lay off.

Krzyzewski's answer: Tell him yourself.

Hurley pouted, moped, and complained when confronted with the challenges all freshmen point guards face. King Rice of rival North Carolina was particularly adept at getting under Hurley's skin. Fans throughout the conference, picking up on Hurley's immaturity, began the plaintive chant of "Hur-ley, Hur-ley, Hur-ley" whenever Duke came to town.

Even Dick Vitale, an unabashed champion of all things pertaining to Duke basketball, found Hurley's childishness hard to take.

"Hey, Bobby Hurley's going to make my All–Bill Laimbeer team," Vitale told a television audience. "A whiner and a moaner and a groaner. I mean, come on, Bobby."

His father admitted he pushed both Bobby and another son, Danny, who played at Seton Hall. Bobby took the criticism personally, never resting as long as there was something else he could do to prove to his father, and to himself, that he was a great player.

"I know I'm a good player, but . . . ," he told Telander of *SI*. "I think I'm constantly looking for ways to improve, to prevent myself from being complacent.

"At times I'm my own worst enemy, but because I'm a point guard, a lot of the team's success depends on how I play, so I have to keep pushing myself."

His self-reflection led to an epiphany of sorts after his trying freshman season.

"I may have been a little bit more of a front-runner my freshman year than a perfectionist," Hurley told Barry Jacobs in *Three Paths to Glory*. "I couldn't turn it around my freshman year. If I had a couple of bad plays in a game, I wasn't able to turn it around and do some positive things. It would just turn out to be a totally bad game for me."

That freshman season ended in about as miserable a fashion as possible for a player in the Final Four. I was sitting courtside at Denver's McNichols Sports Arena watching Duke play Arkansas in the national semifinal when all of a sudden Hurley sprinted from the court to the locker room.

Only later did I learn he was wracked with intestinal flu.

He returned to play in the 97–83 victory over the Razorbacks but contributed little (three points, six assists, and six turnovers) in 36 courageous minutes. He told ACC historian Al Featherston years later that he spent the Sunday between the semifinal and the final against UNLV in bed and missed the Monday-morning walk-through.

He played, but not well, in the Runnin' Rebels' 103–73 blowout, managing only two points and three assists while committing five turnovers.

To be the player Krzyzewski and Duke needed him to be, Hurley recognized he had to get a better grip on his emotions. Helping him reach that conclusion was a video compilation of his less-than-memorable moments, put together by Blue Devils assistant Pete Gaudet.

"I needed to see the tape," Hurley told Bill Brill for *A Season Is a Lifetime.* "I had been getting away from stuff and slipping into bad habits.

"I needed to stop doing those things, and seeing myself doing them really helped."

College is a time for maturation. By steadily following that path, Hurley got better and better. His point totals went up season by season—from 8.8 as a freshman to 11.3 as a sophomore to 13.2 as a junior to 17 as a senior—but more importantly, his turnovers went down. He delivered his career-most assists when he compiled 289 as a sophomore, one more than his freshman total. By his junior season, he learned which gambles he should take and which he shouldn't.

And what a gamer he proved to be. Following that sad performance against Nevada–Las Vegas as a freshman, he and his Duke teammates got another crack at their foils when both teams made it back to the Final Four in 1991. This time, with Hurley nailing a ballsy three-pointer with 2:14 remaining—dubbed by Krzyzewski the game's biggest play—the Blue Devils outlasted the Runnin' Rebels 79–77. Two nights later, Hurley delivered nine points and seven assists as Duke beat Kansas 72–65 for its first of two consecutive national titles.

And in case you're wondering, Hurley was pretty good in the Final Four of 1992 as well, contributing 26 points and four assists in the 81–78 semifinal victory over Indiana and nine points and seven assists in the 71–51 championship rout over Michigan.

Against the Hoosiers in the semis, in an emotional match-up between Krzyzewski and his college coach, Bob Knight, the player the Blue Devils took their cues from, Christian Laettner, was down on himself for his ragged first-half play. So it was left to Hurley to rally the troops at halftime. Apparently, whatever he said worked. The Blue Devils, down five at the break, outscored Indiana 44–36 in the second half.

For his efforts, Hurley was named MVP of the Final Four.

Though selected as the seventh-overall pick by the Sacramento Kings, Hurley had his professional career cut short when he suffered a near-fatal accident while driving home from a game. I can only hope that, in his own mind, Hurley by then had nothing left to prove. There was little more he could prove to me.

Hurley, I was happy to see, became an assistant coach on his brother Danny's staff at Wagner in 2011. And I was even happier that the Seahawks did so well in 2011–12 (25–6, 15–3 in the Northeast Conference) that Danny was hired at Rhode Island of the Atlantic 10.

He took Bobby along as associate head coach. In March 2013, Bobby Hurley was named head coach at Buffalo.

KENNY ANDERSON

6-2 Guard | **Georgia Tech** | **1989–91** | **No. 12**

1990	ACC ROY	100
	First-team All-ACC, third-most votes	350
	First-team All-Tournament	75
1991	First-team All-ACC, unanimous	425
	First-team All-American (with Jimmy Jackson of Ohio State, Larry Johnson of UNLV, Shaquille O'Neal of LSU, and Billy Owens of Syracuse)	200
Awards Points		**1,150**

As good as Kenny Anderson was at Georgia Tech, his life probably peaked at 16.

By then, he was already a legend hotly pursued by every major-college program in America. Recruiters began coming around when he was in the sixth grade and were a constant part of his life long before he became the first freshman to ever be named All–New York City.

And he loved basketball above all else.

"Other kids like to play with toy trucks and wagons and stuff, but I just wanted to play with the basketball," Anderson told Sandra McKee of the *Baltimore Sun*. "I'd just get so much fun out of dribbling to the grocery store for Mom. I just love the basketball."

His father barely passed through his mother's life.

"Kenny's father and I were just lovers," Joan Anderson told the *Sun*. "It was the wrong place, the wrong time. I had a child and we went our separate ways."

Joan Anderson always claimed her son was the reincarnation of her brother James McLaughlin—which would have been quite a trick, considering it was McLaughlin who introduced the five-year-old Anderson to the game on a court in Queens.

McLaughlin died of heart disease at age 25, so it was left to Vincent Smith—the same Vincent Smith who is the older brother of North Carolina

Kenny Anderson

great Kenny Smith, another member of my ACC Basketball Hall of Fame—to help Anderson polish his game.

Because of Anderson's bond with both Smith brothers, many assumed he would play at North Carolina, though he told people he was also considering four other schools—Syracuse, Georgia Tech, Georgetown, and Duke.

Contrary to the time-honored cliché, Anderson was no playground legend, simply because he didn't play much playground ball. He went to school, to the local gym, and back home. But he was serious about the game he seriously loved, and was good enough at it to be the only player other than Lew Alcindor to be named a Parade All-American three times.

"I took my high school career as a job," Anderson told William Rhoden of the *New York Times*. "I knew I had to be here every day practicing. I couldn't miss a practice because I'm saving my mother money [on tuition]."

Anderson was confident on the court but showed a different side to those who got to know him.

"He's never been as cocky as people thought," said Jayson Williams, a longtime NBA player who has known Anderson from their elementary-school days in Queens. "When he was a kid, the bigger guys all wanted to kick his butt, because he always played with this smile, and it looked like he was making fun of them. But you know what? It was a nervous smile."

Bobby Hurley, another budding New York–area star of the day, got along with Anderson far better than he expected. Hurley played for his father at St. Anthony's in Jersey City, while Anderson, like Kenny Smith before him, played for Jack Curran at Archbishop Molloy in Queens. Hurley himself might have ended up at North Carolina if Dean Smith had agreed to stop recruiting other point guards. Smith wanted Anderson—and might have gotten him if a discussion between recruit and coach over latitude had gone better.

Vincent Smith recounted Anderson's version to Rhoden of the *New York Times.*

"Coach Smith said, 'Kenny, we don't mind our players saying things on the floor, but also you have to have some confidence in us; we've been coaching for 30 years.' Then he said, 'If the next day you didn't think things worked out, you can come by the office and we'll point things out.' "

Anderson found Bobby Cremins's recruiting pitch more to his liking.

"He said, 'You're going to have the ball; you're going to run the team,' " Anderson told the *Times.* "It wasn't all recruiting talk. He was true blue. I just knew his word was gold and Coach Curran knew his word was gold."

Anderson had to make a decision to alleviate the pressure, which was severe enough to cause headaches. His mother told him she wasn't enamored of the state of North Carolina, where she had spent some of her childhood during Jim Crow days.

Finally, he called a press conference and told the assembled media he wished he could cut himself into three parts and give his left arm to Syracuse, his right arm to North Carolina, and his body to Georgia Tech.

The heart belongs to the body, so Anderson followed that heart to Atlanta to play for Bobby Cremins.

It's been said the personality of a team reflects that of its coach—which may be why Cremins's Yellow Jackets were as fun to follow as any squad I've watched play. And Anderson sure looked like he was having fun during his two years in Atlanta, especially during the Final Four run of 1990.

The next season, after losing Dennis Scott to the NBA and Brian Oliver to graduation, Tech finished only 17–13 and 6–8 in conference play.

What I'll never forget is how quickly Anderson could push the ball from end line to end line. I've never seen anyone dribble faster.

"His hand speed is incredible, so that's number one," Bobby Hurley said. "His ball-handling ability number two. He can put a lot of different dribble moves together to get guys off him. He can flat out handle the ball."

Anderson, taken by the New Jersey Nets with the second pick of the 1992 draft, played 14 seasons for seven NBA team. He made the All-Star team, but his career never lived up to the outsized expectations. He ended up in Lithuania playing for his final basketball team in 2006.

He was paid a total of $63 million to play basketball. I know that from media accounts of the bankruptcy Anderson filed in 2005. He married three times and fathered seven children with five women. You might recognize one of them, Tami Roman, if you've ever happened to watch the cable-TV show *Basketball Wives*.

William Rhoden caught up with Anderson in 2011. He was coaching the basketball team at Posnack Hebrew Day School in Davie, Florida.

"Maybe this is my route," Anderson told him.

BRYANT STITH

6-5 Forward | Virginia | 1988–92 | No. 20

1989	ACC ROY	100
	Second-team All-Tournament	50
1990	First-team All-ACC, second-most votes	375
	First-team All-Tournament	75
1991	First-team All-ACC, fourth-most votes	325
1992	First-team All-ACC, fifth-most votes	300
Awards Points		**1,225**

From the 1989–90 season through 2001, the one imperative for any sportswriter on the day before the ACC Tournament—known widely as the "workout day"—was to catch up with Coach Dave Odom of Wake Forest.

Of all the coaches who ever sent teams into ACC games, none held the working press (now, there's an oxymoron) in higher regard than did Odom. And to a large degree because of that, no coach was ever as liked and appreciated by me and my cohorts. We never knew what Odom was going to say, but we did know he would keep talking until he said something we could laugh about that night over adult beverages in the hospitality suite.

The story being pursued in 1991 in Charlotte by the Virginia media con-

Bryant Stith

tingent was how a writer for the school paper, the *Cavalier Daily*, had, audaciously enough, given star forward Bryant Stith of the Cavaliers the back of his typing hand. Comparing Stith unfavorably to the other standout wing forwards of the day—Billy Owens of Syracuse, Stacey Augmon of Nevada–Las Vegas, Jimmy Jackson of Ohio State, and Malik Sealy of St. John's—the misguided Russell DePalma wrote the following immortal words: "He may not be great but he's all Virginia has."

Stith was bothered enough at being damned by such faint praise that he called home to the hamlet of Freeman, Virginia.

"They told me, 'That's life,' " Stith informed Doug Doughty of the *Roanoke Times*. "I found my teammates were behind me, as well as the coaches and my parents. More than anything else, I want to win the ACC Tournament for that reason.

"The best always have criticism and I feel I'm no different. I'm susceptible to mistakes. I definitely have fire in my eyes. Every time I step on the floor, I will be thinking of Russell DePalma."

Doughty is the venerable Virginia beat reporter who knew Odom well from the Wake Forest coach's days as an assistant with the Wahoos. And seeing that the Deacons would open the tournament against the Cavaliers, he couldn't wait to ask Odom what impact DePalma's words, and Stith's emotional reaction to them, might have on the game.

Odom's response was classic Dave: "I hope he understands that I didn't write the article. None of our players did. I don't think he has anything to prove to Russell DePalma or anybody else, let alone Wake Forest."

The point of the story is not to set up a recounting of how an enraged Stith took out his wrath on Dave and the Deacons. Sixth-seed Virginia did upend three-seed Wake Forest 70–61, but that had more to do with the play of John Crotty (23 points, four assists) than that of Stith, who made only six of 15 shots from the floor to contribute 14 points along with his six rebounds. Instead, it illustrates to what lengths Stith had to go to prove what a truly great player he was.

Jeff Jones, who coached Stith at Virginia both as an assistant and head coach, addressed that issue after Stith made the team coached by Mike Krzyzewski that represented the United States in the Goodwill Games and the World Championships.

"In the time I've been at Virginia, the only players with a comparable impact are Ralph Sampson and Jeff Lamp," Jones said. "I still sense there are some people who are surprised he made the [United States] team. I hear comments like, 'He's a really nice player,' but they don't mention him with Stacey Augmon, Billy Owens, and Alonzo Mourning. I think they should."

Maybe the lack of recognition stemmed from the fact that Stith was a solid, hardworking, fundamentally sound player not inclined to beat his chest and proclaim to anyone within earshot his magnificence. His values reflected his upbringing in Freeman, just off Route 58 in south-central Virginia between Lawrenceville and Emporia. The nearest theater was 30 minutes away, the nearest mall a 45-minute drive. His father, Norman, drove a long-haul semi for years before becoming the director of engineering at Newport News General Hospital. His mother, Maudriece, was a schoolteacher.

Bryant learned the game on a dirt court shooting at a backboard and basket hung on an oak tree. There, his uncle Gary and Gary's friends taught him a thing or two about toughness and competition. "They didn't take it easy on me," Stith recalled. He didn't drink or smoke and rarely cursed. He began going out with his future wife, Barbara Dilworth, during his sophomore year of high school.

He joked that when he showed up for college, Charlottesville looked like New York City to him.

"I can't imagine anyone being more country than I am," he said.

"Bryant is a homebody," Maudriece Stith told John Galinsky of the *University Journal*. "He always talks about how he wants to come back to Freeman when basketball is over. It's such a good place to settle down and raise a family."

The primary lessons taught in the Stith household were that life is hard and that there are no shortcuts to success. Bryant had to complete his home-work before he could engage in athletic competition. To that end, he was known to rise at three in the morning to study, thus freeing up the afternoons for practice.

Having set his mind on being a great player for Coach Jerry Burke at Brunswick County High School, he ended up scoring more than 2,100 points—while only once taking more than 20 shots in a game. He also set his mind on being the class valedictorian, and accomplished the goal with a GPA of 4.29 while taking college-level courses.

Stith's work ethic served him well in college. Mainly a low-post player as a freshman, he shot 100 three-pointers a day the next summer to expand his game to the perimeter. An offense-oriented player his first two years, he stud-ied defensive principles and did drills after his sophomore season to become more well rounded.

The Virginia coaching staff had plenty of reasons to love and appreciate Stith, the greatest being his fearlessness and will.

Jones recounted to Doughty an example from Virginia's game against Providence in the NCAA Tournament during Stith's freshman season.

"Bryant came to the bench holding his mouth and we asked him what had happened," Jones recalled. "He said he'd broken his tooth and then handed us the pieces. Then we asked him if it hurt or not. He said, 'Only when I breathe.'

"That was the first inkling that he was a big-time, big-game player."

Stith, for the record, scored 16 of his 19 points after returning to the game and led the Cavaliers to a 100–97 victory in Nashville's Memorial Gym.

Krzyzewski, who finished a close second to Virginia in the recruitment of Stith, ate up those qualities while coaching him on the United States team.

"Bryant Stith is the epitome of a competitor," Krzyzewski told Doughty. "I admire who he is, what he's accomplished and the way he's gone about it. He's a great representative for the University of Virginia.

"If they don't realize that, they've got to get their head out of the sand."

Virginia realized it enough to retire Stith's jersey, making him the sixth player afforded such distinction, after Buzz Wilkinson, Barry Parkhill, Wally Walker, Jeff Lamp, and Ralph Sampson. Stith outscored them all, setting a school record of 2,516 points.

Denver realized it enough to take Stith with the 13th pick of the 1992 draft. It proved a solid decision, as Stith played eight of his 10 NBA seasons with the Nuggets (he spent one season each with the Boston Celtics and Cleveland Cavaliers) before retiring in 2002 with a career scoring average of 10.1 points per game.

Afterward, he fulfilled his mother's prophesy by returning with his wife and their four children to be head basketball coach at Brunswick County

High. The Bulldogs, for those keeping track, advanced to the state championship game in Stith's first six seasons at the helm. And two players who helped them get there were sons B. J. and Brandan. B. J. Stith committed to play at his father's alma mater, whereas Brandan chose East Carolina.

To hear the director of athletics at Brunswick County High tell it, the adulation that for Stith was so hard to come by elsewhere continues to grow by leaps and bounds back home.

"It's almost [like seeing] the Pope walking down the street," Mike Barmoy told Matthew Stanmyre in a special to the *Washington Post* in 2008. "Everyone wants to get a glimpse."

CHRISTIAN LAETTNER

6-11 Center | Duke | 1988–92 | No. 32

1989	Second-team All-Tournament	50
1990	Second-team All-ACC, seventh-most votes	250
	Second-team All-Tournament	50
1991	First-team All-ACC, second-most votes	375
	First-team All-Tournament	75
	ACC POY, runner-up	100
	Final Four MVP	150
	Second-team All-American	150
1992	First-team All-ACC, most votes	400
	Everett Case Award	100
	ACC POY	200
	National POY (with fellow first-team All-Americans Alonzo Mourning of Georgetown, Harold Miner of Southern California, Jim Jackson of Ohio State, and Shaquille O'Neal of LSU)	250
Awards Points		**2,150**

My vote for the most arrogant, caustic, infuriating, and enigmatic player to ever play in the ACC?

Christian Laettner.

Christian Laettner
DUKE SPORTS INFORMATION

And one of the most clutch?

Same answer.

Laettner was hard to be around. He made sure of it.

"If I told you how confident he was, you wouldn't believe it," teammate and best friend Brian Davis said once. "Where do you go after arrogance?"

As a Wake Forest beat writer who occasionally covered Duke, I knew Laettner could be a pain in the ass to deal with for his tendency to hurl questions back in the faces of whoever posed them. That was until Lenox Rawlings, my compadre at the *Winston-Salem Journal*, filled me in.

"If he gives you the business, give it right back," Lenox said. "He'll love it, and he'll respect you. And he'll give you good answers."

Years later, I learned from reading the book Bill Brill wrote with Mike Krzyzewski, *A Season Is a Lifetime*, that Krzyzewski gave pretty much the same advice to teammates driven to distraction and beyond by Laettner's psychological, if not physical, battering.

Bobby Hurley asked Krzyzewski to tell Laettner to take it easy on him.

"Tell him yourself," Krzyzewski said.

Cherokee Parks, a freshman center during Laettner's senior season, once became so infuriated at Laettner that he retreated to the locker room for 20 minutes during practice just to get away from his overbearing teammate.

"I didn't want to be around him at all," Parks explained. "He always gets on you. He pisses me off a lot. I don't know if he's doing it to make me play better, but he's always coming at me with the negativity."

Krzyzewski gave Parks the same advice he gave Hurley.

"That's the way Christian would want somebody to talk to him," Krzyzewski observed.

Laettner had an older brother named Christopher who was already the Chris in the family. Brill wrote in his book how Christopher Laettner (who became an umpire in professional baseball) and his good friend Mike Taylor showed absolutely no mercy while schooling young Christian on the court.

"Going through four or five years, losing against them every day, makes you hate to lose, especially when they rub it in and laugh at you," Laettner explained.

He grew up in Buffalo, where his mom taught school and his father worked for the local newspaper. He was named for Christian Diestl, the German soldier Marlon Brando portrayed in the 1958 film *The Young Lions*.

The Laettners were an exceedingly athletic family. Chris played baseball at the State University of New York in Fredonia. Sister Leanne played volleyball at Valparaiso. Sister Kathrine played basketball at Wingate.

At Duke, Christian listened to Prince and read Stephen King (who, upon hearing of Laettner's literary taste, called him up to chat). He also walked across campus holding hands with a male friend, fueling all the rumors that would spread throughout his career that he was gay. During a nationally televised game at LSU, Tiger fans chanted, "Ho-mo-sexual, ho-mo-sexual!"

He never revealed his sexual persuasion one way or the other—not that it was anyone's business. Most people felt that Laettner was just being Laettner, trying to get a rise. Circumstantial evidence from those who knew him at Duke suggests that he got to know many of the coeds around campus quite well. But maybe that's something Lisa, his wife of more than 15 years and the mother of their three beautiful children, might not want to read.

One thing was certain. Laettner was the player any coach would want to have the ball with a big game on the line.

He made two plays that will live forever in the heavily embossed annals of Duke basketball.

One was his running 15-footer at the buzzer to beat Connecticut 79–78 in overtime and pave the Blue Devils' way to the 1990 Final Four.

The other, which I've heard called the most famous play in college basketball history, was the catch and turnaround jumper at the key to knock off Kentucky 104–103 in double overtime in the regional final during Duke's run to the 1992 national title. He took 10 shots from the floor and 11 from the line in that game and made them all.

He was the best player on two of the best teams ever in the ACC, teams that won back-to-back national championships. And whatever anyone says about Christian Laettner—and that's been plenty over the years—it must be acknowledged how good he was and what he meant not just to Duke but to the ACC.

Al Featherston, the ACC historian whose brain I pick concerning all things pertaining to Duke basketball, makes the case that Laettner is the greatest player in the history of the NCAA Tournament. It's a hard point to disprove, given that he holds the record with 407 points and 23 games and was the first player to participate in four Final Fours.

It's almost enough to make you forget his stomping (or laying his foot down on, whichever you prefer) the chest of Aminu Timberlake in the signature 1992 regional championship victory over Kentucky, an incident he admitted being embarrassed about.

I loved watching him play and even enjoyed dropping by his locker afterward—once I learned how to take him.

Although his game was much better suited to college basketball than to the pros, Laettner was the third pick of the 1992 draft, by the Minnesota Timberwolves. He averaged 12.8 points and 6.7 rebounds for six teams over 13 NBA seasons.

RODNEY MONROE

6-3 Guard | N. C. State | 1987–91 | No. 21

1988	Second-team All-Tournament	50
1989	First-team All-ACC, fourth-most votes	325
1990	Second-team All-ACC, sixth-most votes	275
1991	First-team All-ACC, second-most votes	375
	First-team All-Tournament	75
	ACC POY, contested	175
Awards Points		**1,275**

He was the "Ice" to Chris Corchiani's "Fire."

"He was that way on and off the court," Corchiani told Tim Peeler in *Legends of N.C. State Basketball*, describing Rodney Monroe's persistently unruffled demeanor. "Whether he was walking to class or at a nightclub or in the middle of overtime, he was always very, very reserved. Nothing ever got to him."

That being the case, he was never a player who cost Coach Jim Valvano any sleep.

"We don't worry about Rodney," Valvano said. "We just put 20 points in the book."

Monroe honed his game in his hometown of Baltimore, debuting at age six in a summer league run by his mother. A lifelong Orioles fan, he might have ended up at his state university following an All-American career at St. Maria Goretti High School, except that Lefty Driesell was unceremoniously shown the door at Maryland after Monroe's junior season.

Rodney Monroe
N.C. State Athletics

As unflappable as he was, Monroe was no one to rile. B. J. Armstrong and Roy Marble of Iowa made that mistake before the second round of the 1989 NCAA Tournament, when they found themselves on the same elevator as Monroe and teammate Chucky Brown in Providence the night before the game. Armstrong and Marble, without acknowledging the presence of Monroe and Brown, began engaging in some serious trash talk, putting the Wolfpack down for not having beaten anyone that season.

At their floor, after the doors closed behind them, Monroe turned to Brown.

"Let's kick their asses," Monroe said.

The next day, he more than played his part in doing just that, pouring in 40 points in the Wolfpack's 102–96 double-overtime victory. Monroe twice saved the game, hitting the tying basket in regulation and again in the first overtime.

"I don't think I've ever seen anything quite like that," Armstrong said afterward.

His nickname notwithstanding, when Monroe got hot, few, if any, to play in the ACC were ever hotter. He torched Georgia Tech for 48 as a senior, to the utter awe of Yellow Jackets coach Bobby Cremins.

"Monroe played one of the greatest games an opponent has played against one of my teams," Cremins allowed. "He was fabulous, incredible."

Then there was the game in which Monroe outscored Virginia 30–29 in the second half, rallying the Wolfpack from a 20-point deficit to an 83–76 victory.

"The extraordinary is usual for him," Coach Mike Krzyzewski of Duke observed. "He's one of the truly magnificent players to ever play in this league."

Monroe's inclusion in this book begs a question: Where's Corchiani? How can one be in and not the other? That's like peanut butter without jelly, Laurel without Hardy, gin without tonic (and if you don't know what that's like, take it from me, don't try it).

Few tabulations I made for this honor were more surprising than those for Corchiani during his four seasons at N.C. State. The upshot? He wasn't close enough to even try to finagle a way to get him in. The NCAA's all-time leader in assists when he closed his college career, Corchiani never made first-team All-ACC. He barely missed twice, finishing sixth in the voting as a sophomore in 1989 and as a senior in 1991. He still ranks third all-time in the ACC with 328 steals but never received even a protest vote for ACC Player of the Year, never made first-team All-Tournament, and never came within a country mile of being considered for consensus All-American. His only national hardware came his senior year, when the National Association of Basketball Coaches found a spot for him on its third team.

So add up Corchiani's 550 points for twice finishing sixth in ACC voting, his 150 points for being named third-team All-ACC with the 11th-most votes as a junior, and his 50 for making second-team All-Tournament as a senior, and that comes to 750 points.

I can think of only one person whose opinions on matters pertaining to ACC basketball I value as much as those of Barry Jacobs. And he would be Al Featherston, the longtime scribe for the *Durham Sun* and *Durham Herald-Sun* who has been writing books and freelancing for websites since his first newspaper was lost to merger and his second was dismantled by corporate types. Around adult beverages at the ACC Tournament, we've agreed that the one statistic that over the years has not been given its proper due is assists.

Take the ACC's top 10 in all-time assists. The busts of only three—Bobby Hurley, Greivis Vasquez, and Kenny Smith—can be found in this humble volume. Left on the outside looking in are Corchiani, Ed Cota, Steve Blake, Grayson Marshall, Chris Duhon, Muggsy Bogues, and Sidney Lowe.

At no place in this book do I argue that I've concocted the perfect method of picking a Hall of Fame. But I still contend it beats anything anyone else has come up with. Don't like the exclusion of Corchiani and the others? Take it up with the people who don't give enough weight to assists in the All-ACC voting.

Monroe was the second-round pick of the Atlanta Hawks in 1991, but his game did not translate well to the play-for-pay set. He appeared in 38 games for the Hawks and scored a total of 131 points—or 3.4 per game.

Corchiani hung around a bit longer. The second-round pick of Orlando that summer, he played in 112 games for the Magic, Washington Bullets, and Boston Celtics.

J. R. REID

6-9 Forward │ North Carolina │ 1986–89 │ No. 34

J. R. Reid was no typical college freshman. Rival coach Jim Valvano of N.C. State insisted he wasn't a freshman at all.

"I swear I saw him play in the marines somewhere, I think it was 1967 or '68," Valvano maintained. "He's so good already, he should go hardship right now."

J. R. Reid
UNC ATHLETIC COMMUNICATIONS

1987	ACC ROY	100
	Second-team All-ACC, sixth-most votes	275
	Second-team All-Tournament	50
1988	First-team All-ACC, unanimous	425
	First-team All-Tournament	75
	First-team All-American (with Sean Elliott of Arizona, Gary Grant of Michigan, Hersey Hawkins of Bradley, and Danny Manning of Kansas)	200
1989	Everett Case Award	100
Awards Points		1,225

By the time he did in fact leave North Carolina early, after a trying junior season, I remember no flood of tears. In many ways, Reid, an enormous talent who was involved with more off-court incidents than any coach wants to abide, had worn out his welcome.

Yet it should not be forgotten just how big Reid was in 1986, the year he and his trademark haircut—in his own words, a ski-slope box with fade on the sides—showed up in Chapel Hill. Dubbed the best high-school player in the nation, Reid had been featured in the *Sporting News*, *USA Today*, and

People. Early in his ACC career, his photograph was on the cover of *Sports Illustrated* dunking over Wake Forest's Sam Ivy and Ralph Kitley. For his part, Coach Dean Smith would have preferred the magazine hadn't referred to a mere freshman as "North Carolina's Main Man."

His impact on the court was substantial, as witnessed by his 14.7 points and 7.4 rebounds a game and his field-goal accuracy of 58 percent as a freshman.

But Reid's sophomore season got off to a belated start when he and teammate Steve Bucknall were suspended for the opening game against Syracuse for their assault on an N.C. State student in a Raleigh nightclub. And as most of us scribes of the time will attest, the gregarious, if somewhat cocky, freshman wasn't nearly as much fun to deal with as he morphed into a less cooperative and ever more self-absorbed sophomore and junior.

Before the 1989 ACC Tournament, Reid's junior season was most noteworthy for a sign fans held up in Duke's Cameron Indoor Stadium that proclaimed, "J. R. Can't Reid." And with that infamous display of snarky schoolboy/schoolgirl humor, the Crazies blew the lid off the already bubbling rivalry between entrenched power North Carolina and the ever-emerging Blue Devil program it was finding harder and harder to beat.

Coach Dean Smith was never a man to let a slight to himself or a Tar Heel player go unanswered—especially one that registered on his finely tuned racism detector. Smith fired back, revealing that the combined Scholastic Aptitude Test scores of Reid and black teammate Scott Williams were higher than those of Duke's white teammates Danny Ferry and Christian Laettner. Smith's comments—which sent the Duke faithful into convulsions—underscored his long-held belief that standardized tests are culturally biased. Reid and Williams, in fact, had excelled thanks in part to their middle-class backgrounds. Reid's father, Herman Sr., played football at St. Augustine's College in Raleigh and, like his wife, became a teacher. They raised their son in the comfort of a ranch-style home located in a well-manicured upper-middle-class neighborhood in Virginia Beach.

The back-and-forth barbs lanced the spleens of both programs, resulting in what may have been the most brutally contentious ACC Tournament championship game ever. How else can one explain the legendarily graphic exchange between Smith and Mike Krzyzewski as their teams were going at it hammer and tongs?

Krzyzewski, concerned the fray was getting out of hand, yelled at Williams of North Carolina, telling him not to foul so hard.

To which Smith replied, "Don't talk to my players."

To which Krzyzewski responded, "Hey, Dean, fuck you."

My, what times we had.

Duke's prominence by then was every bit as great as North Carolina's, and its star, senior Danny Ferry, was widely recognized as the best player in college basketball, as would be affirmed within weeks when he was named consensus National Player of the Year.

Reid was coming off a disappointing junior season beset by infighting with the team and personal difficulties. But under the bright lights of the Omni in Atlanta, when everything was on the line and the fans of both teams were screaming for blood, Reid gave Ferry all he wanted and more. Though both players scored 14 points, Reid finished with nine rebounds to Ferry's seven. And Ferry struggled with his shot, making only six of 20 from the floor.

One lasting memory from the game was Reid knocking Ferry to the floor and standing over him taunting, "Take that, Mr. Naismith."

The other was Ferry's 90-foot heave at the buzzer that would have sent the game into overtime. It rimmed out, and the Tar Heels, much to the relief of their coach, prevailed 77–74.

"I don't know if this old man's heart could have taken it if Ferry had made that one," Smith said.

The old man's heart was tested again a week later when Reid broke curfew before a second-round NCAA Tournament game against UCLA and was sent home from Atlanta.

"Coach Smith left it up to the seniors, [Jeff] Lebo and Bucknall," reserve Marty Hensley said. "I guess they figured we could win without J. R."

If so, they were right. The Tar Heels advanced past the Bruins 88–81 before getting derailed the next weekend by Glen Rice and Michigan with Reid back in action.

According to Art Chansky in *The Dean's List*, Reid was not pushed out the door. But J. R. did disagree with Smith's new substitution system of allotting predetermined minutes to players in the first half of each game.

So when Reid decided he'd had enough of college basketball, Smith made calls to help him get drafted by the Charlotte Hornets as the fifth overall pick.

Reid was good enough to spend 11 seasons in the NBA with six different teams. But his career averages of 8.5 points and five rebounds didn't exactly live up to what was expected from one who many in the dizzying days of 1986 thought would change the way the game was played.

DANNY FERRY

6-10 Center | Duke | 1985–89 | No. 35

1987	Second-team All-ACC, seventh-most votes	250
1988	First-team All-ACC, unanimous	425
	Everett Case Award	100
	ACC POY	200
	Second-team All-American	150
1989	First-team All-ACC, unanimous	425
	First-team All-Tournament	75
	ACC POY	200
	National POY (with fellow first-team All-Americans	250
	Mahmoud Abdul-Rauf of LSU, Pervis Ellison of Louisville,	
	Sean Elliott of Arizona, and Stacey King of Oklahoma)	
Awards Points		**2,075**

There may never have been another ACC player who had as many advantages as Danny Ferry—whose father, Bob, became vice president and general manager of the Washington Bullets after playing in the league for 10 seasons; whose brother, also Bob, turned down a chance to play for Jim Valvano at N.C. State to compete instead at Harvard; and whose godfather, Gene Shue, coached the Bullets and Clippers after his days as a star at Maryland and in the NBA.

"I don't deny that I've kind of been raised with a silver spoon," Ferry once acknowledged.

From a young age, Ferry was driven to make the most of his considerable blessings. He didn't stop until he became the best player in college basketball.

His favorite childhood haunt was the Capital Centre—except for the time Bullets star Wes Unseld held him by his legs over a staircase with a 15-foot drop. Ferry said he was petrified until he realized that if anyone was strong enough to pull off that stunt, it was Unseld. And besides, he was the boss's son.

Recognizing that the competition at St. Mark's School in Hyattsville, Maryland, might not be up to snuff for an aspiring star, Ferry, at age 15, began catching the subway into Washington to play in a downtown summer league.

Danny Ferry

His teammates, all black, were concerned enough about him that they would meet him at the station and accompany him to the gym.

By then, he had learned to quit playing one-on-one with his older brother. Every attempt seemed to end in a fistfight. He later absorbed the teachings of Morgan Wootten, who won more than 800 games as coach of DeMatha High School.

Mike Krzyzewski observed that Ferry had all the attributes of a classic coach's son.

"He was smart, fundamentally sound, understood the game," Krzyzewski said in Jim Sumner's *Tales from the Duke Blue Devils Hardwood*. "But most coaches' sons are 6-1.

"Danny was 6-10, which made him all the more unique."

Another attribute that set Ferry apart was his sense of humor, which apparently ran in the family. When Harvard played at Duke, his brother talked Coach Frank McLaughlin into allowing him to send a teammate out during pregame introductions. The Crazies of Cameron couldn't miss the put-on when the name Bob Ferry was called and a black player emerged from the Harvard huddle.

Ferry's roommate and best friend at Duke was Quin Snyder. But that didn't prevent Ferry from pulling a fast one on his pal. Snyder had a date one night, so Ferry loaned him his car. But when the lovebirds came out of the restaurant, the car was gone. Snyder just knew Ferry was going to kill him—at least until he learned Ferry had used a second set of keys to move the car. Not only that, Ferry and a confederate had decorated the vehicle with cans and streamers and the words *Just Married* scrawled on the window.

Ferry and Snyder were hell on younger teammates. The two convinced rookies Brian Davis, Christian Laettner, and Crawford Palmer that it was a team tradition for freshmen to carry the seniors' bags on road trips. It wasn't, but the shenanigans worked so well that Ferry and Snyder extended what was concocted as a one-game prank into a season-long practice.

"He's a team guy, a goof-off guy, a guy's guy," Krzyzewski once noted of Ferry. "The main thing is, he's a winner."

Ferry picked up enough tricks along the way to know how to get under the skin of opponents. After playing Duke during Ferry's junior season, Kenny Green of Rhode Island called him the dirtiest player he had ever gone against.

Teammates knew what Green was talking about.

"Danny had an NBA mentality," teammate Robert Brickey told Sumner in *Tales from the Duke Blue Devils Hardwood*. "He knew all the tricks, footwork, ball fakes, that sort of thing. He also knew how to apply a subtle hip check or forearm that would be effective, but wouldn't be obvious."

Ferry's game came together like never before early in his senior year, when Duke visited Miami two weeks ahead of Christmas. The quick but small Hurricanes were willing to run with Duke. Ferry capitalized by scoring 34 points in the first half.

He kept it going all night, hitting 23 of 26 shots from the floor (only two of them three-pointers) and 10 of 12 from the line to score 58 points, breaking the conference record of 57 that David Thompson had scored against Buffalo in 1974.

"I think Danny was a member of the Hall of Justice tonight," Snyder said afterward. "Something divine was going on. Danny could have swallowed kryptonite tonight."

Ferry's road to NBA stardom took a detour to Europe and never really made it back.

Determined not to play for the Los Angeles Clippers, who plucked him with the second pick of the 1989 draft, Ferry signed instead with a professional team in Italy for a reported $2 million and the use of a plush villa.

Cleveland traded for his rights the next summer, after which Ferry began a 13-year career with the Cavaliers and San Antonio Spurs that never really lived up to expectations. Over 917 NBA games, he averaged seven points and 2.8 rebounds.

Ferry's biggest impact on the pro game has been as an executive. He made the same transition from the court to the front office as his father. From 2005 through 2010, he served as general manager of the Cavaliers. He stepped aside at the end of his five-year contract and later became vice president of basketball operations for the San Antonio Spurs. On June 25, 2012, he was named general manager of the Atlanta Hawks.

KENNY SMITH

6-3 Guard | North Carolina | 1983–87 | No. 30

1985	Second-team All-ACC, 10th-most votes	175
	First-team All-Tournament	75
1986	Second-team All-ACC, eighth-most votes	225
1987	First-team All-ACC, second-most votes	375
	Second-team All-Tournament	50
	First-team All-American (with Steve Alford of Indiana, Danny Manning of Kansas, David Robinson of Navy, and Reggie Williams of Georgetown)	200
Awards Points		**1,100**

"If history repeats itself, and the unexpected always happens, how incapable must man be of learning from experience?"
—George Bernard Shaw

The two greatest I have watched coach game in and game out were Dean Smith and Mike Krzyzewski. Both made the same decision in the same situation—which probably was the only one they could have made.

But the decision ended up costing their teams precious mojo when it mattered most, in the win-or-go-home NCAA Tournament. Both brought a star freshman guard back from injury after scorching late regular-season runs, and both went home earlier than anyone expected.

Kenny Smith and Kyrie Irving were two of the most precocious freshmen point guards I've ever had the privilege of watching play ACC basketball. Those who get paid for their opinions apparently agree, in that Smith was the sixth-overall pick of the 1987 draft, while Irving was the very first in 2011.

If George Bernard Shaw had been coaching Duke in 2011 (I know he died in 1950 and probably didn't know a basketball from a tetherball, but play along), maybe he wouldn't have brought Irving back from a toe injury to play in the NCAA Tournament. After all, he would have had the history lesson from 27 years earlier to inform his decision.

North Carolina was well on its way to its 17th victory without a loss when John Tudor of LSU took down Smith beneath the basket in Carmichael Auditorium on January 29, 1984. The Tar Heels were ranked number one at the time, as might be expected for a team that featured Smith, Michael Jordan, Sam Perkins, and Brad Daugherty.

But a funny thing happened in the eight games Smith sat recovering from a broken wrist. Steve Hale moved seamlessly into the lineup, and the Tar Heels reeled off seven wins in eight games, their only loss a 65–64 upset to Arkansas in Pine Bluff.

Dean Smith integrated Kenny Smith back into his plans for the final two games of the regular season—which made the Tar Heels anything but a well-oiled machine over the final six contests of Jordan's career. They needed two overtimes to beat Duke on Senior Day in Carmichael Auditorium, were bounced by the emerging Blue Devils in the semifinals of the ACC Tournament, and then lost to Indiana 72–68 in the second round of the NCAA Tournament in the infamous "Dan Dakich game" in Atlanta, in which the unheralded Hoosier guard held Jordan to 13 points and fouled him out.

Krzyzewski's considerations differed in 2011. Instead of missing eight games, Irving was lost for 26. And Krzyzewski didn't get him back until the first game of the NCAA Tournament.

It's also true that the Blue Devils dropped two of their final three in the regular season, though it's hard to find shame in road losses at Virginia Tech and North Carolina. But the way they put it all together in the ACC Tournament in Greensboro—blowing past Maryland 87–71, Virginia Tech 77–63, and North Carolina 75–58—had to make Krzyzewski wonder if he was right to blend Irving back into the mix. After all, Nolan Smith was never better than in the semifinals and finals, when he burned the Hokies for 27 points and six assists and the Tar Heels for 20 points and 10 assists on the way to winning the Everett Case Award. And given that Smith had settled nicely into the point guard's role, Irving's return was obviously going to shuffle the deck.

After trouncing Hampton 87–45 in the opening round in Charlotte, Duke played two more games. In the second round, a 73–71 victory over Michigan, Smith played well (24 points on 8-of-13 field-goal accuracy) and Irving didn't (11 points, one of four from the floor). In the last game, a 93–77 drubbing by Arizona, Irving was the star with 28 points, while Smith (eight points, six turnovers) just never got going.

I read afterward that Krzyzewski made a mistake, if not for bringing Ir-

Kenny Smith
UNC ATHLETIC
COMMUNICATIONS

ving back to play, then for relying on him so much it wrecked the Blue Devils' chemistry. Shaw might have agreed, but I didn't. When you have a Kyrie Irving, you play him whenever you have the chance. He was that good.

And Dean Smith could have said the same about Kenny Smith 27 years earlier.

The youngest of four children born to William and Annie Smith of Queens, Smith showed enough promise at a young age that his older brother, Vincent, basically sacrificed his own basketball career to bring along young Kenny. Vincent convinced his kid brother to enter the Pepsi Hot-Shot Contest and coached him well enough that Kenny, at 11, won his national age group.

"That's when we began working intensively on my game," Smith said in *Carolina Court: Inside Tar Heel Basketball*. "Each level of competition was held at a different NBA city, and my goal was always to get to the next city. That's when my shooting caught up with the rest of my game."

Smith honed his moves at Lost Battalion Gym in Queens, where he first ignited the retro rockets that earned him one of his two nicknames, "the Jet."

"I used to sneak in and play with the bigger guys and that's how I developed my dribbling," Smith told Draggan Mihailovich of the *Chapel Hill Newspaper*. "I kept working on my speed so I could beat everyone down court to get a layup. That's the only way I could score."

Brother Vincent wasn't the only family member with a special interest in Kenny's game. William Smith took early retirement after 17 years with Consolidated Edison partly so he could see his son play whenever possible.

"My father pushed without yelling like some fathers do," Smith told Gerald Martin, the gone and much-missed writer for Raleigh's *News & Observer*. "My father never yelled. He never embarrassed me, and he has been at every game since I was in high school. He missed [an exhibition in] Greece, but when we got back he came down and watched films."

At Archbishop Malloy in Queens, where he played for the legendary Jack Curran a few years before another Kenny, named Anderson, showed up, Smith received his other nickname, "Special K." When not outracing opponents downcourt, he was rapping along with seven buddies known as "Super Sound," who hired themselves out at parties.

He didn't know how to drive when he reported to Chapel Hill in the fall of 1983 because he didn't have to back home. But his choice of schools did drive to distraction Coach Terry Holland and Assistant Coach Jim Larranaga of Virginia, who had recruited Smith doggedly.

"At Virginia, they were saying they'd contend in two or three years," Smith told Alexander Wolff of *Sports Illustrated*. "Here I could see it for all four years. If that's the goal of everybody in America, why wait?"

To which Larranaga, a Malloy grad, replied, "He's making a mistake."

Holland couldn't resist his own jab: "I don't think Dean knows exactly what he's getting."

What Smith got was a point guard good enough to play 10 years in the NBA, six of them with the Houston Rockets. He played a total of 737 NBA games, averaging 12.8 points and 5.5 assists.

As articulate and fun as Smith was at North Carolina, I'm not surprised to see the career he built for himself as Charles Barkley's foil on TNT's NBA coverage. Nor, given his love of the limelight, was I surprised to read that he founded his own marketing and production company, KSEG (Kenny Smith Entertainment Group), which signed a young artist named Kayla Brianna to a record contract.

Kayla Brianna is also known as Kenny Smith's daughter.

MARK PRICE

6-0 Guard | Georgia Tech | 1982–86 | No. 25

1983	Second-team All-ACC, ninth-most votes	200
	Second-team All-Tournament	50
	ACC ROY	100
1984	First-team All-ACC, fifth-most votes	300
	Second-team All-Tournament	50
1985	First-team All-ACC, third-most votes	350
	Everett Case Award	100
1986	First-team All-ACC, fourth-most votes	325
	Second-team All-Tournament	50
	Second-team All-American	150
Awards Points		**1,675**

Much as Jesus built his church on a rock, Bobby Cremins built the Georgia Tech basketball program on a white guard from Oklahoma too rock-headed to accept the stereotype of being too small and slow to excel in college basketball.

When Mark Price was 16 and growing up in Enid, Oklahoma, he confided to his mother, Mary Ann, his great fear—that he wouldn't grow tall enough to attract a college scholarship.

"I remember one night sitting on the edge of his bed, visiting about things," Mary Ann Price told *Sports Illustrated.* "And he said to me, 'I just hope I get to be good enough that one school will want me. Just one school.' "

That one school, of course, turned out to be Georgia Tech, fighting for respect in a conference it had joined only four seasons before Price's arrival. After averaging just seven victories the previous three years, the Yellow Jackets won 13 when Price was a freshman, 18 when he was a sophomore, 27 (and an ACC championship) when he was a junior, and 27 when he was a senior.

Cremins dispatched Assistant Coach George Felton to find him a point guard. Felton discovered one from an unlikely place.

"We absolutely had to get a point guard," Cremins told Jim Sumner of

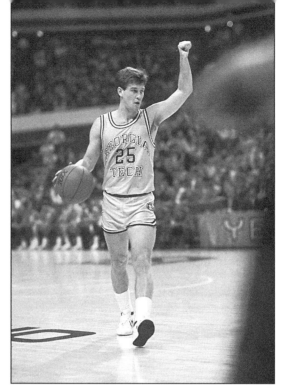

Mark Price
GEORGIA TECH ATHLETICS

theACC.com. "I sent George Felton across the country to find one. He calls me from Jacksonville, Florida, and tells me he's found our guy."

Felton reported, "I'm watching an AAU tournament and the kid we want is from Enid, Oklahoma."

Price grew up a North Carolina fan. Dean Smith even attended one of his practices in high school.

"But they basically told me I was too small," Price explained to the *Charleston Post-Courier* years later. "They never offered me a scholarship."

Cremins recruited other front-line ACC-caliber players as well—power forwards John Salley and Tom Hammonds, guard Bruce Dalrymple, wing forward Duane Ferrell—but Price was the star.

"He's not the average white point guard," Salley told *SI*. "He plays like he's 6-5, a Larry Bird type.

"If coach was to let him go, he'd have 40 a night against anybody."

The 1984–85 Yellow Jackets—who beat sixth-ranked North Carolina 57–54 in the Omni in Atlanta for the program's first ACC title—were as loose and fun-loving a team as any I've ever had the joy to cover. It is said that a team reflects the attitude of its coach, and the Yellow Jackets, like Cremins, were quite a trip to be around.

Price was more reserved than gregarious teammates Salley (who has ridden his gift of gab into a post-basketball career as a television personality), Dalrymple, and Scott Petway, a six-five reserve guard who wore a ducktail that reflected his love of classic rock 'n' roll. But Price was always cooperative, considerate, and easy to talk with.

On the court, he was hard-nosed, determined, and unwilling to back down from anyone, be it Johnny Dawkins, Michael Jordan, Adrian Branch, or Kenny Smith.

One of my indelible memories of Price dates to a night Georgia Tech played at N.C. State's Reynolds Coliseum, which always provided the best seats in the house to the assembled media. Price received the ball on the left wing, directly in front of me, and squared to shoot. Nate McMillan, a six-five player with arms that seemed to stretch past his knees, rushed out to check Price, who leaned so far back I thought he was going to fall over the press-row table. Transfixed, I watched over Price's right shoulder as the shot barely cleared McMillan's fingertips, arced toward the rafters, and swished through the net, dead center.

"He's got more brass than a cannon," Coach Bill Foster of Miami told *SI*. "He just takes it right in your face and he shoots it deep.

"He's the most exciting player I know about."

His father was his shooting coach. Denny Price knew a bit about the game from having played for Phillips 66, a regional power in AAU circles.

"He's the only one who can fix my shot," Price said.

But Price always answered first to a higher power, the one he worshipped every Sunday morning. Cremins even rescheduled practice times around Price's church services. Price occasionally sang in church as part of a quartet with his father and two brothers, Brent and Matt.

Although never a stranger to church, he dedicated his life to his Lord during a revival meeting in 1981.

"All those years I thought I was fine because I was going to church," Price told *SI*. "But just like being in a garage doesn't make you a car, being in church doesn't make you a Christian."

Price agreed to direct Bobby Cremins's first great teams. He asked one thing in return.

"The only thing I've ever done is ask him not to take the Lord's name in vain," Price told *SI*. "That's something I can't tolerate.

"But I don't get in people's faces and tell them they're going to hell. I can't stop loving my teammates if they don't believe the same way I do."

I was lucky to get to know Chris Capo during his days as an assistant sports information director at Wake Forest. He's a smart guy—smart enough to marry another friend of mine who was also an assistant sports information director at Wake, Joanna Sparkman. Capo is as steeped in Georgia Tech sports as anyone I know. He grew up in Atlanta and has now returned with Joanna to raise their family. He agreed to look at what I had written on the three Yellow Jackets honored in this book—Price, Kenny Anderson, and Matt Harpring. What should be remembered about Price, Capo stressed, is just how popular he was, and remains, at Georgia Tech.

The late 1970s were an unsettling time for those who loved Georgia Tech athletics. University president Joseph Pettit openly mulled whether or not the school should de-emphasize athletics and take the route more associated with MIT and the University of Chicago. Bobby Ross's success on the football field helped the Tech sports program regain its footing, but it was the way Bobby Cremins made Yellow Jackets basketball one of the coolest things in town that really solidified the standing of Georgia Tech athletics. And Cremins, everyone recognized, couldn't have done it without Price. In the galaxy of Georgia Tech sports, Capo ventured, Price may well be the brightest star other than Bobby Dodd, the legendary football coach for whom the stadium is named.

When Coach Paul Hewitt was cashiered after the 2010–11 season, there was a groundswell around campus to name Price his successor despite his lack of experience. Maybe he should have been hired. He's been proving people wrong for going on 30 years.

Once Price started proving people wrong, he didn't stop until he'd played 12 NBA seasons for the Cleveland Cavaliers, Washington Bullets, Golden State Warriors, and Orlando Magic. A second-round pick by Dallas (which quickly traded him to Cleveland), Price was better than fans may remember. He averaged at least 15.8 points a game for the Cavaliers for eight straight seasons, topping out at 19.6 in 1991. His free-throw percentages of 90.4 in the regular season and 94.4 in the playoffs remain as of this writing NBA records.

Price's wife, Laura, played tennis at Georgia Tech as a walk-on, so it didn't come as a huge surprise when their daughter, Caroline, became good enough in the sport to play at North Carolina.

But it's back at Georgia Tech, the school he attended once North Carolina turned him down, that Price will be remembered as the great guard who got the good times started.

"We became a hot team," Cremins told Sumner. "We could talk to any recruit in the country. The success of these guys made it possible for us to get the Dennis Scotts and the Kenny Andersons and all the rest.

"We were young and really didn't know what we were doing. We were maybe too naïve to realize that we weren't supposed to win, so we went out and did it."

JOHNNY DAWKINS

6-2 Guard | Duke | 1982–86 | No. 24

1983	Second-team All-ACC, 10th-most votes	175
1984	Second-team All-ACC, seventh-most votes	250
	First-team All-Tournament	75
1985	First-team All-ACC, fourth-most votes	325
	First-team All-Tournament	75
	First-team All-American (with Patrick Ewing of Georgetown, Keith Lee of Memphis State, Xavier McDaniel of Wichita State, Chris Mullin of St. John's, and Wayman Tisdale of Oklahoma)	200
1986	First-team All-ACC, third-most votes	50
	Everett Case Award	100
	First-team All-American (with Steve Alford of Indiana, Walter Berry of St. John's, Len Bias of Maryland, and Kenny Walker of Kentucky)	200
Awards Points		**1,750**

If you take Jay Bilas's word for it, Johnny Dawkins was the most important player ever at Duke.

Bilas, Dawkins's teammate who has carved out an illustrious career as a college basketball analyst, didn't base his observation simply on the 2,556 points Dawkins scored at Duke, a school record until broken by J. J. Redick in 2006. Instead, he was assessing the impact Dawkins had just by casting his lot with young coach Mike Krzyzewski in the first place.

Dawkins was, after all, the one essential recruit in the six-man class that improved Duke's fortunes from 10–17 the season before he arrived to 37–3 by his senior campaign. And other than a couple of backfires, the loudest coming during a 13–18 season in 1994–95, the Blue Devils have been purring along like a Ferrari ever since.

Bilas couldn't see that far ahead the day he met Dawkins. In fact, he couldn't see past the scrawny stranger who opened the door when he, on Krzyzewski's suggestion, dropped by Dawkins's Washington, D.C., home before the two were scheduled to report to Duke.

Johnny Dawkins
Duke Sports Informatiion

"I opened the front door and this kid opens it," Bilas recalled to Jake Curtis of the *San Francisco Chronicle*. "I figure it's Dawkins' little brother, so I ask if Johnny Dawkins is around. He says, 'I'm Johnny Dawkins.'

"I'm thinking, 'Man, we're screwed.' "

What Bilas soon found out was that Dawkins, while wiry, was strong as tempered steel and could run all day without getting winded. He could also take care of himself on the court.

His father and his father's three brothers had made sure of that.

Johnny Dawkins Sr. drove a city bus for 27 years and always requested the 4 A.M.–to–noon shift. That way, he could hit the playgrounds for some basketball in the afternoon.

By age 10, Dawkins was going with his father and uncles to Fort Stevens Recreation Center in D.C. to play against grownups. And few, if any, of the regulars were more grown up than his father, who stood two inches taller than Dawkins and could dunk past the age of 40.

"My father still plays with me," Dawkins told Robert Markus of the *Chicago Tribune* in 1986. "He still can dunk on me, but I think I can handle him now.

"Maybe I better not say that. He might read it."

Another early influence was Tim Sleven, a CYO coach who had the foresight to teach his charges the fundamentals of the game. To that end, Sleven had Dawkins, from the time he was in the third grade, dribble while wearing blinders. Sleven also taught him to improve his hand speed with the use of a paddleball and by trying to grab a ball bounced in front of him.

Dawkins learned early that the world of organized basketball stood apart from the brand found on the playgrounds. Though he respected the blacktop legends, "a number of those guys can't play organized basketball," Dawkins told Markus. "They don't have the structure."

Dawkins was a sharp player, a sharp person, and an exceedingly sharp dresser. Teammate David Henderson once noted that Dawkins never wore an article of clothing that didn't have a name on it.

"Sure, I like to look sharp," Dawkins told Steve Hummer of the *Atlanta Journal-Constitution*. "I iron my clothes. I like my things to be pressed. I iron everything. It makes no difference. It has to have a crease."

His meticulousness was apparent from an early age. His father, who called him "Pooh," said the trait likely came from Dawkins's mother. Peggy Dawkins washed her sneakers so often they came apart.

"In his closet, all of Pooh's hangers are exactly one inch apart," Johnny Dawkins Sr. told Jake Curtis. "He'd say, 'My hangers are off. I can tell you were in my closet.' "

It was equally obvious that Dawkins, even as a young man, was driven to excel. He was known for playing two games in the stifling summer heat, then asking to be dropped off at a neighborhood park on the way home so he could shoot into the night. His wife-to-be, Tracy, spent much of their courtship rebounding the basketball and throwing it back to Dawkins.

Now, that's love.

"Johnny is one of those people with a lot of pride," Krzyzewski told Hummer in 1986. "They are constantly sending out a message: I am really someone worthwhile."

But Dawkins's pride wasn't such that, after a nine-year NBA career with the San Antonio Spurs, Philadelphia 76ers, and Detroit Pistons, he had a problem starting on the ground floor of his new career. Wanting to break into athletics administration, he began in the ticket office back at Duke.

"People would look through the window and say, 'Wow, I can't believe that's you,' " Dawkins told Curtis.

Dawkins's path led him back to the game as a coach. After 11 years as an assistant for Krzyzewski at Duke, he was named head coach at Stanford before the 2008–9 season.

LEN BIAS

6-8 Forward | Maryland | 1982–86 | No. 34

1984	Everett Case Award	100
1985	First-team All-ACC, unanimous	425
	ACC POY, contested	175
	Second-team All-American	150
1986	First-team All-ACC, unanimous	425
	First-team All-Tournament	75
	ACC POY	200
	First-team All-American (with Steve Alford of Indiana, Walter Berry of St. John's, Johnny Dawkins of Duke, and Kenny Walker of Kentucky)	200
Awards Points		**1,750**

Enough has been written, said, and documented about the way Len Bias died. Instead, I'll concentrate on who he was before becoming a worldwide symbol of how much damage drugs can do.

Friends and family called him "Frosty." None of the thousands of words I read about his death and its messy aftermath told me why. I got my answer by returning to *ACC Basketball*, Ron Morris's treasured account of the first 35 years of the conference.

When he was born, Bias had what his mother described as a "little white layer of skin on him."

"And he peeled a lot," she explained.

Lonise Bias worked in a bank. Her husband, James, was an electrician who also repaired heavy equipment. The deeply religious couple raised three sons and a daughter in the Columbia Road neighborhood of Landover, Maryland. Len was the eldest.

Gangly and physically uncertain of himself as a middle-schooler, he showed up as a freshman at Northwestern High School in Hyattsville ready and able to play.

"In eighth grade he was uncoordinated, in ninth grade he was awesome," a friend named Aaron Bell told the *Philadelphia Daily News*. "It seemed like an overnight change."

Len Bias
University of
Maryland Archives

If you happened to attend a Maryland game in Cole Field House in the late 1970s and liked ice cream, Len Bias might have sold you some. Probably not, though. Friends remember how he used the job to get inside to see the games himself, often allowing his product to melt.

He spent his high-school summers working as a counselor at a local facility, Columbia Park. He returned there often, even after becoming a star at nearby Maryland.

James Bias was a father a son could talk with when the need arose—but also one who was rarely reticent when it came to prodding those he loved to be the best they could. Fortunately, Len, who regularly climbed out of bed at six in the morning to run and just as regularly was the last player off the court after practice, didn't need much prodding.

He played at Northwestern High School for Bob Wagner, who said Bias's star got so bright that it outshone even that of Sugar Ray Leonard from nearby Palmer Park. What one AAU coach remembers about Bias was how fast he picked up the game. Show him something in practice on Tuesday afternoon and he would use it in the game Wednesday night.

He was always drawing—on napkins, matchbooks, anything he could find. He told friends he saw himself taking up interior design when his basketball days were done.

He loved winding down with music. He listened mostly to gospel and jazz.

He was a clotheshorse, seeking out the latest fashions in Georgetown for his Greek god–like 195-pound body. He told friends in his last days that he was really getting into the *Miami Vice* look.

He drove an Oldsmobile Cutlass before leasing a Datsun at the end of his career at Maryland. But he planned to buy a Mercedes when the pro and endorsement money came rolling in.

His relationship with the media was rarely anything for long before it became something else. Michael Wilbon, then of the *Washington Post*, remembers a freshman Bias so unsure of himself he could barely finish a sentence. But he got the hang of it, especially when the subject was something that interested him, like music or clothes.

By his senior season, he was pretty much done with all the questions.

Wilbon recalls walking into a preseason Media Day, after Bias had been named ACC Player of the Year the previous campaign, and seeing Bias surrounded while his teammates stood wondering what to do.

"This is crazy," Bias said, apparently to Wilbon. "You've got to tell these guys that they can't just talk to me and leave my teammates sitting there. This is embarrassing. How is it going to look when I'm the only one on television and in the paper?"

Like all the great ones, he burned to be great.

If he drank a beer, he ran extra the next day to melt the calories.

He struggled with his handle as a freshman, so he enlisted the help of his good friend and teammate Keith Gatlin, whose course of action was to blindfold Bias and make him dribble and dribble and dribble by feel alone.

Most of all, he wanted to get the ball inside and dunk. Bias and Gatlin roomed together on the road. As Gatlin remembered it to the *Washington Post*, the two had a ritual every night when it was time to turn out the lights.

"Who you going to throw the ball to?" Bias would ask.

"You, big fella," Gatlin would answer.

"Okay, now I can sleep," Bias replied.

"I think if I did anything else in life, I could become successful at it," Bias once told the *Baltimore Sun*. "I just want to be better than anybody thought I could become. Whenever anybody has criticized me, I've worked harder. When people said I couldn't shoot, I worked on my shot. When people said I wasn't a ball handler, I worked on that."

On the court, he had an edge that veered from time to time into scowling arrogance. He played with sharp elbows but didn't always take as well as he gave. He bitched constantly to officials.

"He was a young 22," Wagner, his high-school coach, told *Sports Illustrated*.

That's one big reason the 21,444 Tar Heel fans who packed the brand-spanking-new Dean Dome had so much trouble stomaching what they saw on February 20, 1986, the night Bias stuck it to them. The top-ranked Tar Heels led the 14–11 and unranked Terps most of the game, but with Bias driving for dunks and pulling up over double teams for jumpers, they couldn't pull away.

In overtime, Bias drilled a jumper from deep on the left wing, dashed in to steal the inbounds pass from Warren Martin, and soared for a reverse flush. He then sealed the legendary 77–72 upset by blocking a driving layup by Kenny Smith.

"Len put on one of the greatest performances I've ever seen by an opposing player when he played [here] last season," Dean Smith said upon the news of Bias's death four months later. "All we could do when it was over was congratulate him."

Gatlin described the performance as literally divine.

"God was with us tonight, and God means Len Bias," he said after the game.

But Terps coach Lefty Driesell was not to be outdone in his hyperbole.

"If Len Bias is not the player of the world," Driesell drawled, "then people just don't know basketball."

The Boston Celtics knew enough basketball to draft Bias with the second pick of the 1986 draft. He stood to make more than $1 million—around $700,000 from the Celtics and $325,000 for an endorsement deal with Reebok.

Two days later, in a dorm room on Maryland's campus, he had an early-morning seizure and died. The cause was deemed to be cocaine intoxication.

Larry Bird, the Celtics' star, told the Boston media, "It's the cruelest thing I've ever heard."

MARK ALARIE

6-8 Forward | Duke | 1982–86 | No. 32

Year	Award	Points
1984	First-team All-ACC, fourth-most votes	325
	First-team All-Tournament	75
1985	Second-team All-ACC, seventh-most votes	250
1986	First-team All-ACC, fifth-most votes	300
	First-team All-Tournament	75
Awards Points		1,025

Mark Alarie

As a lawyer with his *Juris Doctor* from Duke, no less, Jay Bilas knows how to frame and render an argument.

Resolved: Mark Alarie's jersey should be hanging in the rafters of Cameron Indoor Stadium with the 13 others there.

"I think Alarie's number should be retired at Duke," Bilas contended in an interview with LostLettermen.com. "When he left Duke in 1986, Mark Alarie was the third-leading scorer all time behind [Johnny] Dawkins and [Mike] Gminski and one of the [top] five rebounders and I don't think there has been a player that played with somebody else like Dawkins and put up the numbers that Alarie's put up."

Bilas was hardly a disinterested party. He played four years with Alarie and remains proud of what he and the others from the foundation recruiting class of 1982–83 (Bilas, Dawkins, Alarie, David Henderson, Weldon Williams, and Bill Jackman) did to restore the glory to Duke basketball.

Alarie addressed the legacy of his watershed class in the book *Game of My Life* by esteemed ACC basketball historian Al Featherston.

"I was fortunate to play for Coach K when he was a nobody—when we were all nobodies," Alarie said. "Now I look and think that only a handful of programs have approached the success he's achieved at Duke. It might have happened without me, but it wouldn't have happened without the class of 1986. We were the cornerstones.

"Danny Ferry said he came here because he liked the way I played. Christian Laettner came because of Danny Ferry and so on. It's like we're all part of one big family tree."

Krzyzewski, a largely unknown coach with a perpetually mispronounced name upon his hiring in 1980, was barely hanging on when he landed the class. A lynch mob that went by the name Concerned Iron Dukes had formed. Its mission, conducted mostly in secret, was to run Krzyzewski out of town.

"We found out who our friends were," Bilas said. "Even the students didn't come around until our sophomore year. One Iron Duke actually showed me a petition demanding that Krzyzewski be fired. I don't know if he expected me to sign it or not."

Gene Banks and Kenny Dennard were seniors Krzyzewski's first year, and the only other All-ACC-quality player in the program, Vince Taylor, was a junior. So Krzyzewski needed talent, and he needed it fast. And the NCAA did him no favors by instituting an early-signing date in November.

"We didn't forecast that," Krzyzewski said. "We were undergoing a recruiting revolution, and the people who were out there recruiting juniors were way ahead of us."

Intensifying the pressure on Krzyzewski was his maddening propensity for getting in really, really good with the top prospects in the country, only to come away empty. Duke's own John Feinstein, five years before attaining literary stardom upon the publication of *A Season on the Brink*, chronicled in *Sport* magazine the frustration of Krzyzewski (and no doubt himself) stemming from near-misses with the likes of Chris Mullin, Bill Wennington, Uwe Blab, and Jimmy Miller.

Bilas has called Johnny Dawkins the most important player ever at Duke. His point is that securing Dawkins's name on a letter of intent broke the logjam and resulted in the fateful recruiting class that included Bilas.

Alarie, who attended the private and highly competitive Brophy Prep in Phoenix and was considering Stanford and Notre Dame as well as Duke, said he was swayed by Krzyzewski's confidence and passion. But he also took note of who he would be playing with.

"They already had Jay Bilas and Bill Jackman and Weldon Williams and Johnny Dawkins," Alarie said in *Game of My Life*. "I saw that the class was already ranked in the top 5 or top 10. I thought I could put us over the top. And then we got David [Henderson], after I signed. That was the nucleus of a top club. It helped convince me that I was getting in on the ground floor."

Though raised in Scottsdale, Alarie had Midwestern roots. His father was from Fort Wayne, Indiana. Like pretty much every Hoosier, transplanted or otherwise, he loved his hoops. Alarie couldn't remember a time when a goal wasn't attached to the family's carport.

His coach, John Chambers, was there for him when his father died during his freshman year at Brophy.

His big rival in high school was Brad Lohaus, who played for Greenway High in Phoenix on his way to Iowa and eventually the NBA. Alarie emerged on the national scene with his play at the Basketball Congress Invitational in Provo, Utah.

Two trips during the summer between his freshman and sophomore seasons at Duke helped elevate him from a solid starter to an All-ACC player.

Coming off a dismal 11–17 season, Krzyzewski had the good sense to take his team on a tour of France.

"The trip brought us together," Alarie said in *Tales from the Duke Blue Devils Hardwood* by Jim Sumner. "Our state of mind wasn't very good after the 1983 season. The trip gave us a chance to play some winning basketball. When everybody in the place is against you—the other team, the fans, the referees, the scorekeeper, the ballboys, everyone—you have to pull together. We left our freshman year behind."

Even more helpful from a personal standpoint was the trip to the Far East with a select team from the National Sports Festival. During those intense sessions against the best in the land, he learned he was a pretty deadly shooter from 18 feet and in. The result was that Alarie blossomed into what is known today as a "stretch four." In Featherston's mind, he was the forerunner of Duke inside-outside forwards such as Ferry, Laettner, Shane Battier, and Kyle Singler.

"I feel when we need a basket, I can score," Alarie said during his sophomore season. "And that's really important, to have that confidence. Last year, I would look at someone like a [Ralph] Sampson or [Sam] Perkins and I'd be intimidated, being a freshman. This year, I don't shy away from that. I love the challenge of playing against people like that."

Bilas's summation of why Alarie's jersey belongs in the Cameron rafters along with those of Dick Groat, Mike Gminski, Dawkins, Ferry, Art Heyman, Laettner, Bobby Hurley, Grant Hill, Jeff Mullins, Battier, Jason Williams, J. J. Redick, and Shelden Williams: Alarie made first-team All-ACC twice and second-team once, averaged 16.1 points and 6.3 rebounds for his career while shooting 55 percent from the field and 79.7 percent from the line, and helped make Duke basketball relevant (and then some) while starting every game of his career.

The hole in Bilas's case should also be noted. Alarie's 833 career rebounds didn't rank him in the school's top five at the close of his career. He was actually eighth, behind Gminski, Randy Denton, Mike Lewis, Gene Banks, Ronnie Mayer, Bernie Janicki, and Heyman.

But it sounds good, and Bilas is, after all, a lawyer.

MICHAEL JORDAN

6-6 Guard | North Carolina | 1981–84 | No. 23

1982	ACC ROY	100
	First-team All-Tournament	75
1983	First-team All-ACC, unanimous	425
	Second-team All-Tournament	50
	ACC POY, close runner-up	125
	First-team All-American (with Dale Ellis of Tennessee, Patrick Ewing of Georgetown, Keith Lee of Memphis State, Sam Perkins of North Carolina, Ralph Sampson of Virginia, and Wayman Tisdale of Oklahoma)	200
1984	First-team All-ACC, unanimous	425
	Second-team All-Tournament	50
	ACC POY	200
	National POY (with fellow first-team All-Americans Akeem Olajuwon of Houston, Ewing, Perkins, and Tisdale)	250
Awards Points		1,900

The greatest player to take the floor for ACC basketball was Michael Jordan. That's not to say he was the greatest ACC player ever, because if you watched ACC basketball in the 1970s and 1980s, you know he wasn't.

David Thompson was.

If Jordan had returned for his senior season, led North Carolina to its second national title in four years, and maybe repeated as consensus National Player of the Year, a strong case could have been made that he was indeed the greatest ACC player ever.

I don't blame him for forgoing his last year to turn pro. It certainly appears he was ready.

And I most strenuously disagree with those who feel that Jordan,

Michael Jordan
UNC ATHLETIC
COMMUNICATIONS

constricted by the hidebound system of Dean Smith (yeah, I know, the only man to hold Jordan to fewer than 20 points a game), never really showed what he could do in college.

He showed me a hell of a lot. Jordan was a rangy wing who prowled the court like a big cat, dunking, draining jumpers, rebounding, passing, and locking down any opponent from a six-foot water-bug point guard to a six-eight beef-eating power forward.

By 1983–84, Jordan's junior season, Smith refined his defense to where Jordan was allowed to freelance, and the results were devastating—so devastating that the Tar Heels were 27–1 (remember that?) before the unsuccessful integration of injured freshman Kenny Smith back into the lineup upset the chemistry to the point they lost two of their final three.

Hard Work, Roy Williams's autobiography, written with the help of Tim Crothers, is a good book. I enjoyed it for several reasons, one being that Williams and I are both North Carolina mountain grills who had similar childhood experiences. But it isn't a great book because those kinds of books just never are.

It contains, however, one passage that anyone who ever aspired to be the best really, really needs to read. It captures the essence of who Michael Jordan was, what he became, and how he did it.

Williams, then an assistant for Smith, was sitting with Jordan at the track cooling down from a conditioning session when Jordan said he wanted to be the best to ever play at North Carolina. Williams told him he'd have to work harder than he did in high school.

Jordan, brought up short, protested that he worked as hard as anybody.

"Oh, excuse me," Williams replied. "I thought you just said you wanted to be the best player to ever play here."

"Working as hard as everybody else is not going to come close, son."

Two days later, Jordan came back around.

"He said, 'Coach, I've been thinking about what you said. I'm going to show you. There will never be anyone who will outwork me,' " Williams recalled. "He did that. From that day on, Michael tried to kick everybody's rear end in every drill. We had James Worthy, Sam Perkins, Matt Doherty and Jimmy Black and he was trying to destroy all of them.

"That's when I knew we had something special."

Michael Jordan was the greatest player to take the floor in the ACC because he wanted so badly to be just that. He had to be, because that's who he was. He couldn't take being second-best.

The Michael Jordan story is one of the best-known in the history of American popular culture partly because it's so good. Born in New York City but raised in Wilmington, he realized early in life that to be the best in just his family, he had to beat his big brother Larry. And that, according to his father, wasn't easy.

"Back then Larry was a little taller and much stronger," James Jordan said in Ken Rappoport's *Tales from the Tar Heel Locker Room*. "Larry would beat Michael unmercifully. As Michael got older, he got bigger, and the games became much closer."

The son of a sharecropper, James Jordan bettered himself by training on the GI Bill to become a supervisor at General Electric. His wife, Deloris, worked in a bank. The couple had five children—three boys and two girls. Michael was the third son and fourth child.

He wore number 23 at North Carolina because Larry Jordan's number in high school was 45, and that's as close as Michael could come to half that. As you may remember, he took jersey number 45 when he came out of NBA retirement.

His early love was baseball. He was a good enough pitcher to throw no-hitters and, over his hottest streak, post 42 straight scoreless innings. But beating his big brother became an obsession, so he turned to basketball.

If you lived in ACC country in 1982, you knew who Michael Jordan was as a freshman. But most people's first memory of him is his ballsy 17-foot jumper that beat Georgetown for Dean Smith's first national title.

"The kid doesn't even realize it yet, but he's part of history now," said Eddie Fogler, then an assistant for Smith. "People will remember that shot 25 years from now."

Jordan flourished in the professional game—and by *flourished* I mean he made the All-Star team 14 times, was named regular-season MVP five times and playoff MVP six times, and absolutely willed the Chicago Bulls to six championships. Nor should I forget to mention his Olympic successes. He first won the gold with amateurs in Los Angeles in 1984, then with the Dream Team in Barcelona in 1992.

And if possible, he was even more successful as the greatest pitchman any American product—in this case Nike—has ever had.

It takes a special person to accomplish 1 percent of what Jordan has. What enabled him to do so was the furnace that burned inside. Jordan's was lit by a flamethrower.

But when flames are thrown, people—usually those standing closest—get burned.

For every story about how often Jordan won, another told how he just couldn't lose. He took failure personally and lashed out at those he felt were responsible.

Roommate Buzz Peterson, one of the friendliest, most amiable players ever at North Carolina, once beat him in Monopoly. Jordan blew up, first by throwing the money he owed at Peterson, then storming out of the room. According to the story, he crashed with his sister that night because he was ashamed to face Peterson.

Williams has remained a close friend over the years but still knows how to get Jordan's goat by mentioning that day three decades ago when he beat him in pool.

Never one to let any grievance go unaired, Jordan trotted them out one by one in his widely panned acceptance speech into the Basketball Hall of Fame in 2009. Everyone in attendance at Symphony Hall in Springfield, Massachusetts, heard all they wanted, and then some, about how Peterson beat him out for North Carolina High School Player of the Year, how Smith did not allow him to pose for the cover of *Sports Illustrated* because he was a freshman (even though he has gone on to grace 51 *SI* covers), how Coach Doug Collins of the Bulls wouldn't let him play in the summer, how Coach Pat Riley of the Knicks wouldn't let Charles Oakley and Patrick Ewing hang out with him, how Assistant Coach Tex Winter told him there was no *i* in *team* (to which Jordan responded by noting the *i* in *win*), and how he gave Byron Russell of the Utah Jazz what-for for having the temerity to suggest he could contain His Airness.

Everyone has heard the story of Jordan's getting cut from the varsity as a sophomore at Laney High School in Wilmington, and how the humiliation provided all the motivation he would need to become a great success. It's in all the books and documentaries about Jordan. It's the defining vignette of the great and glorious Michael Jordan saga.

I won't dignify the folk tale by recounting any more about it here. But I will refer anyone who wants to know the real story of what happened at Laney High in the fall of 1978 to the exquisitely written, excruciatingly sad 7,000-word myth-buster Thomas Lake wrote for the June 16, 2012, edition of *Sports Illustrated.* The article details the wreckage left in the painful life of Pop Herring, the coach who made the call to give a 5-10 guard named Mike Jordan a chance to play full time as a sophomore on the junior varsity.

Michael Jordan has played well with others only on the rarest of occasions. I've never seen the movie, but I have it on good authority from others that, in the movie *Space Jam*, he gets along just fine with Bugs Bunny.

SAM PERKINS

6-9 Center │ North Carolina │ 1980–84 │ No. 41

1981	ACC ROY	100
	Everett Case Award	100
1982	First-team All-ACC, third-most votes	350
	First-team All-Tournament	75
	Second-team All-American	150
1983	First-team All-ACC, third-most votes	350
	Second-team All-Tournament	50
	First-team All-American (with Dale Ellis of Tennessee, Patrick Ewing of Georgetown, Michael Jordan of North Carolina, Keith Lee of Memphis State, Ralph Sampson of Virginia, and Wayman Tisdale of Oklahoma)	200
1984	First-team All-ACC, unanimous	425
	First-team All-American (with Ewing, Jordan, Akeem Olajuwon of Houston, and Tisdale)	200
Awards Points		2,000

Sam Perkins, a tremendous rebounder and low-post defender, was a pleasure to watch play. And fans weren't the only ones who had that reaction.

"He was a great pleasure to coach, and every one of his NBA coaches have told me the same thing," Dean Smith said in his autobiography, *A Coach's Life*, written with John Kilgo and Sally Jenkins. "Bob Knight truly enjoyed coaching Sam on the 1984 Olympic team as well."

Knight, who led Perkins and company to a gold medal, actually took it one giant step farther.

"One of the finest human beings I've ever been around," he said of Perkins.

Perkins might never have made it out of Bedford-Stuyvesant—much less been around Knight or any major-college coach—if it hadn't been for a social worker named Herb Crossman.

Perkins's father died when he was one. He and his three sisters were raised by their mother and their devout grandmother, Martha Perkins. Sam would tag along when his grandmother handed out literature of the Jehovah's Witnesses.

He went to school when he felt like it, which wasn't often. He spent way too many days on the B-46 bus circling from Kings Plaza in Brooklyn to the Williamsburg Bridge.

"I'd try at first," Perkins told *Sports Illustrated*. "And then I'd say, 'What's the use? I won't get the grades to make the team.'

"I'd stop going to school. I just didn't have much discipline."

When he did show up at Tilden High School, his basketball was confined to pickup games and gym class. But friends convinced him to play in a summer schoolyard tournament. And as fate would have it, Crossman was around that day.

"It was hard to miss Sam's obvious height, but Herb also noticed that he had quickness, excellent hands, and an even temperament," Smith wrote in *A Coach's Life*. "Nothing seemed to bother him. Herb began working out with Sam and discovered that he also had a bright mind and was a good listener."

When Crossman moved to the Albany area, he talked Perkins's family into allowing him to become Sam's legal guardian and take him along. The winning pitch was not the opportunity to play basketball but the sterling academic reputation of Albany's Shaker High School.

"You don't understand," Crossman replied to *Sports Illustrated* when asked why he accepted such a responsibility. "I saw this kid's smile when he was 14."

Upon arriving at North Carolina after picking the Tar Heels over Syracuse, Houston, UCLA, and Notre Dame, Perkins was measured at nine-four from his flat feet to his highest reach—the greatest at North Carolina until Eric Montross was measured at nine-five and Warren Martin at nine-six.

Sam Perkins
UNC Athletic Communications

Great players don't come more low-maintenance. Smith marveled over Perkins's absence of ego.

"In fact, when he was a freshman, he told me after a month of practices that senior Pete Budko should start ahead of him and that he just hoped to come off the bench and contribute," Smith recalled in *A Coach's Life*. "Sam went on to become MVP of the ACC Tournament that year, and an All-American for three straight years."

Perkins was a pleasant guy to be around, but never the best of interviews. Apparently, he said what he had to say to his coach. Smith made it a practice to talk with his players for 30 to 45 minutes every season just to find out what was going on in their lives. When scheduling a time for Perkins, he told his secretary to allot an hour and a half.

"I knew we would talk about everything, not just basketball," Smith explained.

The one thing I remember Perkins saying during his career blew up in his face. After beating James Madison and Ohio State in the first two rounds of the 1983 NCAA Tournament, the Tar Heels were pitted against Georgia in the Sweet 16 in Syracuse. Asked about his team's prospects, Perkins happened to mention he didn't know what league the Bulldogs played in.

Given the reaction from the Georgia players, one would have thought Perkins had defected on the state flag. The crowing could be heard across the nation when Coach Hugh Durham's Bulldogs held Perkins to 14 points—only four in the first half while Georgia was taking control—in an 82–77 upset.

"Yeah, we heard those remarks in our room," Vern Fleming said. "We thought we'd just show him what conference Georgia plays in."

Terry Fair was flabbergasted.

"I don't know how he can say something like that. I mean, we played North Carolina last year," he said. "He's got to remember."

What the Bulldogs didn't know was what we who covered ACC basketball did. Sam Perkins was the kind of person who concerned himself only with what he needed to be concerned about. He could have made the same comment about Kentucky, Indiana, or UCLA, as he tried to explain after the loss.

"I said I didn't know what league they were in," Perkins said. "I really don't care either. You give me a team now and ask me about it, and I wouldn't know their league. I'm honestly telling the truth.

"I pay attention to the Atlantic Coast Conference. I don't pay attention to those other leagues."

Taken by Dallas with the fourth pick of the 1984 draft, Perkins played 17 NBA seasons with the Mavericks, Los Angeles Lakers, Seattle SuperSonics, and Indiana Pacers, averaging 11.7 points and six rebounds. His unruffled demeanor and unselfish nature made him a favorite not only of his coaches but his teammates as well. His nicknames were "Easy," "Sleepy Sam," and "Big Smooth."

"He's just so smart," George Karl, who coached Perkins in Seattle, told Glenn Nelson of the *Seattle Times*. "I think in pro basketball, in the playoffs, you win as much with your brain and your heart as your talent. And he's a winner.

"His confidence and his strength come from winning. Players who are driven by winning have an inner strength. It's a foundation that coaches always want to have around their teams."

I've never met Glenn Nelson, but he's obviously a good sportswriter. He got Perkins to say more about himself than I've ever heard or read elsewhere.

"Everyone wants some attention," Perkins told Nelson. "But I never want the light to shine so bright that it becomes an ego thing. If you get the light shining on you all the time, other people start tripping off that."

RALPH SAMPSON

7-4 Center | Virginia | 1979–83 | No. 50

Year	Award	Points
1980	ACC ROY	100
1981	First-team All-ACC, most votes	400
	ACC POY	200
	National POY (with fellow first-team All-Americans Danny Ainge of BYU, Isiah Thomas of Indiana, Mark Aguirre of DePaul, and Steve Johnson of Oregon State)	250
1982	First-team All-ACC, unanimous	425
	First-team All-Tournament	75
	ACC POY	200
	National POY (with fellow first-team All-Americans James Worthy of North Carolina, Quintin Dailey of San Francisco, Sleepy Floyd of Georgetown, and Terry Cummings of DePaul)	250
1983	First-team All-ACC, unanimous	425
	First-team All-Tournament	75
	ACC POY, heavily contested	150
	National POY (with fellow first-team All-Americans Dale Ellis of Tennessee, Keith Lee of Memphis, Michael Jordan and Sam Perkins of North Carolina, Patrick Ewing of Georgetown, and Wayman Tisdale of Oklahoma)	250
Awards Points		**2,800**

Any excuse is a good excuse to call Dave Odom. No coach who has ever patrolled the ACC sidelines was ever as helpful as Odom, for none ever held media types like me, justifiably or not, in higher regard.

As a result, we in the media loved him. From 1989 through 2001, I was known as the luckiest beat guy in the conference because I was assigned to cover the Wake Forest program Odom coached. I've regaled ACC Tournament hospitality suites with Dave Odom stories ever since.

We've remained good friends, so I warned him I'd be calling with one express purpose. In the interest of fairness, I wanted to give Odom every chance to convince me that Ralph Sampson, whom he coached as an assistant in 1982 and 1983, wasn't the biggest asshole to ever play in the ACC.

Ralph Sampson
<small>UNIVERSITY OF VIRGINIA MEDIA RELATIONS</small>

It was a tall order, I knew. It stood seven-four and wore a constant scowl.

Everyone who covered the conference in the early 1980s remembers what a pain it was dealing with Sampson and Terry Holland, his inherently decent but woefully thin-skinned and overprotective head coach. The guys I knew on the Virginia beat got so tired of the friction—the wrangling it took to get five minutes with Sampson, the football player named Jerry Glover who was stationed at Sampson's locker to hold the media at bay until Sampson deigned it was time to talk, the way he looked across the room over everyone's head while giving his predictably rote responses—that they gave up going to Holland and Sampson and sought from Odom information on what was happening with the team.

The word that best described Sampson was *petulant*. He came off as perpetually put-upon. And he could be that way on the court as well, lashing out at opponents and officials he felt were doing him wrong.

Every ACC player feels at some time in his career that he is being abused. That's human nature. It's how he deals with it that tells you who he is.

How Ralph Sampson dealt with it was by swinging elbows, as he did against Maryland as a senior, knocking Len Bias to the floor during one particularly unhinged display that ended with teammate Othell Wilson laying his shoulder into Sampson's midsection to keep the screaming giant from getting at the officials.

Working for a paper a lovely three-and-a-half-hour drive to the south, I fortunately didn't have many reasons to talk with Sampson. But I do remember an assignment my editor, Terry Oberle, gave me for the 1983 ACC Tournament, the season the conference experimented with a 30-second shot clock and a three-point line a mere 19 feet from the back of the rim. My charge was to poll all 40 ACC starters on two questions: Were they for or against the shot clock, and were they for or against the three-point line? Getting 39 of the starters—among them Mark Price and Johnny Dawkins and Sam Perkins and Michael Jordan—on the record proved no problem.

As for the 40th . . .

The first three days, counting the workout day, I was unable to penetrate the crush around Sampson to ask my questions. So I tried to enlist a member of Virginia's sports information office, telling him my assignment. If he could ask Sampson the questions and report back, that would be fine.

On Sunday, after the Cavaliers lost to N.C. State in the final, Sampson went to the podium at the media conference, returned to the locker room, and headed straight to the showers. I made eye contact with the sports information assistant I'd talked to, and he just pointed to Sampson.

"There he goes," he said. "You ask him."

So there I was, a sweaty, rotund Lilliputian chasing a skinny, towel-draped Gulliver down the hall to ask my two questions before he stepped into the shower. Yea or nay, Ralph? That was all I needed.

To see the look of disdain on his face, good Lord, you would have thought I was hitting him up for money.

"I'm for the shot clock but not the three-point line," Sampson practically spat. "Okay?"

Why, I asked Odom 30 years later, did it have to be so hard?

"The thing is, to whom much is given, much is expected," Odom explained. "He was given great athleticism, a great athletic body, and a lot of talent, and people expected an entrée into his world, and he resisted that. That didn't make him a bad person, it really didn't. He just didn't know how to deal with it at that time. Each year I've known him, he's gotten better at it, he really has."

Of all the players honored in this book, Sampson is probably the one I've researched the deepest to find out who he was and what made him tick. I read the book *Sampson: A Life Above the Rim* by Roland Lazenby, published in 1983, at the end of his college career. Alexander Wolff wrote an insightful cover story for *Sports Illustrated* in September 1986, during Sampson's third season with the Houston Rockets. And Ron Morris did himself proud with a feature on Sampson in *ACC Basketball*.

Much of what I learned about Sampson cast him in the best light. He was born to two solid, loving parents. His father, Ralph Sr., was a working man who rose to foreman at Kawnee Company, Inc., a local Harrisonburg business that turned out aluminum window frames. His mother, Sarah, one of 12 children raised by George and Josephine Blakey on a 300-acre farm outside nearby McGaheysville, was a pretty, vivacious woman with enough smarts and drive to work herself up from seamstress to the personnel department at a Harrisonburg pants factory. The family lived in a brick-and-frame split-level in Harrisonburg bought from Sampson's grandfather, the five-eight Hampton Lee Sampson.

Ask the townsfolk about Ralph and they invariably offer the proverbial, "As great a player as he was, he was an even better person." Polite, though shy, he was well liked by his teachers and coaches, who recognized he had overcome a reading disability to make grades high enough to qualify him to play major-college basketball.

He wore number 50 because that was what his cousin Raymond Williams had worn at Harrisonburg High in the days he lived with the Sampson family and, for a while, even shared Ralph's bed. Williams was a promising basketball player before moving north to Boston, messing around with drugs, and ending up in jail. Learning his lesson, Sampson was never much of a drinker and was infamously adamant against taking drugs.

He showed up for his freshman season at Virginia in the fall of 1979 in his father's pickup—the one with the eight-foot bed in the back. By then, "Stick"—the nickname given to him by his high-school coach—had experienced one of the most intense recruiting battles in the history of college basketball. He had been licked by the flames of fame and already felt burned.

"He grew up under a microscope and never got out from under it," Odom said. "Even to this day, to some extent, everything he does is measured. That's a hard cross to bear, particularly for a guy who grew up in a small Shenandoah Valley town. He was so very comfortable where he was that he had a hard time moving from that environment and atmosphere to where everything he did was measured and evaluated. To him, he deserved the same opportunity to be private at times as others."

He was a legend long before he arrived in Charlottesville, so much so that when he was given a helicopter ride across campus on a recruiting visit, he looked down and saw the words *Ralph's House* on the dome of the basketball arena, University Hall.

My good friend Jerry Ratcliffe of the *Charlottesville Daily Progress* wrote that when Sampson, at a media conference held in the Harrisonburg High gym, announced he was choosing Virginia over North Carolina, Kentucky, and Virginia Tech, "loud cheers broke out in the parking lot, with the roar spreading all over the Commonwealth."

Nothing about Sampson impressed me more than reading of his college life at Virginia—how engaged he was in his classes, how he loved participating in campus high jinks, how he applied for and earned the privilege to live in one of the 54 rooms on "the Lawn" before the hassles his presence caused prompted him to move out at midyear.

Nor should it be underestimated just how overwhelming the media requests became. Every newspaper, magazine, and television network in the free world jockeyed for access. In hindsight, maybe Holland and Virginia did everything they could.

"You got people coming by to bang on his door at midnight or 2 o'clock in the morning," Holland explained in *ACC Basketball*. "It was very difficult to explain to people.

"We'd have 10 or 15 calls a day and people would say, 'We'd like to come over and just take a picture of Ralph.' And we'd say, 'Well, it's like he's an animal in the zoo. He's not an exhibit all day long.'"

Odom was not the first to tell me that Sampson was a trusted and valued teammate who did what it took to become a great basketball player.

"I can tell you without any fear of contradiction that behind closed doors, in terms of working with him on the court, nobody worked harder and nobody cared more," Odom maintained. "Nobody was a better teammate than Ralph. And in terms of working with him off the court, he was also equally easy to work with, except when it came to doing things with people that he didn't really know."

I don't know Sampson, but I do know Tim Duncan. What does it say that Odom, the easiest coach with whom I've ever dealt, coached the two players I had the hardest time covering?

"They were both similar in that they didn't feel like they needed more exposure," Odom explained. "In their mind, 'Just let me play, let me do my deal, and you can write it or say it or whatever.' "

There's something to be said for that philosophy. It's just that it was my job to get them to say it—which, in the end, was my problem and not theirs.

"He's a good guy," Odom said of Sampson. "He really is."

If Dave Odom says it, I believe it.

JAMES WORTHY

6-9 Forward | North Carolina | 1979–82 | No. 52

1981	Second-team All-ACC, eighth-most votes	225
	First-team All-Tournament	75
1982	First-team All-ACC, second-most votes	375
	Everett Case Award	100
	Final Four MVP	150
	First-team All-American (with Terry Cummings of DePaul, Quintin Dailey of San Francisco, Sleepy Floyd of Georgetown, and Ralph Sampson of Virginia)	200
Awards Points		**1,125**

Different lads pass into manhood at different points in their lives. Some grow up early, while others take their own sweet time.

I met James Worthy when he was 17 years old, the summer before his senior year of high school. In my capacity as sports editor of the *Chapel Hill Newspaper*, I interviewed him while he was on break at Dean Smith's basketball camp in Woollen Gym. Not only was he already a man, but judging from his heavy growth of beard, his chiseled physique, his basso profundo voice, and his striking self-assurance, he had been one for quite some time.

Smith noticed the same thing while watching Worthy star for Ashbrook High School in Gastonia. He mentioned it in his autobiography, *A Coach's Life*.

"James Worthy was one of the few young men I ever looked at as a high schooler and felt certain he was going to be a college star and pro player,"

Smith recounted. "It was a long wait, watching him grow up. I used to joke about Worthy, 'We were hoping he would go hardship and leave high school after his junior year so he could come in and help us out.' "

Smith also couldn't help noticing Worthy's uncommon quickness for his size and his ability to finish plays. And from getting to know the young man and his parents, he understood Worthy came from a solid home. His father, Ervin, known affectionately to the Tar Heel staff as "the Big E," was a Baptist minister.

By the time I made it over to Woollen, Worthy had been dominating his fellow campers for years. He first showed up as an eighth-grader. Smith recalled how Doug Moe, a former UNC star who was responsible for directing the action, told him that Worthy was simply too strong, too advanced, and too good for others his age.

"Get him out of here," Moe implored Smith. "He ruins the competition."

James Worthy
UNC Athletic Communications

So they bumped Worthy up to the ninth-grade level, which solved little. It wasn't until he was put up against 10th-graders that he faced any challenge worth his time.

Worthy, for his part, said he didn't even like basketball as a kid and took up the sport only because he thought college tuition might be a hardship on his family. It turned out he had no worries on that score. Colleges all over threw offers at him.

Smith felt good about his chance of landing Worthy, based on the strong relationship he and his assistants had with Ervin Worthy and James's mother, Gladys. But Worthy took the grand tour anyway, making visits to Kentucky, Michigan State, and UCLA, in addition to North Carolina.

The day the North Carolina staff realized Worthy was likely Chapel Hill bound is covered in both *A Coach's Life* and *Hard Work* by Roy Williams and Tim Crothers. Worthy was on one of his official recruiting trips (Smith remembers it being at Michigan State, Williams at Kentucky) when he called his father. Only he played a trick on "the Big E." Having perfected Smith's infamously nasal Kansas twang, Worthy fooled his father into believing it was the Carolina coach calling, worrying over some rumor that James had committed to the Spartans.

Ervin Worthy told Smith and the Tar Heel assistants the story, describing how he had talked with his son for several minutes before he realized the ruse.

"When James' dad told me that story, I knew his son was coming to UNC," Williams wrote.

Smith noted that the pieces began coming together for his first national championship the day Worthy arrived. And having had the good fortune of watching Worthy play his two and a half years at North Carolina, I can see why he felt that way. I recall games when Worthy would simply not allow the Tar Heels to lose. One was the national semifinal game of 1982, when his driving dunk over Houston's Larry Micheaux right in front of the Tar Heel bench helped spark North Carolina to a 68–63 victory.

But it was the next, and last, game he played for the Tar Heels that solidified his standing as "Big Game James," a nickname bestowed by legendary North Carolina play-by-play announcer Woody Durham.

Smith recalled running into Danny Worthy, James's brother, at the team hotel on the way to the pregame meal before the title game against Georgetown. The coach asked the brother how the star was doing. The brother told the coach he had never seen the star so zeroed in. Worthy had lost to Indiana in the national final the season before and didn't want to repeat that painful experience. Also, fellow Gastonian Sleepy Floyd was playing guard for Georgetown, and Floyd's Hunter Huss High team had upended Worthy and Ashbrook for the state championship.

The rest—the 13 field goals on 17 attempts for 28 points, many scored on fearless drives into the teeth of the Hoyas' Patrick Ewing–anchored defense—is one of the most told and retold accounts in North Carolina basketball history. The monkey was off Smith's back, and it was Worthy who kicked it down the hall.

After ascertaining that Worthy would be the first player chosen, Smith advised him to take his talents to the NBA. That he did, beginning a fabled 12-year career with Los Angeles during which the Lakers played in the championship series seven times and won three titles. Worthy was named MVP of the playoffs in 1988, the last season the Lakers won the championship with him on the court. Over his career, he averaged 17.6 points and 5.1 rebounds. In 2003, he was inducted into another Hall of Fame—the one named for James Naismith in Springfield, Massachusetts.

Worthy received an even greater honor in 1996 when he was named one of the top 50 players in NBA history.

AL WOOD

6-6 Forward | North Carolina | 1977–81 | No. 30

Year	Award	Points
1979	First-team All-ACC, fifth-most votes	300
	Second-team All-Tournament	50
1980	Second-team All-ACC, 10th-most votes	175
	First-team All-Tournament	75
1981	First-team All-ACC, second-most votes	375
	Second-team All-Tournament	50
	Second-team All-American	150
Awards Points		**1,175**

Mention *"the Al Wood game"* and everyone automatically thinks of the national semifinal of 1981, when Wood, drilling 14 of 19 shots from the floor and 11 of 13 from the line, burned Virginia for a career-high 39 points. The box score shows he piled up 10 rebounds to boot, as the Tar Heels thumped Ralph Sampson and the Cavaliers 78–65.

In London in the fall of 1967, a graffiti artist infamously scrawled "Clapton is God" on the wall of the Islington underground station. Fourteen years

Al Wood
UNC Athletic Communications

later, it was impossible to walk down Franklin Street in Chapel Hill without seeing another work of street art: "Al Wood, 39."

Years later, in an interview with Scott Fowler for the book *North Carolina Tar Heels: Where Have You Gone?* Wood gave some of the credit for scoring the most points ever in a national semifinal to Roy Williams, then an assistant on Dean Smith's staff.

Fowler asked Wood if he had ever been hotter.

"No," Wood replied. "And thank God for Roy Williams being on the sidelines that night.

"Roy had seen me when I got into a zone in pickup games and couldn't miss. That game, for me, turned into a pickup game. I completely went away from the norm of what we always did—the number of passes we made and all that.

"But after I'd shot five in a row, Roy pretty much grabbed Coach Smith by the arm when he was about to pull me out and said, 'Aww, leave him alone.' "

Coach Terry Holland of Virginia would have rather bragged about a primo performance from Sampson, but the big guy made three of 10 shots from the floor to contribute just 11 points and nine rebounds. So Holland's postgame praise was reserved for number 30 of the other team.

"Al Wood is a truly fine basketball player who had a truly great day," Holland said. "We tried everything to stop him except throwing the kitchen sink at him, but nothing worked."

Wood played another game at North Carolina, though, that may have meant as much to him, if not to the Tar Heel nation at large. That was the only game his mother saw him play in person.

His mother was an alcoholic, as Wood himself would become before finding both his maker and sobriety, in that order. Wood's father was not part of his childhood in Gray, Georgia, located 14 miles northeast of Macon along Route 129, commonly known as the Gray Highway. Wood's mother couldn't take care of him, so he was adopted by his grandmother. The city coroner came tapping on her window at four o'clock one morning to report that Wood's mother, in a drunken rage, had stabbed to death her common-law husband of 15 years.

So while Wood was starring at North Carolina, his mother was serving a prison sentence. But it was arranged during his senior season that she would be allowed to attend a game in Chapel Hill.

What she saw was a young man who had matured considerably since his early days of playing ball, back when few who mattered in the world of college basketball knew who he was.

Wood had been so impressed by the Tar Heel connection to the 1976 Olympic team that won the gold medal in Montreal (Smith was the head coach, Bill Guthridge an assistant, and Walter Davis, Phil Ford, Mitch Kupchak, and Tommy LaGarde on the roster) that he asked his high-school coach to write Smith a letter describing his game. Smith, taking a flyer, sent an assistant, Eddie Fogler, to watch Wood, who rose to the occasion by pouring in 58 points.

That's how Wood ended up in Carolina blue.

Smith may have never had a player who bought more completely into his system. Wood's greatest fear was that he would someday break Smith's cardinal rule of always showing up on time. Being late, Smith was known to say, was to imply that your own time was more important than that of others on the team.

Once when Wood was on his way to a pregame meal, his car broke down. In a panic, he ditched the car and hitchhiked.

Smooth and easygoing, Wood was never one of the most dominant personalities on the team. His hobbies were shooting pool, dancing, playing softball and tag football, swimming, listening to music, and watching television. His favorite show was *Sanford and Son*.

But by his senior season, he knew he had to take on a broader leadership role.

"I used to be more of a laid-back player, but this fall I decided it was time to stop watching other people do it," Wood said that season. "I'm playing harder and asserting myself more. As a senior, the other players looked to me for leadership, and I think the role fit me well."

I covered many of Wood's games, but I had forgotten that his shoulder was known to pop out of joint on occasion, a condition that has also afflicted other ACC stars, Randolph Childress among them. In fact, Wood's shoulder popped out in the final minutes of his 39-point performance against Virginia.

"There was a lot of pain, but it's not a lasting thing," Wood explained back then. "It pops out and it pops in again."

His future appeared bright when he was picked fourth overall in the 1981 draft by the closest thing he had to a hometown team, the Atlanta Hawks. But midway through his rookie season, he was traded along with Charlie Criss to the San Diego Clippers for Freeman Williams.

He lasted six seasons in the NBA, playing for the Hawks, Clippers, Seattle SuperSonics, and Dallas Mavericks. He averaged 11.8 points and three rebounds for his career while shooting 46.5 percent from the floor.

A social drinker for years, Wood began climbing deeper and deeper into the bottle, until he finally faced the realization that he suffered from the same disease that had wrecked his mother's life.

He and his wife, Robin, had their third child, daughter Candace, in October 1989. Wood is proud to say that Candace has never seen alcohol in their family home.

When he knew it was time to get sober, he gave his ex-coach a call.

"Coach Smith didn't belittle me or put me down," Wood told Fowler in *North Carolina Tar Heels*. "He told me how much he loved me, and how he appreciated me giving him a call."

Today, Wood is an ordained minister at Morningstar Ministries in Fort Mill, South Carolina, and the principal and director of athletics at the Comenius School for Creative Leadership, a private Christian school for children from kindergarten through high school.

He's also the proud father of a Tar Heel athlete. Candace signed to play for North Carolina before the 2008–9 season but endured four knee surgeries. She was a redshirt senior in 2012–13.

JEFF LAMP

6-6 Guard | Virginia | 1977–81 | No. 3

1978	Second-team All-ACC, seventh-most votes	250
1979	First-team All-ACC, second-most votes	375
	Second-team All-Tournament	50
1980	Second-team All-ACC, sixth-most votes	275
1981	First-team All-ACC, third-most votes	350
	Second-team All-Tournament	50
	Second-team All-American	150
Awards Points		**1,500**

Told he wasn't good enough to make his school's junior-high basketball team as an eighth-grader, Jeff Lamp had two choices. He could give up the sport and find another endeavor, or he could take the advice of a wise older friend in the neighborhood and find the right person to make him better.

To the eternal gratitude of Terry Holland and Virginia basketball fans, Lamp chose the latter course.

The man he picked to make him the player he became was Richard Schmidt. The head coach at Ballard High School in Louisville, Kentucky, Schmidt had two tenets for success. One was commitment and the other hard work.

Lamp proved more than capable of both. Along the way, he gained weight and confidence, developed a deadly jumper, and led a Ballard team that also featured Lee Raker, Jerry Eaves, and Norman Miller to the 1977 state championship.

Lamp scored 43 points in the 68–59 title-game victory over Valley High School and was named Mr. Basketball in the state of Kentucky. Raker committed to Virginia, Eaves to Louisville, and Miller to Mississippi. As for Schmidt, he accepted a position on the Virginia staff in time to convince Lamp that he belonged not at Indiana playing for Bobby Knight but in Charlottesville playing for Holland. The pipeline kept pumping when another player from Ballard, six-eight forward Terry Gates, joined the Cavaliers a year later.

Virginia had stunned the ACC in 1976, when the Cavaliers, led by Wally Walker and Billy Langloh, won the school's first ACC title by knocking off

Jeff Lamp
UNIVERSITY OF VIRGINIA MEDIA RELATIONS

North Carolina in Landover, Maryland. But it wasn't until he landed Lamp and Raker—and Ralph Sampson two years later—that Holland built the Wahoos into a true national power. More help arrived from Kentucky when Jeff Jones, succumbing to the hard sell of Lamp and Raker, joined the Cavaliers in 1979.

Jones, who succeeded Holland as head coach at Virginia, roomed with Lamp in Charlottesville. He remembered Lamp as a person who paid little attention to basketball when he wasn't playing. What Lamp was well known for, however, was an unsurpassed work ethic and an overriding desire to have the ball in his hands with the game on the line.

"When you've got someone like that who is one of your best players and works as hard as Jeff did, it really sets the tone for the rest of your team," Jones told Sean McLernon of TheSabre.com.

Lamp began his career by scoring 24 points against James Madison in his first college game and ended it by scoring 25 against LSU in the consolation game of the Final Four. Along the way, he made one big shot after another as Virginia enjoyed its most successful run in school history. In Lamp's time, the Cavaliers played in the NIT three seasons and the NCAA Tournament once, won a postseason game for the first time by beating Northeast Louisiana 79–78 in the first round of the 1979 NIT, won their first postseason title by beating Minnesota 58–55 for the 1980 NIT championship, and soared all the way to number one in the nation by winning their first 23 games of the 1980–81 season.

Lamp contributed 2,317 points to Holland's reclamation project, breaking a school record by Buzz Wilkinson that had stood since 1955. Lamp's record, incidentally, was broken in 1992 by Bryant Stith, also honored in this book. But Stith, lest anyone forget, played after the three-point shot was introduced in 1987, six years after Lamp was done at Virginia.

"Lamp was a leader in the huddle and a leader on the bus," Mac McDonald, a play-by-play announcer for Virginia, told McLernon. "He was the big man on campus.

"Ralph [Sampson] was a sophomore [in 1981] but it was still Jeff Lamp's team." Accordingly, Lamp's jersey was retired that season, right after his 18 points lifted Virginia to an 84–73 victory over Maryland in his final home game.

Though never the quickest player on the court, Lamp was tall for a guard. He was also tough enough to take care of himself. And most of all, he was fearless.

A first-round pick (15th overall) by Portland in the 1981 NBA draft, Lamp played six seasons with the Trailblazers, Milwaukee Bucks, San Antonio Spurs, and Los Angeles Lakers. He logged 291 NBA games all told, averaging 5.1 points.

After knocking around awhile in Europe, Lamp returned to the NBA in an administrative capacity. His job entails advising players how to prepare for life after retirement from the league.

ALBERT KING

6-6 Forward | Maryland | 1977–81 | No. 55

1980	First-team All-ACC, second-most votes	375
	Everett Case Award	100
	ACC POY	200
	Second-team All-American	150
1981	Second-team All-ACC, seventh-most votes	250
	First-team All-Tournament	75
Awards Points		**1,150**

For a while, back when any college basketball recruiter who could scrape together the cost of airfare or gas money was beating a path to Brooklyn, Winston Karim was the most popular shipping clerk from Trinidad around.

And then he wasn't.

Karim, as those in college basketball circles knew, held the key to recruiting the nation's hottest prospect, Albert King. That's because Karim held the key to the East Flatbush apartment where King spent most of his days and many of his nights.

Besieged from the day he scored 36 points and pulled down 23 rebounds in his first game for Fort Hamilton High School, King preferred that recruiters not flock to his parents' apartment in a less-than-swanky Brooklyn neighborhood called Fort Greene. Thomas and Thelma King, who had already survived the ordeal of sending their older son, Bernard, to the University of Tennessee, had endured quite enough.

So King holed up with Karim, who became his de facto gatekeeper, fielding phone calls from one overwrought assistant coach after another, often deep into the night.

King, a springy, explosive forward who averaged 30 points and 20 rebounds over his career at Fort Hamilton, was considered about as sure a bet as one could make on a high-school All-American.

"We're interested in three kinds of players—good, great and super," Leonard Hamilton, at the time an assistant at Kentucky, told Kent Hannon of *Sports Illustrated.* "Better than super is where I would classify Albert King. He can deliver the goods."

Albert King
UNIVERSITY OF MARYLAND ATHLETICS

To deliver the player who could deliver those goods, Karim, it was widely reported, received all kinds of enticements. The reports, however, didn't indicate from where those under-the-table offers came. Ultimately, it was big brother Bernard who convinced King his future belonged at Maryland, mainly because the next most logical choice, Arizona State, was too far away.

None of which stopped friends, family, and anyone else who followed King's high-school exploits from blaming Karim for the choice of school. As Hannon wrote in a follow-up story for *SI*, the Maryland program King joined in the fall of 1977 was a dysfunctional mess beset by selfishness, jealousy, and woefully unfulfilled promise. Coach Lefty Driesell had recruited highly regarded guards Jo Jo Hunter and Bill Bryant, who were more concerned with being go-to guys than with where the team actually went.

King, by all accounts a genuinely decent and well-grounded individual, didn't grumble. Instead, he just tried to make the most of his opportunities every time he got the ball—which, unfortunately for a Maryland team sliding to last place in the ACC, wasn't nearly enough.

Marty Blake, one of the NBA's most celebrated assessors of talent, took up for King.

"People expect one of the best high-school players in the country to come in and tear up the college ranks," Blake said. "But realistically, that just can't happen."

At least it couldn't when said player wasn't getting the ball.

"In high school, I wasn't playing with a really good team, so I had to shoot the ball a lot," King explained two years later. "But when I came here, I hesitated shooting a lot. I played as hard as I could. I just didn't play well."

King called it hesitation. Coach Terry Holland of Virginia, looking into the eyes of a frustrated freshman after King scored 15 points in a losing cause against his Cavaliers, called it something else.

"I thought he looked scared," Holland observed.

King finally got a break his junior year, mainly because Greg Manning, a junior who actually knew what the job description of point guard entailed, got a firm grip on the reins of the Maryland offense. With Manning consistently feeding him the ball where he could do something with it, King saw his scoring average soar from 15.9 points a game to 21.7 and his field-goal accuracy from 49.4 percent to 55.3.

If King had made his last shot in the ACC Tournament that season, Driesell would have clinched his first conference title and King would have won the everlasting acclaim of Maryland fans everywhere. King had, after all, scored 27 points in the game.

But his 17-foot jumper on the final possession caught too much iron, Kenny Dennard of Duke wheelbarrowed a leaping Buck Williams out of bounds underneath the basket, and the Blue Devils gathered at midcourt for the trophy celebration.

"When the whole season comes down to one last shot, it can go either way," King recalled. "It really hurt. I tried, and if I had the same opportunity again, I know I would make it."

King and Williams both left Maryland for the New Jersey Nets 12 months later, King as a senior drafted 10th overall and Williams as a junior plucked with the third-overall pick.

After Williams established a solid and at times standout NBA career while King faded from third option to role player to journeyman, sportswriters across the Northeast flocked to a Wendy's restaurant on Palisades Avenue in Englewood, New Jersey, to get a bead on what happened. There, they found the proprietor, one Albert King of Brooklyn, doing all the things an owner of a fast-food establishment does. And if they looked around, they couldn't miss a

Sports Illustrated cover photograph of the proprietor in his glory days posing with Mark Aguirre and Ralph Sampson.

The headline of the article: "That Old School Spirit."

"Some people gravitate to the limelight, to stardom," Williams told sportswriter-author Mike Lupica. "Albert always shied away from it. I'm not even sure how much Albert ever loved playing ball. He was extremely gifted, at an extremely young age, and he took advantage of it.

"But I used to think sometimes that he was always a prisoner of his own talent."

GENE BANKS

6-7 Forward | Duke | 1977–81 | No. 20

1978	ACC ROY	100
	Second-team All-ACC, sixth-most votes	275
	First-team All-Tournament	75
1979	Second-team All-ACC, seventh-most votes	250
1980	Second-team All-ACC, seventh-most votes	250
	First-team All-Tournament	75
1981	First-team All-ACC, fifth-most votes	300
Awards Points		1,325

Mary Garber was an iconic figure in sportswriting in general and ACC basketball in particular who, I'm proud to say, became a close friend during the two decades we worked together at the *Winston-Salem Journal*. She told many unforgettable stories, but my favorite was probably her account of Senior Night at Duke in 1981.

Arriving early, as always, Garber found the lobby of Cameron Indoor Stadium both crowded and abuzz. She had almost made it through the maelstrom when she came face to face with Gene Banks, decked out in a tuxedo and accompanied by two lovely lasses carrying roses.

"A rose for Miss Mary," Banks proclaimed, taking a flower from one of the budding Vanna Whites and handing it to Garber with a low bow.

Garber, decked out in her customary tennis shoes and toboggan, certainly knew bullshit when she saw it.

Gene Banks
DUKE SPORTS INFORMATION

And as Kenny Dennard revealed in *Forever's Team* by John Feinstein, nobody served up a higher grade of bullshit than Gene Banks.

"Remember this about con men," Dennard said. "The best ones are the
ones who you know are conning you but you want to believe them anyway.
They look right at you, tell you something you know can't be so and you believe it anyway. That was Gene. He is without doubt the most charming person I've ever met. I've never met anyone Gene couldn't charm."

Coach Bill Foster got into the Banks derby because Gene's high-school
coach, Joey Goldenberg, worked at Foster's summer camp. He had to outlast
both Digger Phelps of Notre Dame and the Duke admissions board to win the
prize.

Phelps, who refused to back off even after Banks committed to Duke, was
quite an adversary. He worried the Duke staff to distraction when he maneu-
vered Banks aside for a 15-minute pitch after an All-Star game in Washington.

"All I can go by is what the kid tells me," Phelps said, as Art Chansky recounted in *Blue Blood*. "And he hasn't told me to stop recruiting him."

A bigger challenge might have been the admissions board. Banks had good grades at West Philadelphia High School, but his standardized test scores set off warning bells. Frustrated, and still worried about Phelps's shenanigans, Foster suggested Banks force the admissions board's hand by holding a press conference to announce his decision. Banks was eventually admitted, but not until Foster promised to never again request as much latitude.

Banks's decision rocked a campus that had been less than gaga over basketball. Within 24 hours of the announcement, all the season tickets for the 1977–78 campaign were sold—and Cameron has remained sold out every season since. The brothers in Mike Gminski's fraternity printed T-shirts proclaiming, "Gene Is Coming."

Upon arrival, he certainly looked the part. Teammate Bob Bender remembered in *Forever's Team* his first impression of Banks from preseason pickup games: "It was like being in the presence of a god. First of all, he had this body that was chiseled from stone. I mean the guy had never lifted a weight in his life and he was Adonis. Then when we started playing, he was just amazing. He never said anything, because he still wasn't comfortable with the rest of us yet. But he was as gifted a basketball player as I've ever been around."

He was also a bit of a flake, as his nickname, "Tinkerbell," might suggest. He carried a stuffed dog to every game, leaving it in his locker. And he wore the same pair of socks all season.

Banks's life didn't turn out like most people expected. Foster left for South Carolina after Banks's junior season, and the adjustment to Mike Krzyzewski was a trying one.

After the Blue Devils tied for fifth in the ACC with a 6–8 conference mark and were eliminated at Purdue in the third round of the NIT, Banks was drafted in the second round (28th overall) by San Antonio. He played six seasons for the Spurs and Chicago Bulls, averaging 11.3 points and 5.8 rebounds.

What fans have to remember him by was as great a night as any player in ACC history ever experienced. The same night he handed a rose to Mary Garber in the lobby of Cameron, Banks went out to score 25 points in a storybook 66–65 victory over North Carolina. After nailing a 20-footer over Sam Perkins to force overtime, he scored six points in the extra period, including the winning basket with two seconds remaining off a missed shot by Vince Taylor. Students swarmed out of the stands to loft Banks on their shoulders and carry him around the court.

"This is the closest I've ever been to heaven," Banks said afterward.

HAWKEYE WHITNEY

6-5 Guard | N.C. State | 1976–80 | No. 43

1977	ACC ROY	100
1978	Second-team All-ACC, ninth-most votes	200
1979	First-team All-ACC, fourth-most votes	325
	Second-team All-Tournament	50
1980	First-team All-ACC, most votes	400
Awards Points		**1,075**

One's first impulse is to remember Whitney for what he became—a drug addict living on the streets of Kansas City and Washington, D.C., who in 1996 was sentenced to prison for kidnapping.

But doing so would diminish the drive and resolve he displayed while transforming himself from a butterball 234-pound freshman into one of N.C. State's greatest players.

"I've never known anybody to work so hard to get ready to play," his coach, Norm Sloan, maintained.

Whitney was plenty good his first two years, averaging 14.6 points and 5.8 rebounds as a freshman and 15.3 points and 5.4 rebounds as a sophomore. During his first season, he burned Virginia for 21 points and 15 rebounds in a 73–57 road victory that turned when Whitney hustled downcourt to block a dunk attempt by the Cavs' six-nine center, Marc Iavaroni.

But it was not until Whitney committed himself to the weightroom before his junior season and trimmed down to a cut 213 pounds that the ACC really got a look at what he could do. He went on to average 18.3 points, 5.5 rebounds, 3.1 assists, and 1.5 steals over his final two seasons, becoming what Coach Bill Foster of Clemson described as "the greatest clutch player in the league."

Kelly Tripucka wasn't one to argue after Whitney amassed 23 points and 11 rebounds in a 63–55 Wolfpack victory at Notre Dame in 1980.

"That was the best game anyone played against us in a long time," Tripucka said. "Whitney was just incredible. He was too much. We didn't give him much easy, he just took it."

Hawkeye Whitney
N.C. STATE ATHLETICS

He was even better against rival North Carolina on Senior Day in Raleigh, making all eight field-goal attempts in the first half and 11 of 12 for the game to pour in 26 points in a resounding 63–50 victory.

His game was similar to that of two stars from the previous decade, Art Heyman and Larry Miller, in that he was powerful enough to bully perimeter players and too mobile for most forwards. Only once did he fail to make at least half his field-goal attempts in a season, and that was as a sophomore, when he shot 46 percent from the floor. For his career, he shot 50.7 percent.

His impact on the Wolfpack program transcended his on-court production. By landing Whitney, a third-team high-school All-American, Sloan was able to repave the D.C.-area inroads he'd built by signing Kenny Carr out of DeMatha High School two years earlier. Those inroads led to the recruitment of Sidney Lowe and Dereck Whittenburg from D.C. and Thurl Bailey from nearby Seat Pleasant, Maryland. All played integral roles in the Wolfpack's magical run to the 1983 national championship three years after Whitney departed.

"He's like a father image to us," Bailey said while playing with Whitney in 1980. "He motivates us, and he does it in such a way that we all love him for it."

On second thought, it might be worth remembering Whitney for what he became.

Selected by the Kansas City Kings with the 16th pick of the 1980 draft, Whitney experienced a terrible break before he could get established as a pro. Skying for a dunk midway through his rookie season, he tripped over Sidney Moncrief's shoulder and wrecked his knee. He never really recovered. His professional career lasted but 70 games. He averaged 5.8 points and 2.1 rebounds.

Cocaine was starting to become a scourge of the league. When Whitney started freebasing, he was really in trouble, whether he knew it at the time or not.

The death of friend Len Bias rocked him, but not hard enough.

"When that happened, I had to ask, why him and why not me?" Whitney wondered. "I was doing exactly what he was doing."

By 1989, after failing at efforts toward gainful employment in construction and retail, he found himself homeless, crashing in any abandoned building on any grungy mattress he could find.

He made one serious attempt at recovery, returning to N.C. State in the early 1990s with every intention of earning his degree, marrying for a second time, and performing various duties for the Wolfpack athletics program. He even helped Phil Spence, another ex-Wolfpack player, coach the East Wake High School basketball team.

At every opportunity, he preached the evils of addiction.

But the grip drugs had on him wouldn't let go, and by 1993 he was back home in Washington doing what he knew he shouldn't.

What was left of his world came crashing down around him on January 26, 1996, when he and a drug dealer kidnapped a man off the street and forced him to withdraw funds from various ATMs around the city.

Two extenuating factors probably cost Whitney his freedom. One, the kidnapped man happened to be Mark Fabiani, the personal lawyer of Hillary Clinton. And two, the other kidnapper, whom Whitney maintained made him go along at gunpoint, proved to be too young to try as an adult.

So Whitney took a hard fall, landing in a medium-security federal prison in Ashland, Kentucky, to begin a 69-month sentence.

Luckily, his second second chance proved to be his ticket out of his personal purgatory. He kicked his habit during his two years behind bars, got right with God, remarried, and moved back to Kansas City to become the residential technician at Niles Home for Children. He was eventually promoted to coordinator of physical activities and recreation at the facility, which provides shelter and sustenance for around three dozen young victims of neglect and abandonment.

"He brings a special touch, almost a magic touch," Valerie Nicholson Watson, the president and CEO of Niles Home for Children, told Tim Peeler of GoPack.com. "Just the way he had that magic touch with the ball, he has the same magic touch with our kids."

At every opportunity, he counsels potentially wayward youth of the perils that await them on the lost highway.

"I want to see if there is someone I can help from going down the road I went down," Whitney explained.

MIKE O'KOREN

6-8 Forward | North Carolina | 1976–80 | No. 31

1977	First-team All-Tournament	75
1978	First-team All-ACC, fifth-most votes	300
1979	Second-team All-ACC, sixth-most votes	275
	First-team All-Tournament	75
	Second-team All-American	150
1980	First-team All-ACC, fourth-most votes	325
	Second-team All-American	150
Awards Points		**1,350**

To hear Jerry Tarkanian tell it, Dean Smith might have been the greatest recruiter in the history of college basketball.

"Forget about signing Michael Jordan, James Worthy, and the rest," Tarkanian said. "Dean Smith beat Frank Sinatra on a kid from Jersey City.

"Impossible."

Of all the recruiting stories I've come across, my favorite might be the one Tarkanian told about getting his good buddy Sinatra to drop by Mike O'Koren's home to pitch the eternal benefits of playing basketball at Nevada–Las Vegas.

Sinatra, as you might have heard, grew up in Hoboken. O'Koren's hometown of Jersey City is right next door, along the west bank of the Hudson. Rose O'Koren, Mike's mom, grew up a big fan of Ol' Blue Eyes. Can't say for sure, but she might have even been a bobby-soxer.

Mike O'Koren
UNC ATHLETIC COMMUNICATIONS

So I understand why the Shark got so excited when Sinatra agreed to help him out.

"I figured if we got Frank into that living room in Jersey City, there was no way we wouldn't get Mike O'Koren," Tarkanian wrote in his autobiography, *Runnin' Rebel*.

He recounted in his most sardonic fashion how Sinatra made his grand entrance, met the family, signed an autograph or two.

"He might have even sung them a couple of songs," Tarkanian ventured.

If so, one should have been "Don'cha Go 'Way Mad," because that's all he had to say to Tarkanian when word came that O'Koren had committed to North Carolina.

Dooby dooby doo.

I happened to be working for the *Chapel Hill Newspaper* when O'Koren showed up in town, and I can attest that he was, as we said back then, quite a piece of work—freewheeling, quick-witted, effervescent, a smartass.

"I'm as New Jersey as it gets," he once said.

The way the Tar Heel staff remembered it, Tarkanian never had too good a shot at O'Koren, Frank Sinatra or no Frank Sinatra.

Bill Foster at Duke assumed he had an inside track because his star guard, Jim Spanarkel, had played with O'Koren at Hudson Catholic High and the two were friends. Notre Dame was a serious player, but O'Koren's brother, Ronald, was dead set against Mike's heading to South Bend.

Assistant Coach Eddie Fogler of North Carolina risked Tommy John surgery for all the elbow bending he did in Jersey City bars selling O'Koren's colorful assortment of neighborhood pals on the unsurpassed beauty of Chapel Hill in the springtime. Smith remembered in *A Coach's Life* a raucous night spent with several of that crowd at a party after O'Koren cast his lot with the Tar Heels. Three of them—Eddie Ford, Gibby Lewis, and Ron Steinmitz—became fast friends who brooked no ill word in their presence about Smith and the Carolina basketball program.

In the end, O'Koren wanted to win. He noticed that Duke had finished last in the ACC in 1976, while the Tar Heels won the regular season by four games. So he headed to Chapel Hill, where he became the second freshman (after Phil Ford two seasons earlier) to start his first game under Smith.

He played 30 minutes, contributing six field goals on eight attempts for 15 points, in a 78–66 victory over N.C. State in the Big Four Tournament. The performance was no fluke. O'Koren averaged 13.9 points and 6.6 rebounds that season while shooting 57.7 percent from the floor. He proved an indispensable cog in the Tar Heels' run all the way to the championship game against Marquette.

At North Carolina, O'Koren quickly learned the value of a good shot.

"We were playing Virginia during my freshman year," he recalled to Ken Rappoport in *Tales from the North Carolina Tar Heels Locker Room*. "I got hot. I took a couple of shots, and then I took a bad shot. I came over to the bench and Coach goes, 'That was a bad shot.' I said, 'But Coach, I felt it.' He said, 'Oh. Go feel the bench.'"

To help the Tar Heels make their date with destiny and Al McGuire's Marquette Warriors in Atlanta, O'Koren had to get past an old acquaintance. North Carolina played the Nevada–Las Vegas Runnin' Rebels in the national semifinals. O'Koren rubbed in his decision to turn down Tarkanian by going off for 31 points in a wild 84–83 victory.

After the game, O'Koren was asked if 31 points were the most he'd ever scored.

"So far," he replied.

That was my first Final Four. I also remember O'Koren holding up his jersey and saying, "This is the only 31 I know."

Years later, Tarkanian was still smarting from the episode.

"Every time he scored, I was ready to curse Sinatra for not closing out that recruiting deal," he wrote. "If we had gotten O'Koren instead of Carolina, we would have won the national title.

"That Frank Sinatra, he could really sing, but he sure couldn't recruit."

For the most part, O'Koren's wisecracking, irreverent ways fit into the structured confines of the North Carolina basketball program. Except for one notable time they didn't.

Smith created quite a flap in 1979 when he went into the four-corners offense following the opening tap at Duke, a move that resulted in the Tar Heels trailing 7–0 at halftime and eventually losing 47–40. Among the many who objected to Smith's strategy was O'Koren, who told the *Durham Morning Herald* that he, for one, wanted to run against the Blue Devils.

Art Chansky wrote about the repercussions in *Blue Blood*. O'Koren was called onto the Carolina blue carpet. He found Smith in his office, holding a cigarette in one hand and a copy of that day's Durham paper in the other.

"Michael," Smith said, "you play and I'll coach."

Anyone passing through Carmichael Auditorium that afternoon couldn't miss seeing O'Koren running the steps in a weighted jacket.

A first-round pick (sixth overall) by New Jersey, O'Koren played his entire eight-year NBA career with the Nets except for 15 games with the Washington Bullets. He averaged 8.2 points and 3.4 rebounds. He remained in the league as an assistant coach of the Nets and an associate head coach of the Washington Wizards.

MIKE GMINSKI

6-11 Center | Duke | 1976–80 | No. 43

The back pages of ACC basketball are crammed with bad decisions by even the best of coaches. No less a light than Everett Case passed on Dickie Hemric and Lenny Rosenbluth—and spent many days and nights regretting it.

So perhaps Dean Smith can be partly excused for not seeing the potential of a 16-year-old center from a small school in Connecticut who dropped by for an informal visit with his family after attending a basketball camp at Davidson. Or maybe Smith saw what he didn't like in Mike Gminski's father, Joe,

1977	ACC ROY	100
	Second-team All-Tournament	50
1978	First-team All-ACC, third-most votes	350
	First-team All-Tournament	75
1979	First-team All-ACC, unanimous	425
	First-team All-Tournament	75
	ACC POY	200
	First-team All-American (with Larry Bird of Indiana State, David Greenwood of UCLA, Magic Johnson of Michigan State, and Sidney Moncrief of Arkansas)	200
1980	First-team All-ACC, third-most votes	350
	First-team All-Tournament	75
	Second-team All-American	150
Awards Points		2,050

the ultimate Little League parent, who made Coach Bill Foster's life miserable during Gminski's four years at Duke.

Gminski offered a guess as to why he received a rejection letter from North Carolina assistant Bill Guthridge.

"I wanted to play a lot as a freshman, and I think that played a part of it," Gminski said in *Blue Blood* by Art Chansky.

A year later, Tommy LaGarde tore a knee ligament during North Carolina's run to the Final Four, forcing Smith to fashion, Frankenstein-like, one serviceable center out of the three freshmen he had recruited instead of Gminski.

His handiwork was dubbed "Yonwolfsin" by clever scribes of the day. Rich Yonakor of Euclid, Ohio, averaged 3.7 points and 2.5 rebounds; Jeff Wolf of Kohler, Wisconsin, averaged 1.7 points and 1.4 rebounds; and Steve Krafcisin of Chicago Ridge, Illinois, averaged 2.9 points and 1.5 rebounds.

Eight miles away at Duke, Mike Gminski of Monroe, Connecticut, averaged 15.3 points and ranked second in the ACC with 10.7 rebounds a game.

Foster was giddy about Smith's loss becoming his gain.

"He's here," Foster gushed. "The big guy is here."

Duke lore reveals that Terry Chili, his career averages of 4.7 points and 2.7 rebounds notwithstanding, was one of the most important players in school history. While working Lefty Driesell's summer camp at Maryland, Chili became acquainted with the then-15-year-old Gminski. Duke was paying scant attention to Gminski because the Blue Devils, like everyone else, thought he was entering his junior season of high school. But when Chili reported to Foster that Gminski planned to consolidate his junior and senior years and graduate early, Foster went to work and convinced Gminski to visit.

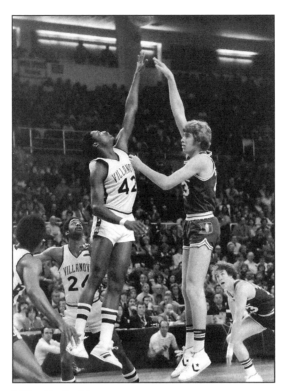

Mike Gminski

He arrived the same spring weekend as Mike O'Koren and Jim Graziano, both more highly regarded recruits. But after a well-oiled night of partying with Jim Spanarkel described in *Forever's Team* by John Feinstein, Gminski canceled all his other visits and cast his lot with Duke.

Feinstein also chronicled the combustible relationship between Foster and Joe Gminski, who quit his job to devote his life to developing his son into a great player. He took his endeavor so seriously that he was moved to write a letter to the local paper castigating Foster's coaching acumen.

The elder Gminski, who had a brief and less-than-memorable basketball career at the University of Connecticut, defended his involvement in his son's life.

"You're looking at a man who doesn't give a damn about what other people say," Gminski told the *Schenectady Gazette*. "Mike has been rewarded for his work.

"I fail to see the difference between bringing an athlete along and someone with musical ability."

The work for which Gminski was rewarded was prodigious, according to Lou Goetz, an assistant for Foster who took a special interest in Gminski.

"One thing people forget about Mike is how hard he worked," Goetz said in *Forever's Team*. "Except for the shooting, which he always did well, things don't come naturally for him on a basketball court. Everything he's become is because he's consistently worked his tail off to get better."

Gminski's impact on the Duke program was incalculable, but I'll give it a good college try. The Blue Devils were 11–37 in the ACC from 1973 through 1976, and 13–47 through Gminski's 2–10 freshman season of 1976–77. Over the next three seasons, they were 24–14. And they really put the hammer down in ACC Tournament play, winning championships in two of those seasons and losing to North Carolina in the title game of the other.

Before 1978, Duke hadn't won a game in the ACC Tournament since 1972. Foster, who took over the program in 1975, was 0–3. Emboldened by the addition of Gminski, Spanarkel, Gene Banks, and Kenny Dennard, Foster approached the 1978 tournament with more confidence.

"We usually lose and I go home," he cracked on workout day. "In the past, I've just packed a handkerchief, and that's about it. But this time, I packed for the whole week, and so did the team."

The Blue Devils, as it turned out, needed all their threads, rolling past Clemson 83–72, Maryland 81–69, and Wake Forest 85–77 to the school's first conference title since 1966.

There were plenty of reasons Duke was 8–1 in ACC Tournament play in 1978, 1979, and 1980, but none was bigger than Gminski, who over his career averaged 19.1 points and 11.8 rebounds in the tournament while shooting 54 percent from the floor and 83 percent from the line. He ranks seventh all-time in points scored in the tournament (191) and third in rebounds (118).

In 1980, Duke retired Gminski's jersey, making him the first Blue Devil so honored since Dick Groat three decades earlier.

Sportswriter Al Featherston, whom I imagine knows more about Duke basketball than any living soul (especially now that the other preeminent Duke hoops historian, Bill Brill, has passed), explained in a piece for dukebasketballreport.com how Eddie Cameron, the longtime director of athletics, was Groat's most influential fan. Convinced there could never be an equal to old number 10, Cameron nixed all attempts to have more jerseys retired. That's how Gary Melchionni, Mark Crow, Greg Wendt, and Thomas Hill ended up wearing the number 25 of the great Art Heyman, and Pete Kramer, Todd Anderson, Phil Henderson, and Cherokee Parks got number 44, worn by Jeff Mullins.

By 1980, Tom Butters was calling the shots for the Duke athletics department. When Foster came to him suggesting that Gminski's jersey be raised to the rafters, Butters said, "Sure, why not?"

Since the logjam was broken, 11 more Duke jerseys have been retired over the past 32 seasons—including those of Heyman and Mullins.

Gminski wasn't a Dream Teamer in the pros, but he was good enough to play more games (938) and pull down more rebounds (6,480) than any other player from Duke. Only Jack Marin, who was good enough to be traded for Elvin Hayes, scored more points, totaling 12,541 to Gminski's 10,953.

Taken by New Jersey with the seventh-overall pick, Gminski played 14 seasons with the Nets, Philadelphia 76ers, Charlotte Hornets, and Milwaukee Bucks.

"A lot of my career, I've been the guy people didn't think could make the transition to the next level," Gminski said in *Forever's Team*.

Dean Smith, lest it be forgotten, was one of those people. And that's how he got stuck trying to win a national championship with an aggregate named Yonwolfsin at center.

JIM SPANARKEL

6-5 Guard | Duke | 1975–79 | No. 34

Year	Award	Points
1976	ACC ROY	100
1977	Second-team All-ACC, seventh-most votes	250
	Second-team All-Tournament	50
1978	First-team All-ACC, fourth-most votes	325
	Everett Case Award	100
1979	First-team All-ACC, third-most votes	350
	First-team All-Tournament	75
	Second-team All-American	150
Awards Points		**1,400**

Jim Spanarkel may be the only player in ACC history whose name was fashioned into a verb. When faster and more athletic opponents were beaten by smarts, verve, and savvy, they were said to have been Spanarkeled.

Considered a step or two slow by most major colleges, the pigeon-toed Spanarkel picked the Blue Devils over Wake Forest, Holy Cross, Ohio University, and William & Mary because of Duke's academic reputation. But Coach Bill Foster also dangled the promise he could play baseball as well as basket-

Jim Spanarkel

ball. Spanarkel did actually pitch and play shortstop for two seasons at Duke before the demands of major-college basketball and classes became so staggering he retired from the diamond.

"I can't say we knew Jim would be as good as he became, but I think we deserve credit for seeing the potential," Foster said in Jim Sumner's *Tales from the Duke Blue Devils Hardwood*. "We knew we had something special early in practices. No matter how we divided up the teams, the team that Jim was on always seemed to win. He just had a knack for doing the right thing."

In *Forever's Team*, John Feinstein wrote about the backhanded scouting report Duke assistant Bob Wenzel got from Rocky Pope, Spanarkel's coach at Hudson Catholic High School in Jersey City.

Wenzel recalled, "I said, 'Tell me about this Spanarkel kid,' and Rocky says, 'Well, he's about six-foot-five inches, he's not very fast or quick, he can't jump, and he's not a very good shooter. But when the other team presses, we give him the ball. When we need a basket, we give him the ball. If we're having trouble stopping a big man, we put him on the guy. If we're having trouble with a guard, we put him on that guy. About the only thing he can do for you is win.'

"Four years later, when Jimmy was a senior at Duke, I got a call from a pro scout and he said, 'Tell me about Spanarkel.' I gave him the same speech Rocky had given me four years earlier because it was still true."

Foster and his staff celebrated when Spanarkel committed. They felt they had Duke on the path back to national relevance.

The Blue Devils struggled Spanarkel's freshman and sophomore seasons, winning only five of 24 ACC games. Following the arrival of Mike Gminski in 1976 and Gene Banks and Kenny Dennard in 1977, however, they caught fire.

In 1977–78, with both Spanarkel and Gminski making first-team All-ACC, the Blue Devils finished second in the league at 8–4, beat Wake Forest 85–77 in Greensboro to win the school's first ACC title since 1966, and kept rolling until they reached not just the Final Four but the championship game against Kentucky. The magical run ended in St. Louis, where Jack "Goose" Givens erupted for 41 points to spark the Wildcats to a 94–88 victory.

According to teammates, Spanarkel, Duke's captain his final two seasons, was the player all the others looked up to.

"He had an unbelievable basketball IQ," Gminski said in Sumner's *Tales from the Duke Blue Devils Hardwood*. "He had a great sense of what we needed and when we needed it.

"No question it was his team."

Spanarkel played during wild times at Duke, when the Cameron Crazies were cementing their reputation as one of the zaniest and most creative student bodies ever. Whenever anybody goes off about how wild the Blue Devils' student section is today, I tell them they should have been there in the late 1970s, when no topic was off-limits and no joke too off-color.

Guard Moe Rivers of N.C. State was charged with stealing aspirin, so of course he was pelted with Bufferin and other brands when he visited Cameron.

Forwards Tony Warren and Tiny Pinder of the Wolfpack were charged with changing the price tags on underwear, so during pregame introductions a sign appeared: "Warren, Pinder, You Can't Switch the Numbers on the Scoreboard."

That was one of two signs involving Pinder to show up in the Duke cheering section. The other was the classic, "Mrs. Sloan Loves Norm's 'Tiny Pinder.' "

After getting picked up for breaking into a pinball machine, Tommy Burleson was serenaded by a rousing rendition of the Who's "Pinball Wizard" from the Duke pep band.

When Maryland visited Cameron just after the *Washington Post* published a report on the need of several Terps to improve their grades to remain eligible, Duke students sat behind the visitors' bench wearing dunce caps.

I got a sneak peek at my own personal favorite when I stepped into the bathroom off the Cameron lobby and saw a student wearing a red scarf on his head and a red dress. He was carrying a piece of aluminum foil fashioned to look like a microphone. Some may not remember, but Coach Norm Sloan's wife often sang the national anthem before N.C. State's home games. On this occasion, Sloan was left to stare daggers at the student in drag as he stood at midcourt lip-synching, "Oh, say can you see . . ." In case anybody missed it, the prankster had "Mrs. Norm Sloan" stenciled on his back.

Spanarkel, for his part, was a model of decorum in a sea of insanity. His calm, steady game reflected his personality.

"He's my wind-up toy," Foster said. "Wind him up and he plays all day."

Spanarkel continued to confound conventional wisdom over the five years he spent in the NBA. A first-round pick (16th overall) by the Philadelphia 76ers in 1979, he was plucked by the Dallas Mavericks in the expansion draft before the 1980–81 season. He led the Mavs in scoring that year and was the team's second-leading scorer the next. He retired at age 27 to take a job with Merrill Lynch back home in New Jersey but remains close to the game as a color commentator for college basketball.

ROD GRIFFIN

6-6 Forward | Wake Forest | 1974–78 | No. 32

1976	Second-team All-ACC, 9th-most votes	200
1977	First-team All-ACC, most votes	400
	ACC POY	200
	Second-team All-American	150
1978	First-team All-ACC, unanimous	425
	First-team All-Tournament	75
	Second-team All-American	150
Awards Points		**1,600**

Revisionist history has never held much fascination for me. Why spend time wondering about "what ifs" when it's so hard to keep up with what actually was?

But in researching Rod Griffin, I couldn't help spinning in my head what might have happened if Dean Smith had decided one night to remain at a

Rod Griffin
WAKE FOREST ATHLETIC COMMUNICATIONS

small, out-of-the-way gymnasium an hour or so longer.

Smith had tooled his Carolina blue Cadillac down to Fairmont, a country town in Robeson County a dozen miles from the South Carolina border, to see another prospect play in a Class A tournament. Richard Bass, the coach at Fairmont High, took the opportunity to suggest that Smith remain long enough to see Griffin, the pride of Fairmont, in a later game.

Bass was well aware that Griffin, while hoeing, plowing, and feeding livestock on his grandparents' farm, daydreamed about playing basketball for Smith at North Carolina. But Smith, for whatever reason, declined the invitation and headed back to Chapel Hill before Griffin took the floor. I hope for his sake he had important business to tend to.

Imagine what might have transpired if Smith had hung around, liked what he saw, and offered Griffin a scholarship. The impact on ACC basketball, if not college basketball as a whole, might have been monumental.

Smith brought in two recruits for 1974–75, Griffin's freshman season. One was Phil Ford, the other Tom Zaliagiris. Ford became an instant starter, while Zaliagiris played little until his senior season.

Manning the Tar Heels' front line in 1974–75 were junior Mitch Kupchak, senior Ed Stahl, and sophomores Tommy LaGarde and Bruce Buckley. If Griffin had played as well for North Carolina that season as he did for Wake Forest, for whom he averaged 13.9 points and 7.6 rebounds, that would have been bad news for Stahl, LaGarde, and Buckley and good news for North Carolina.

Griffin was good enough as a sophomore to make second-team All-ACC. By his junior season, he was Player of the Year. North Carolina remained strong without him, finishing 23–8 in 1975 (though a disappointing 8–4 in ACC play), 25–4 in 1976, 28–5 in 1977 (the season it lost to Marquette in the NCAA championship game), and 23–8 in 1978.

But say Griffin ended up at North Carolina and played four years with Ford, the best point guard in the history of the ACC. How would that have changed the course of Tar Heel basketball history?

For one thing, the Tar Heels wouldn't have had as much trouble beating Wake Forest, which won five of 11 games against North Carolina those four seasons despite being prohibitive underdogs almost every time. And when North Carolina did pull a game out, it was rarely easy. Four of the Tar Heels' victories during that stretch were by three points or fewer, one coming in overtime.

"The best thing Wake Forest has going for it is we're Carolina," Smith said at the time, in typical Carolina-centric fashion. "They do a good job getting up for us."

Smith had himself to blame for that. In his 11 games against the Tar Heels, Griffin averaged 17.7 points and 8.5 rebounds while shooting 58 percent from the floor. That's a tad more production than Smith could count on from the likes of Stahl, Buckley, and Chickie Yonakor.

Further, it's a safe bet that when the ACC revealed the 50 players named to its silver-anniversary team in 2003, Griffin's name would have been on it. His omission and that of Bob Verga of Duke were easily the two most egregious.

Lest I be accused of being as Carolina-centric as Smith, it's possible Coach Carl Tacy would have sold Griffin on the advantages of Wake Forest even had the Tar Heels' head man been interested. Tacy did have an ace in the hole—a merchant back in Fairmont named Linwood Rich. It was Rich who had steered Griffin to Tacy's basketball camp in Winston-Salem during the summer of 1973, unbeknownst at the time to Tacy himself.

Griffin was a man-child whose mother threw him alley-oops in the backyard. That's when she wasn't in New York City trying to make a living while she left Rod to help out on the farm.

"Here comes this big, strapping youth with arms as big as my legs," Tacy recalled years later. "I thought he was maybe a counselor who had come. And I was quick to ask him in the hallway if he was one of our counselors. He said no, he had come to be a part of our camp as a player."

Recognizing Griffin's ability, Tacy was left to hope that no one else stumbled across the diamond in the rough.

"Clemson and Maryland sent me their brochures and a letter or two, but they never came to see me," Griffin said.

After picking Wake Forest over offers from UNC-Charlotte, UNC-Wilmington, Campbell, and Pembroke State, Griffin needed little time to prove he belonged in the ACC. Nine games into his career, he blocked a shot by David Thompson in the semifinals of the Big Four Classic, the night Wake knocked off the defending national champions and broke the Wolfpack's 36-game winning streak.

He quickly became known for his power and strength, his deadly mid-range jumper, and his superstition of eating a bowl of lime sherbet before every game.

He grew in college in every way.

Wake Forest in those days was not the exclusive institution it would later become. But it was still a different world from the family farm back in Fairmont.

Tacy recognized that Griffin's biggest adjustments came not on the court, but off it.

"Every day, you could see a change in Rod for the better," he recalled. "He just gained so much confidence, and everybody loved him. He was one of the standouts in my mind."

Listed at six-six and 225 pounds, Griffin was caught between positions after being selected by the Denver Nuggets with the 17th pick of the 1978 draft. He never played a game in the NBA but ended up doing quite well for himself and his family while playing for years in the top professional league in Italy.

PHIL FORD

6-2 Guard | North Carolina | 1974–78 | No. 12

Year	Award	Points
1975	Everett Case Award	100
1976	First-team All-ACC, third-most votes	350
	First-team All-Tournament	75
	Second-team All-American	150
1977	First-team All-ACC, second-most votes	375
	First-team All-Tournament	75
	First-team All-American (with Kent Benson of Indiana, Otis Birdsong of Houston, Rickey Green of Michigan, Marques Johnson of UCLA, and Bernard King of Tennessee)	200
1978	First-team All-ACC, unanimous	425
	Second-team All-Tournament	50
	ACC POY	200
	National POY (with fellow first-team All-Americans Butch Lee of Marquette, David Greenwood of UCLA, Larry Bird of Indiana State, and Mychal Thompson of Minnesota)	250
Awards Points		**2,250**

Phil Ford was the one player who made Coach Dean Smith almost sorry for the other team whenever he directed the Tar Heels into their infamous four-corners spread offense.

The operative word of that sentence: *almost.*

"I admit it was unfair with Ford," Smith said years afterward. "He hit the foul shots, he could drive, he could take it in, bring it out, and pass it off. He was unstoppable."

A multi-sport star in Rocky Mount, North Carolina, Ford was the focus of a recruiting war so fierce that, as one unverified account from Art Chansky's *The Dean's List* has it, a Clemson booster visited his home and left behind a suitcase filled with cash. An equally unverified account from Chansky's book has it that when Ford's father called Smith to ask what he should do, Smith suggested, "Have Phil sign with Carolina and keep the money."

To anyone who offered illegal inducements, Ford's father had a stock reply: "You can have my son for a nickel, if that's where he wants to go to school.

Phil Ford

If he doesn't, there's not enough money in the world."

Smith recalled in *A Coach's Life* the white-hot recruiting battle. Lefty Driesell of Maryland offered to put the ball in Ford's hands the day he arrived at College Park and leave it there all four years. Norm Sloan of N.C. State dangled the opportunity to play a season with David Thompson.

Smith went to work selling the star's parents, Phil Sr. and Mabel, both of whom were educators with master's degrees, on the value of a North Carolina diploma. He wrote how, when Mabel Ford first heard he was visiting, her response was, "Isn't it nice that North Carolina is sending one of its deans to our house?"

In his autobiography, *Hard Work*, Roy Williams claimed at least a modicum of credit for Ford's deciding on North Carolina. Williams, who had helped pay his way through North Carolina by refereeing intramural games, recalled the summer of 1973, when Ford attended Smith's basketball camp.

Smith asked Williams to referee the games in which Ford played, mentioning in passing that Ford was a player the Tar Heels really, really, *really* wanted.

"Phil Ford enjoyed himself at basketball camp that summer because every time Phil drove to the basket, Phil got fouled," Williams wrote. "On the defensive end, Phil got a charge call in his favor every time. Phil played great.

"Phil came to UNC."

The cocky kid with the Little Richard look found the college game a little more demanding than he expected. Ron Morris's *ACC Basketball* tells of a despondent Ford.

"I called home crying," Ford recalled. "It was the first time that basketball was so hard."

Smith apparently was more impressed with Ford than Ford was with himself. Taking advantage of the freshman eligibility rule instituted just two seasons before, Smith installed Ford at the point and let him run the show. One story has it that in Ford's four years, he only once called a play of which Smith did not approve.

Buddies back home kidded him about the two front teeth that had been knocked out playing basketball, calling him "Bunny Rabbit." The nickname followed him to Chapel Hill because of the crackling energy with which he played. On the court, he gave no quarter and asked for none.

"He was the fiercest competitor I've ever seen in the ACC," Lefty Driesell said. "If you could get every player to play as hard as Phil Ford did, you'd never lose a game."

Perhaps because of the reckless abandon with which he played, Ford suffered some of the most ill-timed injuries in conference history.

As a sophomore, he sprained his ankle in a pickup game back home just before the Tar Heels were to play, and lose to, Alabama in the NCAA Tournament.

As a junior, he hyperextended his elbow in the East Regional victory over Notre Dame and was hindered in the regional championship victory over Kentucky and the Final Four run in Atlanta. Smith later said Ford's injury convinced him to make his ill-fated move to the four corners while tied with Marquette in the national championship game.

"If Ford hadn't hurt his elbow, and could shoot from outside, we would have continued to play against their zone," Smith revealed.

And as a senior, Ford sprained his wrist late in the regular season and sat out a loss to N.C. State that the Tar Heels didn't need to win to finish first. He had entered the season saying he wanted to play one perfect game. He may have succeeded in his final game at Carmichael Auditorium, when he shook off the injury to score a career-high 34 points with five assists and three turnovers in an unforgettable 87–83 victory over Duke.

"He was just taking it down and spinning it off his feet or under his legs or hooking it," Coach Bill Foster of the Blue Devils lamented. "We didn't have any defense for that."

Although the Ford-driven Tar Heels never fulfilled their promise in the NCAA Tournament, losing in the first round twice and the second round once and the 1977 championship game, Ford did earn a gold medal as the point guard of the 1976 United States Olympic team, coached by Smith.

Drafted by the Kansas City Royals with the second pick, Ford paid immediate dividends when he was named NBA Rookie of the Year. By his second season, he was All-NBA. His career stalled, however, when he suffered both a serious eye injury and the effects of alcoholism.

"I abused alcohol, and there's no excuse," Ford acknowledged.

Rehabilitated, he returned to North Carolina as an assistant coach and was on the staff in 1993 when the Tar Heels won Smith's second national championship.

"If I had to choose the ideal qualities I'd want in a guard, the result would be Phil Ford," Smith said. "Because of his special blend of talent and desire, I don't know of any guard anywhere in the world who is as suited to the role."

KENNY CARR

6-8 Forward | N.C. State | 1974–77 | No. 32

1975	First-team All-Tournament	75
1976	First-team All-ACC, most votes	400
	ACC POY, close runner-up	125
1977	First-team All-ACC, fourth-most votes	325
	First-team All-Tournament	75
Awards Points		**1,000**

From the day I began this project, I could hear the outcry from those whose heroes were spurned—the inevitable "I know what a Hall of Famer looks like, and (fill in the blank) was a Hall of Famer."

Well, this is the point when I mention that I, too, know what a Hall of Famer looks like. And Kenny Carr was a Hall of Famer.

My problem arose when I first tabulated the totals needed for induction

Kenny Carr
COURTESY OF ED CARAM

and Carr came up shy. Now, he could have made it easier on me (and on his coach, Norm Sloan) by returning for his senior season. But even with his early departure for the NBA, I knew he belonged in this book. Here was someone who was judged to be one of the ACC's four best players twice, who in the eyes of many was the best player in the league as a sophomore, who was first-team All-Tournament twice, and who (although the honor doesn't factor into my Hall of Fame tabulation) won a gold medal with the United States Olympic team.

But even after adding the points I was at the time awarding to those who received half as many Player of the Year votes as the actual winners, Carr fell short. And that just wasn't right.

So I began messing around with the Player of the Year voting, justifying myself with the rationalization that few tools were more valuable for culling the good—and even the very good—from the great. I remembered Sloan's irate reaction when Mitch Kupchak edged out Carr for POY, 74 votes to 50. Stormin' Norman chalked it up to "old-school loyalties," an obvious shot at what he perceived to be a light blue bias among the working press.

I revisited the issue and decided that a hotly contested POY vote should be seen in a different light. What I came up with was a sliding scale in which a runner-up who finished with two-thirds as many votes as the POY received 125 Awards Points (to the POY's 150). Fault my rationalization if you like, but it's hard to fault the results, at least in Carr's case.

On Super Bowl Sunday in 1976, during one of the mildest winters of my lifetime, the balmy weather outside matched the sunny mood inside Carmichael Auditorium. The customary crowd of around 10,000 packed into the 12-year-old facility with the three sides of permanent seats and one side of roll-out bleachers to celebrate a new day in the red-hot rivalry with N.C. State.

The Wolfpack's streak of nine straight victories over the Tar Heels had been snapped the season before. And North Carolina, led by precocious freshman point guard Phil Ford, had knocked off N.C. State in the ACC Tournament championship for good measure.

Now, the scourge of Tar Heel brethren everywhere, David Thompson, had taken his high-flying ways to Denver of the ABA. The Wolfpack had enjoyed its run against North Carolina, but it was officially over.

So what was guard Al Green of the visitors doing on the foul line hitting the winning free throw? He was only adding the period to the statement sophomore teammate Kenny Carr made that afternoon by contributing 29 points and 16 rebounds to the Wolfpack's stunning 68–67 upset. Thompson or no Thompson, N.C. State was still a force to be reckoned with.

"Kenny Carr was one of the best athletes I ever coached," Sloan said in Douglas Herakovich's *Pack Pride*. "He was a real joy to coach and an outstanding student.

"David Thompson was the best athlete I ever coached but Kenny wasn't too far behind."

Frank Weedon, an institution at N.C. State for his decades of service as sports information director and associate director of athletics, went one step farther.

"Kenny was a great, great player," Weedon told Tim Peeler in *Legends of N.C. State Basketball*. "But he was so stoic and never showed any emotions, and I think people forget about him. He may have been the second-greatest player to ever play here, behind David."

Growing up in Washington, D.C., Carr didn't take up basketball until he was 14. As a youngster, he preferred football.

He came of age playing for the legendary Morgan Wootten at DeMatha. Eddie Biedenbach, an N.C. State assistant, was visiting DeMatha while recruiting Adrian Dantley when Wootten pulled him aside and advised him to keep an eye on the strapping sophomore named Carr across the way. Carr played little as a high-school junior while recovering from a knee injury. But he emerged as the real deal as a senior, and the inroads Biedenbach had made paid off.

A chance to play with David Thompson helped as well. Carr was infatuated with Thompson after watching him take a spill over Phil Spence's shoulder in the famous NCAA Tournament game against Pittsburgh.

"I had a heads up on everybody because of recruiting Dantley and sitting there with Morgan," Biedenbach said in *Legends of N.C. State Basketball*. "I think they gave me an honorary degree for the number of hours I spent up there for two years.

"Kenny Carr ended up being a truly great college player. He was one of the toughest, strongest forwards ever. I'm not sure people really ever appreciated him, and what he accomplished."

Carr replaced Thompson, but he wasn't Thompson. No one was. The two had different games, Thompson relying on explosiveness and aerobatics and Carr on strength, mobility, and a surprising touch.

Ford of the rival Tar Heels considered Carr ahead of his time, a bruising, powerful inside player with the ability to knock down the 20-footer.

It was to Sloan's credit that he allowed a player of Carr's size and physicality the latitude to play an all-around game.

It was to Carr's credit that he was able to do so when few could.

"Kenny Carr is a real player, a whale of a player," Red Auerbach of the Boston Celtics said in *Pack Pride*. "He's a complete player. He can drive, shoot, run, rebound and play defense. He does it all."

Those were precisely the qualities that convinced Dean Smith to pick Carr for the 1976 team that won the gold medal in Montreal. Carr, who averaged 6.9 points and 3.1 rebounds for the United States, is one of two Wolfpack players (along with Tommy Burleson) to play in the Olympics and the only one to bring home the gold.

"As far as I am concerned, our team won the last legitimate gold medal there was for the United States," Carr said in *Legends of N.C. State Basketball*. "In 1980, we boycotted Russia. In 1984, they boycotted us. In 1988, we lost it [to Yugoslavia].

"And in 1992, we started the Dream Team."

Carr led the ACC in scoring for his second-straight season as a junior but grew frustrated by what he considered a lack of suitable competition. So he left after his junior year for a tougher challenge.

The sixth pick overall of the 1977 draft by Los Angeles, Carr played 10 NBA seasons with the Lakers, Cleveland Cavaliers, Detroit Pistons, and Portland Trailblazers, averaging 11.6 points and 7.4 rebounds for his career.

Along the way, he found time to return to N.C. State to complete his degree. His jersey hangs in the rafters at the Wolfpack's home arena.

SKIP BROWN

6-1 Guard | Wake Forest | 1973–77 | No. 15

1975	First-team All-ACC, second-most votes	375
	Second-team All-Tournament	50
1976	Second-team All-ACC, seventh-most votes	250
1977	First-team All-ACC, third-most votes	350
Awards Points		**1,025**

In an era of sportswriting known for its flowery prose, perhaps no one covering the ACC piled the compost higher than Bruce Phillips, a hell of a guy I was proud to know in the days he wrote for the *Raleigh Times.*

Early in Skip Brown's sophomore season, when he was emerging as one of the most dynamic players in the league, Phillips sat at his typewriter to bang out the following homage, datelined Greensboro:

> In a grouping of the best basketball guards in the world, don't Skip Brown.
>
> Friday and Saturday, in the Big Four Tournament here, the Wake Forest sophomore took his place among the game's grandiose with a performance that should be hanging in the Louvre.
>
> He wears Skip on the back of his jersey and scoots across the hardwood like a bar of wet soap. He is so quick the only way to stay with him is with a camera. By the time a defender gets to him, he's moved to a new address.
>
> His shooting range is anywhere inside the city limits. He has amazing body control.
>
> Skip Brown is the total guard: Leader, shooter, defender, ball handler, inspirer. And his work is almost sleepy effortless perfection that marks all the good ones.

Brown wasn't expected to be all that when he chose Wake Forest over N.C. State, Florida State, Virginia Tech, and Tennessee. But it was a good thing for Coach Carl Tacy he was, because the program Brown joined had won only six ACC games over the previous two seasons—and was destined to win just five more in Brown's first two years.

The Deacons climbed to fourth place at 5–7 in conference play Brown's

Skip Brown

junior season, after Rod Griffin emerged as a sophomore to give Tacy an inside-outside axis. Wake Forest then enjoyed Tacy's first really good season in Brown's senior campaign of 1976–77, tying for second in the ACC at 8–6, finishing 22–8 overall, and riding Brown's 25 points and eight assists to an 86–81 victory over Southern Illinois in the Midwest Regional semifinal in Oklahoma City.

Standing in the way of the Deacons' trip to the Final Four was Marquette, the team destined to win it all the next weekend in Atlanta. With Brown managing just 10 points and six assists (while committing five turnovers), the Warriors rolled 82–68.

A native of Kingsport, Tennessee, Brown might well have played for the state university if Coach Ray Mears hadn't pushed for him to redshirt as a freshman. That's why he passed up an opportunity to play with Bernard King and Ernie Grunfeld in Knoxville.

Instead, he took the advice of local banker Bill Green, who would in time become the owner of the Bank of Tennessee. Green convinced Brown to attend Wake Forest and pursue a career in banking.

He got his nickname because his sister didn't like the name given him, Simpson Ollie Brown, which also happened to be that of their father. So Alma started calling him "Skip" shortly after he was born.

Growing up with six sisters, five of them older, Brown learned early to take up for himself. That trait was on full display his junior season, when he was relegated to second-team All-ACC after having made first team as a sophomore. He played the year with a bruised kneecap and finished seventh in the voting, behind guards Phil Ford, John Lucas, and Tate Armstrong.

"I'm the best guard in the ACC," Brown proclaimed at the outset of his senior season. "On one leg last year, I was quicker than Phil Ford and Tate Armstrong. I deserve a little more credit than I have been getting."

Tacy was Brown's biggest supporter from the time he exploded onto the conference and national scene as a sophomore.

"I don't think any coach likes to feel that his program is built around one player, but there is no way we can measure Skip's value to us," Tacy remarked. "I said before the season that he was one of the most exciting guards in the country, and it looks like he may be better than even our staff recognized."

Brown was selected by the Boston Celtics in the third round of the 1977 draft, but any visions of a long, profitable NBA career never materialized. So he fell back on Plan B—which stood for Banking.

He completed the management training program at First Federal Savings and Loan in Winston-Salem and a commercial training program at NCNB, then spent almost 20 years with Bank of America.

In 2004, he started TriStone Community Bank, which was purchased by First Community Bank in 2009. That year, Brown was also named chairman of the North Carolina Bankers Association.

JOHN LUCAS

6-3 Guard | Maryland | 1972–76 | No. 15

What do you do when John Wooden, Hubie Brown, and Dean Smith tell you you're not good enough to play for their college teams?

What do you do when Wooden flies all the way from Los Angeles to see you play, then flies back without offering a scholarship? When Brown, as an assistant at Duke, says you can't play for your hometown team at a time when the guards are Gary Melchionni and Richie O'Connor? When Smith main-

John Lucas

1973	First-team All-Tournament	75
1974	First-team All-ACC, third-most votes	350
	First-team All-Tournament	75
1975	First-team All-ACC, fourth-most votes	325
	Second-team All-Tournament	50
	First-team All-American (with Adrian Dantley of Notre Dame, Scott May of Indiana, Dave Meyers of UCLA, and David Thompson of N.C. State)	200
1976	First-team All-ACC, fourth-most votes	325
	First-team All-American (with May and Kent Benson of Indiana, Dantley, and Richard Washington of UCLA)	200
Awards Points		1,600

tains you don't have a jumper or the ability to go to your right, and suggests maybe you should check out Elon or High Point?

Well, if you're John Lucas of Hillside High School in Durham, you go on to score more points than anyone before in the history of Maryland basketball.

Lucas was raised in a middle-class section of town. His father, John Sr., was the principal of Hillside High, and his mother, Blondola, was an assistant principal at Shepard Junior High who in 1975 was named Durham's Mother of the Year.

"All the stories about blacks are the same," Lucas told Barry McDermott of *Sports Illustrated*. "They all come from the ghetto. They all grew up with roaches and rats and pimps and pushers.

"All blacks aren't like that, and my family background is not like that. I had to be home when the streetlights came on. The first time I didn't, I got whipped."

Lucas's extraordinary hand-eye coordination was apparent from the time he strolled into a fire station while a game of table tennis was being played. He picked up the sport fast enough to win the state championship in his age group shortly afterward.

He swapped the paddle for a tennis racket in high school and was all but invincible, winning 92 straight matches while losing one set. He played against the legendary Arthur Ashe, who critiqued Lucas's game by saying he probably started out too late to ever become great. But Ashe speculated that Lucas could have made enough money in tennis to never worry about paying for his next meal. He would have been an All-American at Maryland if he had never played basketball. In fact, he earned the distinction in both sports, winning the ACC singles title his junior and senior seasons.

"Look, tennis is a game played mostly by white rich kids," Lucas explained to *SI*. "When they lose, they shrug and walk away. When I lose, I die."

He found more competition in basketball, where he had one advantage over many of his opponents. His father was the principal, so he could borrow the keys to the gym anytime he wanted.

But having an edge is not the same as taking advantage of it. Many was the night Lucas turned out the lights after another long, exhausting workout.

He was a senior when Hillside played a Rocky Mount High team featuring a sophomore named Phil Ford at the point. Ford took it to Lucas early.

"C'mon All-American," Ford taunted. "You can't play."

"Young man, I'll teach you the game of basketball," Lucas responded on his way to 57 points.

The NCAA change allowing freshmen to play varsity came one season too late for David Thompson, who was forced to compete a season with the N.C. State freshman team despite being possibly the best player in the league. But Coach Lefty Driesell took full advantage of the change, installing Lucas in the lineup for his first game and leaving him there all 110 contests Lucas played in college.

He made an immediate impression at College Park, where junior Len Elmore, after playing against Lucas in pickup games at Cole Field House, predicted that in two years he could be the first- or second-best guard in professional basketball.

"Two years?" Lucas said. "That long?"

He was razzed constantly by Coach Lefty Driesell for having "white man's disease," as he could barely jump over a College Park phone book. But Lucas compensated with strength, combativeness, courage, and quicksilver hands.

His affliction aside, Lucas won over his coach and teammates in no time. After missing his first shot in college, he made his next 12 while leading the Terps to a 127–82 rout of Brown and an 85–50 shellacking of Richmond.

The Terps, featuring a front line of Tom McMillen, Len Elmore, Owen Brown, and Tom Roy, were a good team in 1972–73, but Lucas made them better.

"John was the kind of guy that everyone loved," Driesell told John Feinstein of the *Washington Post*. "He could order the big guys around, and they never minded.

"When he was a freshman, Tom McMillen and Len Elmore were already juniors. But he ran things, and they never minded.

"He just had that kind of personality."

His aversion to losing was never more evident than in the painful aftermath of the 103–100 loss to N.C. State in the 1974 ACC championship game, considered by pretty much all of us who were there to be the greatest game in conference history. Lucas missed a critical one-and-one with nine seconds left. The heart-wrenching scene in which he cried in Driesell's arms afterward prompted conference officials to change a tournament policy. No longer would members of the losing team be required to remain on the court for the postgame trophy presentation.

But that was a rare failure against the Wolfpack. Throughout his career, Lucas drove Coach Norm Sloan of N.C. State to distraction, so much so that Sloan once told a reserve guard attempting to dribble against Lucas to stand in the corner and not touch the ball.

"I can never remember him having a bad game against us," Sloan said. "But I never realized how complete he is, what kind of defensive ability he has, until I saw him guarding David Thompson last season."

Lucas was actually only an inch shorter than Thompson, and every bit as chiseled. At least the wives of ACC coaches thought so when they voted him "Best Body" in the conference.

He carried that body with all the self-assurance of a young god. Impressed with freshman Steve Sheppard, Lucas told him that one day he would be remembered as the second-best player ever at Maryland.

"Guess who will be the first," Lucas said.

Maybe, maybe not. But Lucas did become in 1976 the first guard ever chosen with the first pick of the NBA draft. Houston selected him before Chicago picked Scott May of Indiana second.

Mine wasn't the only jaw to drop when Lucas, always considered a solid citizen, fell prey to substance abuse during his NBA career and voluntarily entered drug and alcohol rehabilitation to remain in the league.

"I would have bet all the money in the world that the last person who would ever have a drug problem would be John Lucas," Driesell told Feinstein. "I guess that shows how much I know about drugs.

"But when I heard, I called him and I told him to go to the hospital and get treatment. I told him it was no different than cancer. If you don't get treated for it, you die, simple as that."

After playing 14 NBA seasons for the Rockets and six other teams, Lucas began his own program to treat athletes struggling with substance abuse. In 1992, he made a triumphant return as head coach of the Spurs. He has since also coached the 76ers and Cavaliers.

One son, John III, played for the Houston Rockets after a standout career at Oklahoma State. Another, Jai, played college basketball at Florida and Texas.

MITCH KUPCHAK

6-10 Center | North Carolina | 1972–76 | No. 21

1975	First-team All-ACC, third-most votes	350
	First-team All-Tournament	75
1976	First-team All-ACC, most votes	400
	First-team All-Tournament	75
	ACC POY, heavily contested	150
	Second-team All-American	150
Awards Points		1,200

In the interest of full disclosure, I am happy to see Mitch Kupchak enshrined in these hallowed halls. I got to know him fairly well while we were both in Chapel Hill in the mid-1970s and found him to be a thoughtful and engaging

Mitch Kupchak
UNC ATHLETIC
COMMUNICATIONS

guy who was easy to like and fun to watch play basketball.

Truth is, he was the subject of one of the first extended profiles I ever wrote for the *Chapel Hill Newspaper*. The piece was so long that it had to be published in two installments. As a happy coincidence, the second installment ran the day it was announced Kupchak had been named ACC Player of the Year.

Art Chansky wrote in *The Dean's List* that a big reason Kupchak outpolled N.C. State's Kenny Carr—once again rankling the ever-irascible Norm Sloan—was because of his popularity with the media. I don't doubt that was the case.

One point I would pick with Chansky is his characterization of the vote being a runaway. Carr pulled in 50 votes to Kupchak's 74, making it the fourth-closest race to that time, in terms of percentage of votes cast.

Kupchak's first love was baseball. Growing up on Long Island, he dreamed of playing third base for the New York Yankees.

"I'd sit in our kitchen on a Sunday afternoon listening to a doubleheader on the radio," he told Steve Springer of the *Los Angeles Times*. "My mom thought there was something wrong with me."

In an interview with Bruce Newman of *Sports Illustrated* during his playing days with the Los Angeles Lakers, Kupchak explained that he never played basketball until the eighth grade, and then made the team only because of his height.

"I was awful," Kupchak said. "I think when I was growing up I was self-conscious about my height, and I felt as if playing basketball would be like admitting I was tall. For a long time, when people would ask me if I played basketball, I took real pleasure in saying no."

He actually got a good break when a collapsing trampoline broke his wrist in three places.

"That was the end of my eighth-grade [basketball] career," he told Newman, "and to be honest, I was really relieved."

But as he grew, his strike zone kept getting bigger. And also as he grew, he couldn't escape the notice of Steve Kellner, the basketball coach at Brentwood High School. Kupchak was already six-four at age 14 when Kellner spotted him walking the halls of a junior high.

"He grabbed me right there and became one of the most influential people in my life," Kupchak told the *Los Angeles Times*.

He attended Kellner's camp after his freshman season at Brentwood High, the same year he sprouted three more inches. By his senior season, he was a big man on campus in more ways than one, averaging 30 points and 24 rebounds a game and drawing the intense interest of college coaches throughout the land.

His name is of Ukrainian origin, but Kupchak is of Polish stock as well. His father was an engineer of construction equipment who raised his family in tract housing in a Hicksville, New York, neighborhood where one couldn't swing a dead polecat without hitting a kid. Kupchak said he counted them once and came up with 70 young people in the 12 houses on his block.

He was sold on North Carolina because of the family atmosphere Dean Smith fostered there but admits he was also partial to the V-neck uniforms worn by the Tar Heels.

"They mocked me for two years at Carolina because of the way I talked," Kupchak told *SI*. "I vowed that I wouldn't say y'all while I was there, and I never did. Now I say it all the time. It really makes more sense to say y'all than youse guys."

Kupchak played the game wide open. His unbridled desire made him one of the ACC's best rebounders. He ranked third in the league (behind Tree Rollins and Tom Roy) with 10.8 as a junior and first with 11.3 as a senior.

"Mitch is very methodical," Smith told Chansky. "He was lost as a freshman, mainly defensively. He's very bright, with high college boards. But as a basketball player, he was slow to grasp what we wanted him to do. Once he started the habit of, say, boxing out, you could count on him 100 percent of the time.

"He was always going to the boards, and he played as hard as he could play every time out. He was an unbelievable pleasure to coach, diving for loose balls all the time. As a rookie in the NBA, he sprinted to the bench at timeouts. They kidded him, but pretty soon those other guys were moving a little faster too."

His ideal player was Bobby Jones, with whom he played two seasons. For all his production in a 36-point, 21-rebound, four-overtime performance against Tulane in 1976, Kupchak was most proud of a steal that led to a break-away dunk.

"Just like Bobby, just like Bobby!" he yelled to teammates as he ran back on defense.

He developed a reliable face-up jumper but was always best grinding away under the basket. His shot selection, and the fact he played his junior and senior seasons with Phil Ford, were two reasons he finished his career shooting 59 percent from the floor.

The play I remember that exemplified how Kupchak played the game was Walter Davis's legendary bank shot that climaxed the Tar Heels' rally from eight points down with 17 seconds remaining against Duke in March 1974. The basket sent the game into overtime, in which North Carolina prevailed. Kupchak threw a long inbounds pass to Davis. In the many photographs taken of the play, he can be seen arriving on the scene at full gallop as the ball car-omed through the goal.

Kupchak, who along with Tar Heel teammates Phil Ford, Walter Davis, and Tommy LaGarde helped Dean Smith bring home the gold medal in the 1976 Olympics in Montreal, may be the Hall of Famer best known for some-thing other than playing basketball. Although Kupchak was a solid pro who averaged 10.2 points and 5.4 rebounds over nine seasons with the Washington Bullets and Los Angeles Lakers, it wasn't until he retired and earned an MBA from UCLA's Anderson School of Management that he found his true niche in the NBA. During the decade beginning with the 2000–2001 season, following Jerry West's departure for the Memphis Grizzlies and Kupchak's elevation to full general manager duties, the Lakers won six NBA titles.

DAVID THOMPSON

6-4 Forward | N.C. State | 1972–75 | No. 44

1973	First-team All-ACC, unanimous	425
	First-team All-Tournament	75
	ACC POY	200
	First-team All-American (with Doug Collins of Illinois State, Ernie DiGregorio of Providence, Dwight Lamar of Southwestern Louisiana, Ed Ratleff of Long Beach State, and Bill Walton and Keith Wilkes of UCLA)	200
1974	First-team All-ACC, unanimous	425
	First-team All-Tournament	75
	ACC POY	200
	Final Four MVP	150
	First-team All-American (with Marvin Barnes of Providence, John Shumate of Notre Dame, and Walton and Wilkes)	200
1975	First-team All-ACC, unanimous	425
	First-team All-Tournament	75
	ACC POY, unanimous	250
	National POY (with fellow first-team All-Americans Adrian Dantley of Notre Dame, Dave Meyers of UCLA, John Lucas of Maryland, and Scott May of Indiana)	250
Awards Points		**2,950**

Of all the really good guys I've known in my years of covering ACC basketball, one of the best was Tom Mickle, who was Duke's assistant sports information director in 1972 when I met him.

Mickle, who later became assistant ACC commissioner and executive director of the Florida Citrus Bowl before passing of kidney cancer in 2006, was sitting in the lobby of the Embassy Suites near the now-abandoned Charlotte Coliseum, where the ACC Tournament was being held one year in the early 1990s. I walked up and asked if he had ever heard a reasoned discussion among people who were there and knew what they were seeing as to who was the greatest ACC player ever.

He said no.

David Thompson
<small>COURTESY OF ED CARAM</small>

"Thompson?" said I.

"Of course," said he.

To know how good David Thompson was, and to know the impact he had on the ACC, you had to be there when he burst into the conference in 1972 and surprised even some of the men who had strived so hard to recruit him.

"I just thought he was really good," said Bucky Waters, whose Duke program received a year's NCAA probation for improprieties stemming from Thompson's recruitment. "The best in the country? The best ever in the ACC? I didn't see that. How could a kid from Shelby be that good?"

His impact can best be measured by what happened after January 14, 1973, the day the kid from Shelby had the whole country abuzz over the brand of basketball being played in the ACC.

C. D. Chesley, the visionary who escorted the league into the television age, had convinced league officials to pit Maryland against N.C. State on

Super Bowl Sunday to give the sporting public something to watch while killing time waiting on the kickoff between the Miami Dolphins and Washington Redskins. As Chesley's and the ACC's luck would have it, the Wolfpack was ranked number three and the Terps number two, and both were undefeated. While a national television audience watched breathlessly, the teams (featuring four players honored in this book) were tied at 85 when Thompson soared over 6-11 Tom McMillen and six-nine Len Elmore to tip in the winning basket and stun the home crowd.

ACC basketball to that point was a cottage industry compared to the conglomerate of today. Over the league's first 18 seasons, through 1972, seven conference players were voted consensus first-team All-Americans. Over the next 18, after the kid from Shelby captured the imagination of basketball fans everywhere, the number of times ACC players made consensus first-team All-American more than tripled to 22.

My favorite claim to fame as a sportswriter is that I saw that kid from Shelby play. I never saw Babe Ruth, Johnny Unitas, or Muhammad Ali in their glory, but I did see the great David Thompson. More than just seeing him play, I covered him semi-regularly as a junior and senior in college working for the *Chapel Hill Newspaper* and as a first-year full-time writer in 1975, the year after I graduated.

It would be fudging to say I knew him. I interviewed him many times and found him to be cooperative and decent. But Thompson, the youngest of 11 kids born to Vellie and Ada Thompson and raised in a cinder-block house at the end of a dirt road, was never one to give away too much of himself, at least to those he didn't know well.

He was shy. His father, a church deacon who made $6,000 a year as a janitor at a fiber plant, said he came by that quality naturally.

"I guess all of us are like that," Vellie Thompson told Bob Padecky of the *Charlotte News* in 1973. "We like to be calm outside. Inside we are burning. It's just that we don't show it."

Teammates remember how sensitive and vulnerable to criticism Thompson could be. After the Wolfpack lost to UCLA in St. Louis in 1974, the only setback of his first two seasons, he was walking along a Raleigh street with teammates when a fan approached and, unbelievable as it seems, hounded him about his 7-for-20 performance against the Bruins.

Barry Jacobs set the scene in *ACC Basketball* through the eyes of Phil Spence, one of the teammates who was there.

"David just broke down and told the guy, 'I tried to do my best,' " Spence recalled. "Me, I would have told him where to go. David wanted people to love him.

"He told the guy he was sorry. It was coming from the heart."

After the NCAA busted N.C. State for its recruitment of Thompson, forcing the Wolfpack to miss the 1973 NCAA Tournament after going 27–0, Thompson clipped the headline—"State Placed on Probation for Recruiting Violations"—out of the paper and taped it on his door. He said it reminded him to play harder.

"I owe that much to the fans," he said.

The kindnesses Thompson showed others were, like the young man himself, the stuff of legend. While being recruited, he saw to it that different players from his Shelby Crest team made at least one trip with him, to share the experience. He spent time with the inmates at Central Prison in Raleigh. He once drove to Raleigh-Durham Airport, a dozen miles west of downtown Raleigh, to be interviewed by a reporter stuck on a layover.

Douglas Herakovich wrote in *Pack Pride* about the time Thompson was asked to talk with a vision-impaired six-year-old fan after a game. He did the kid even better, picking him up in his arms to walk the length of the Reynolds Coliseum court.

On the court, Thompson burned to excel and to win, and he always seemed to know how to do both. He played 86 college basketball games and walked into a losing locker room only seven times.

"He will just not let them lose," Bobby Jones of North Carolina said. "If State needs something, Thompson will get it for them. He's just the best I've ever been around."

From my fellow writers, Thompson commanded awe.

Wrote Bob Lipper of Norfolk's *Virginian-Pilot*, "Words—no matter how flowery, how precise, how flattering—cannot do justice to his artistry."

Wrote Ron Green of the *Charlotte News*, "He can hit from anywhere inside the city limits, climb the backboard without benefit of a ladder and he's learning to dribble 'Flight of the Bumblebee' on the piano with a basketball."

Wrote Curry Kirkpatrick of *Sports Illustrated*, "It was not stretching credibility to note that a 19-year-old junior could actually be a combination of Oscar Robertson and Julius Erving, at once casual and cataclysmic."

From opposing players, Thompson commanded the utmost respect.

"I still think David Thompson is the greatest player ever in college basketball," Len Elmore, who competed against Thompson while at Maryland, told Tim Peeler in *Legends of N.C. State Basketball*. "David was the queen on the chessboard. He could go everywhere, inside, outside, rebounding. His impact was felt all over the floor. He changed the game.

"Everybody from then on wanted to be a Skywalker."

His coach, Norm Sloan, said that the regard opposing players had for Thompson came as much from who he was as what he could do.

And what Thompson could do was what others could not.

He practiced for a day for a track event, took a running start, lifted off a foot and a half before the takeoff line, and broke the school record with a triple jump of 47¼ feet, a distance long enough to qualify him for NCAA championship competition.

He soared for an errant pass from Monte Towe one day in practice, cradled the ball, and laid it in the basket. Sloan said, "Let's see that again." The Will Ferrell movie *Semi-Pro* notwithstanding, that's how the alley-oop came to be.

"He always wanted to give credit to other people and was gracious with the media," Sloan said in *Pack Pride*. "When we represented the ACC in the post-season, even though we had tremendous rivalries with Duke, Wake Forest and North Carolina, I think most people from those schools pulled for us because of David's demeanor on the court. He was a great player, but they couldn't get upset with David because he didn't talk or point fingers, he just played."

And from N.C. State fans, Thompson commanded a love I had never seen before and have not seen since. The adoration came pouring out that harrowing day in Reynolds Coliseum in the 1974 NCAA Tournament game against Pittsburgh, after Thompson tripped over the shoulder of the six-eight Spence and crashed headfirst to the court to lie unconscious in twin puddles of blood and urine.

"That was something that I'll never forget," longtime Pack radio announcer Wally Ausley said. "We were sitting up in the booth, and we didn't really know if he was dead or alive. And we weren't alone."

Thompson came to in time to be carried to Rex Hospital, where 15 stitches were woven into the back of his head. He got back to Reynolds by the final moments of the Wolfpack's victory. The place went absolutely bonkers from equal parts admiration and relief.

"It was probably the greatest feeling I've ever felt," Thompson said in *Pack Pride*. "I can't really describe it. It really showed love by the people. It really made it all worthwhile. They were really concerned about me as a person, and not only as a basketball player."

Thompson was no more perfect than the Wolfpack's efforts to recruit him. But whereas he saw the transgressions that may well have cost N.C. State the 1973 national title as nitpicky, he took a serious view of the twin cocaine and alcohol addictions that—along with a knee injury incurred in a fight on the steps of New York's infamous Studio 54—ended what was a star-studded professional career at age 30.

Thompson reverted to the Christian ways of his upbringing and kicked the habit. After doing so, he made up with ex–N.C. State teammate Tommy Burleson, from whom he had been estranged for eight years.

"God brought me to my knees so I could look up to Him," Thompson says in the inspirational speeches he often gives. "When I was at the top of my career, the more successful I became, the further I got away from the Lord."

TOM McMILLEN

6-11 Forward | Maryland | 1971–74 | No. 54

1972	First-team All-ACC, third-most votes	350
	First-team All-Tournament	75
1973	First-team All-ACC, fourth-most votes	325
	First-team All-Tournament	75
	Second-team All-American	150
1974	Second-team All-ACC, seventh-most votes	250
	First-team All-Tournament	75
Awards Points		**1,300**

Did Dean Smith really lose the recruiting battle of the century because the Tar Heels' play-by-play man wrote pornographic books on the side?

Well, that was Norm Sloan's story. And being the hard-headed Hoosier he was, Stormin' Norman was sticking to it.

The reasons Tom McMillen ultimately picked Maryland have been told and retold so many times they've become a particularly juicy chapter of ACC basketball lore.

His dentist father, Dr. Jim McMillen, wanted him to go to Maryland, where Tom's brother Jay had played four years earlier and where one of the assistant coaches, Joe Harrington, was such a close family friend that he had spent two summers as a McMillen house guest.

His mother, Margaret, wanted him to go to Virginia, which was so serious in its recruiting efforts that it arranged for McMillen, while on his official trip, to observe knee surgery performed by the school's orthopedic surgeon.

As for Tom himself, he wanted to go to North Carolina after building a strong relationship with Smith.

Throughout the spring and summer of 1970, it was generally assumed McMillen was headed to North Carolina, because that's what he told Smith.

Tom McMillen

But along the way, for whatever reasons, his parents developed a deep dislike for the North Carolina coach.

A man who helped me get started in this business, Ladd Baucom, entered the story when, as sports editor of Greensboro's afternoon paper, the *Record*, he called the McMillen household at 6:30 one June morning. Baucom's doggedness earned him one of the greatest scoops ever in ACC basketball. Dr. McMillen told him that he and his wife were adamantly opposed to their son's attending North Carolina. He even suggested underhanded actions by Smith, saying he and his wife had "valid reasons" for their sentiments. Prodded by Smith, they eventually explained the "valid reasons" as (1) Margaret McMillen felt Smith chased her out of the family kitchen while delivering his recruiting pitch (Smith countered that it was Tom who wanted to be left alone with the coach), (2) Smith had urged McMillen to play in the Dapper Dan All-Star Game against his parents' wishes, and (3) the parents wanted the signing to take place in one restaurant and Smith and McMillen preferred another.

The whole episode came to a head in classic cloak-and-dagger fashion after a family debate that raged through the night and into the morning. Jay drove off with his brother to College Park to enroll McMillen and make Lefty Driesell the happiest man in America.

Other reasons were given along the way, such as a medical condition that prevented Dr. McMillen from flying to see his son play all the way down in North Carolina. Before the smoke completely dispersed, Sloan, who didn't have a dog in the fight, couldn't resist stirring things back up. Bill Currie, the infamous "Mouth of the South" who called Tar Heel basketball games on the radio, was said to have written pornographic novels under a non de plume. According to Al Featherston in his unpublished work on the ACC Tournament, "Every Game a Feast," Sloan had it on good authority that Driesell sent Margaret McMillen a copy of Currie's handiwork with the question, "Do you want your son to be around a man who can write this kind of stuff?" Margaret McMillen, the story goes, vowed never to allow her son to play at North Carolina.

Smith was in Europe conducting basketball clinics when he received probably the most famous telegram in ACC basketball history. From Tom McMillen, it read, "Coach Smith, going to Maryland for reasons you know."

If they had been bestowed on a less-celebrated player, Tom McMillen's accolades at Maryland would be considered quite substantial. He was judged one of the seven best players in the ACC three times, during a period when the league was absolutely stacked with talent. He was judged to be one of the four best twice. He was the first Maryland player in 12 seasons to be named first-team All-ACC, and the first ever to make a consensus All-American squad. And he was named first-team All–ACC Tournament all three seasons he was eligible.

So it seems sad, if not cruel, that he had to read in the student newspaper, the *Diamondback*, how many at Maryland felt they had been "cheated" by McMillen's play, in that he hadn't dominated the college game the way so many expected.

Such was the price he paid for his appearance on the cover of *Sports Illustrated*, complete with a caption that christened the product of Mansfield High in Pennsylvania as "The Best High School Player in America."

If classroom accomplishments carried the same weight as basketball prowess, McMillen would probably deserve distinction as the ACC's greatest player ever. In high school, he was named by Richard Nixon to the President's Physical Fitness Commission. He finished first in his class academically, was elected president of the student council, and played trombone well enough to snare first chair in the school band. At Maryland, he was a Phi Beta Kappa chemistry major and a Rhodes Scholar, later spending a year at Oxford. He earned a master's degree in politics, philosophy, and economics.

Between sessions at Maryland, he represented his country on the ill-fated

1972 Olympic basketball squad, which refused to accept the silver after its controversial loss to the Soviet Union in the finals.

After playing professional basketball in Italy while pursuing his master's, McMillen joined the NBA and competed 11 seasons for the Buffalo Braves, New York Knicks, Atlanta Hawks, and Washington Bullets, averaging 8.1 points over 729 games.

He ended his pro career to run for Congress and was elected the Democratic representative of Maryland's Fourth District. He was defeated in 1992 after three terms.

Along the way, he served on both the Board of Regents and Board of Visitors at Maryland, where his scoring average of 20.5 points a game remains the school's all-time benchmark.

McMillen has not ruled out a return to Congress.

"President Obama may need a center," he told Jim Sumner of theACC.com.

TOMMY BURLESON

7-4 Center | N.C. State | 1971–74 | No. 24

1972	First-team All-ACC, fifth-most votes	300
1973	First-team All-ACC, second-most votes	375
	Everett Case Award	100
	Second-team All-American	150
1974	Second-team All-ACC, sixth-most votes	275
	Everett Case Award	100
Awards Points		1,300

Earnest and unfailingly affable, Burleson was an easy player to like. David Thompson enjoyed playing with him so much he put his basketball future in Burleson's giant hands.

"David came to me and asked where I was going to school," Burleson said in Douglas Herakovich's *Pack Pride*. "I told him North Carolina or North Carolina State. He said, 'You choose the school and I'll follow you there.' "

So Burleson's impact on the historic run by the Wolfpack in 1973 and 1974 extended beyond his on-court contributions, which in themselves were considerable.

Tommy Burleson
<small>Courtesy of Jim Holcombe</small>

A good ol' country boy from the North Carolina mountain town of Newland (population 550, one traffic light) who showed livestock in 4-H competi-
tions, Burleson stood five-eight by the sixth grade, six-four by the eighth, and
seven feet as a high-school sophomore.

An aunt gave him some of the best advice he ever received.

"When you're that tall, throw your shoulders back, don't stoop your
shoulders," she said. "So be proud. Walk tall."

He was seven-four by his senior year of high school and drew the interest
of 386 schools. Luckily for N.C. State, Burleson got lost wandering around
campus on his visit. He met so many friendly people that he felt right at home.

His good nature and unselfishness masked an intense inner drive. Though
surprisingly agile, Burleson was so frail when he arrived at college that he
could have easily been little more than a curiosity. Except he wouldn't have
that.

"Tommy was basically a 7-4 stick when he first came to State," teammate
Rick Holdt said in *Pack Pride*. "He was just very weak physically. But he had
all the abilities and talent he needed. It was just a matter of developing his
strength. He had a lot of potential, and he worked hard to make the most of it."

Burleson's resolve was most evident when the stakes were highest. And the stakes were never higher than during N.C. State's 103–100 overtime victory in the fabled 1974 ACC championship game against Maryland, back when only the winner qualified for NCAA Tournament play. After watching Burleson make 18 of 25 shots while piling up 38 points and 17 rebounds against his team, Coach Lefty Driesell sought him out in the victorious Wolfpack locker room to shake his hand.

"Son, that's the greatest game I've seen a big man play," Driesell drawled.

The performance was no fluke. Burleson also came through with 20 points and 15 rebounds in the seminal 1973 Super Bowl Sunday victory over Maryland, scored 26 points against Pitt in the 1974 East Regional final, and then delivered 20 points and 14 rebounds against Bill Walton and UCLA in the national semifinal.

"I'm aware he has room for improvement," Sloan said at the outset of Burleson's senior season. "But I'm also aware of what he means to us. He hasn't gotten full credit for what he's done here. And more than any other player, he's turned our program around. People just don't realize how valuable he is to our team."

Those who didn't know found out the following year, when a team with basically the same roster—sans Burleson, but with the addition of freshman Kenny Carr—finished 8–4 in the ACC, lost to North Carolina in the conference championship game, and ended up 22–6.

No longer could the Wolfpack resort to one of the most unstoppable plays in ACC history. Many was the time I saw Burleson float out to the foul line, take a pass from Monte Towe or Moe Rivers, and tower over the defense while teammates cut toward the basket or darted to open spots on the floor. Unfortunately, assists weren't kept as part of N.C. State's official statistics, but I was always struck by how well Burleson passed the ball and how willing he was to do it.

"I was a self-made player to the point that I developed some skills," Burleson recalled in Ron Morris's *ACC Basketball*. "But God gave me the physical ability and He gave me a big heart and the desire to want to go out there and win.

"That's something you can't teach."

I also give Burleson much of the credit for N.C. State's being an exception to a rule I've observed over my years of covering college sports. Almost invariably, if a coach has trouble with the media—the kind of trouble that fosters distrust, miscommunication, and way too often contempt on both sides—then the team does as well. Players seem to take their cues on such matters from their coach.

Sloan got along well with certain sportswriters but had a legendarily stormy relationship with the media at large—hence the nickname "Stormin' Norman," which he apparently detested. He responded by calling the likes of me "the Worm Brigade."

When a young sportswriter these days remarks how a coach comes off as contentious during a press conference, I have to laugh. And then I describe what it used to be like covering Wolfpack postgames, when if a question happened to be asked a second time, in that the questioner didn't accept Sloan's first explanation, he would bristle. And if the question was thrown his way a third time, Sloan was known to storm out of the room.

"It doesn't matter what I say," he would rail. "I answer your question and you ask it again. So it doesn't matter what I say."

One of my favorite fellow sportswriters was Joel Chaney, a Good-Time Charlie kind of fellow who covered Wake Forest for the *Raleigh Times* and, post-merger, the *News & Observer*. Chaney was scurrying around postgame at Wake Forest's old Memorial Coliseum, ducking into the locker rooms downstairs before hustling up to catch Sloan's conference. He made it only halfway up the stairs when there came Sloan stomping down. He had already left the press conference in one of his infamous huffs. Sloan looked up from his muttering to catch Chaney eyeball to eyeball on the landing.

"If it wasn't for A. J. Carr," he snarled, "every one of you sportswriters would be assholes."

Carr, for the uninitiated, was the big-hearted, friendly writer for the *News & Observer*, known among ACC sportswriters as the nicest man who ever lived.

From what I could tell, Burleson wasn't far behind. I remember walking into the Wolfpack locker room—back when we could invade the players' inner sanctum—after another Sloan tirade and being amazed by how warm, friendly, and forthcoming the players were. Instead of taking their cue from their coach, I believe the Wolfpack players in those wonderful days took it from their seven-four center.

Burleson played seven seasons in an NBA career cut short by a knee injury. He returned to the mountains to buy a spread on Rhoney's View, about three miles up the slope from Newland.

BARRY PARKHILL

6-4 Guard | Virginia | 1970–73 | No. 40

1971	Second-team All-ACC, sixth-most votes	275
	First-team All-Tournament	75
1972	First-team All-ACC, unanimous	425
	First-team All-Tournament	75
	ACC POY	200
	Second-team All-American	150
1973	Second-team All-ACC, seventh-most votes	250
	Second-team All-Tournament	50
Awards Points		**1,500**

Ralph Sampson notwithstanding, the Virginia basketball program is beholden to no man more than Barry Parkhill.

Sampson took the Cavaliers to unprecedented heights in his four years in Charlottesville, but he might never have deigned to play at Virginia if Parkhill hadn't helped pull the program out of the ACC ditch earlier. In the 17 seasons of ACC basketball before Parkhill became eligible in 1970–71, the Cavaliers finished last seven times and never as high as the first division. Their conference record was 60–169.

And on his visits back, Sampson might not have had the opportunity to watch his old team play in John Paul Jones Arena if it hadn't been for the tireless efforts of Parkhill, whose primary charge as Virginia's associate director of athletics for development was to raise money to build the glittering showplace known as the finest home facility in the league.

"It's very challenging and very overwhelming," Parkhill told Sean McLernon of TheSabre.com. "But the best part about it is trying to make our athletic program better for the kids coming in than it was for the kids before."

Parkhill has twice been there when his school needed him most. Both times, he succeeded in a big way.

What's worth noting, though, is that he might never have ended up in Charlottesville if it hadn't been for University Hall, the arena he was largely responsible for replacing. He first got a glimpse of U-Hall when he came down

Barry Parkhill
UNIVERSITY OF VIRGINIA MEDIA RELATIONS

from State College, Pennsylvania, for a recruiting visit, and he was agog. The arena had opened only three years earlier.

"I was not highly recruited and that was one of the biggest, nicest new arenas I had seen," Parkhill told McLernon. "Back then it was, 'Wow, this is really neat. It's a big building and it's clean.' "

The problem with U-Hall was not what was in it but what wasn't. Home games back then were sparsely attended—so sparsely that Jim Hobgood, a teammate of Parkhill's, described a sad scene that left his mother in tears. His mom showed up his freshman season to take in a varsity game. Hobgood, ineligible for varsity, sat with her until she suddenly disappeared. He found her sobbing in the lobby.

"There were more empty seats than fans," Hobgood told Jim Sumner of theACC.com. "My high school had sell-outs every game and now this. My mother wondered what I had gotten myself into."

Fortunately for Virginia, Parkhill's hometown school, Penn State, didn't give a hoot for him—which was how Coach Bill "Hoot" Gibson was able to land the player who first filled the seats. Coming off a 13–9 season in his first campaign as Penn State's head coach, John Bach had no need for the local kid, though Parkhill had honed his game on the campus and his father had played for the university.

"They weren't interested in me," Parkhill recalled. "I would have gone there in a heartbeat, but they didn't give me the time of day."

He wasted little time making the Nittany Lions regret their oversight. By his sophomore season, the first he was eligible, Parkhill was already one of the ACC's best players. The Cavaliers, coming off a stunning 95–93 upset of second-seeded North Carolina in the 1970 ACC Tournament, plugged Parkhill into the lineup and proceeded to win their first six games, capping the joyride with a 94–91 victory at West Virginia.

Losses to North Carolina and Virginia Tech over the next three games set the stage for the most significant home stand Virginia basketball had ever experienced. Over an eight-day span, from January 9 through January 16, 1971, the Cavaliers won four straight over Clemson, South Carolina, Wake Forest, and Georgia Tech. Guilty as he might have been of hyperbole, Gibson dubbed it "the week that saved Virginia athletics."

Cavalier fans had certainly never been treated to a spectacle like that on January 11, when a crowd of 9,550 packed U-Hall to see the Cavaliers take on Frank McGuire's big, bad boys from South Carolina, ranked number two in the nation. And a spectacle it was, what with McGuire receiving a technical for his distasteful in-game repartee with reporter John Hedberg of the *Staunton Leader*, enforcer Tom Riker shoving photographer John Atkins of the *Charlottesville Daily Progress*, and the crowd getting into the ugly act by littering the court with debris, thus incurring a technical of its own.

Instead of attacking the Gamecocks' vaunted zone defense, Gibson decided to see what would happen if he pulled the ball out. What happened was the stubborn McGuire refused to force the action.

"At one point, I dribbled six minutes off the clock," Parkhill recalled to McLernon. "South Carolina didn't come out and chase."

Gibson twice called time in the final minute, his team trailing 49–48. During the second, which came with 19 seconds left, he made sure everyone knew the plan.

"I know it's a gamble to hold the ball and go for the last shot with us one point down," Gibson acknowledged. "But we had confidence in Barry."

Parkhill bided his time, dribbled to his right, and elevated for the jump shot that sent South Carolina to defeat and reduced U-Hall to pandemonium. Amid the maelstrom, Parkhill could be seen riding on the shoulders of delirious revelers. He had played only 11 varsity games, yet his status as a school legend was secure.

"First of all he was incredibly competitive," Hobgood explained to Sumner. "He had a burning desire to be the best. He was very dedicated to the gym, had a great work ethic. He understood the game, loved the pressure and wanted to have the ball in his hands with the game on the line.

"He was a quiet leader. He could give you a look that would stop you in your tracks, but he usually led by example. He was a great teammate."

Parkhill's best season was 1971–72, when he received every vote for first-team All-ACC. He got rolling early, pouring in 51 points against Baldwin-Wallace on December 11, 1971, to break the school record of 48 Buzz Wilkinson had scored in 1955.

"I just couldn't miss that night," Parkhill recalled to McLernon. "Every now and then you have a night when you just can't miss and that was mine. In the second half, Coach Gibson called a timeout and said, 'Listen, you're close to the record and I'm going to let you get it.'

"Well, at that point I started missing. I think if he hadn't told me that, I probably could have gotten 61."

Parkhill faced disappointment in 1973, when, after winning Player of the Year as a junior, he was relegated to second-team All-ACC with the seventh-most votes. The fifth spot on the first team went to Gary Melchionni, whose Duke team, as fate would have it, was matched against Virginia in the first round of the ACC Tournament. Parkhill responded with 22 points and five assists, while Melchionni managed only 14 points and two assists.

After Virginia pulled out a 59–55 victory, neither coach could resist a jab at those who selected the All-ACC teams.

"You guys didn't do us any favors by voting [Parkhill] to the second team," Bucky Waters of Duke groused. "It looked like he had something to prove. He just dominated the game."

Gibson's barb was not-so-thinly veiled.

"Barry Parkhill—who didn't make first-team All-ACC—was super," he said.

After his jersey was retired at Virginia, Parkhill played three seasons in the ABA and embarked on a coaching career during which he was an assistant to his brother Bruce at Penn State and head coach at William & Mary. He returned to Virginia in 1992 to raise money for the school he loved.

"My college experience was great," Parkhill told Sumner. "We proved that Virginia could win in the ACC, and that's not a bad legacy to have."

JOHN ROCHE

6-2 Guard | South Carolina | 1968–71 | No. 11

1969	First-team All-ACC, unanimous	425
	First-team All-Tournament	75
	ACC POY, heavily contested	150
1970	First-team All-ACC, unanimous	425
	Second-team All-Tournament	50
	ACC POY, heavily contested	150
	Second-team All-American	150
1971	First-team All-ACC, second-most votes	375
	Everett Case Award	100
	Second-team All-American	150
Awards Points		**2,050**

To understand the visceral hatred and contempt rival fans felt for John Roche and his Gamecock teammates, you had to be there.

I was, sitting in the Carmichael Auditorium student section as a fresh-faced freshman in January 1971, when South Carolina hit town ranked second in the nation and undefeated, having won 17 straight ACC games. I booed lustily throughout and reveled when North Carolina, using stall tactics to pull USC from its zone, roared away to a 79–64 victory.

But Roche and the Gamecocks got their revenge two months later, administering maybe the most bitter loss of my life (back before I became a sportswriter and sacrificed the right to root). In the finals of the ACC Tournament, six-three Kevin Joyce beat 6-10 Lee Dedmon to a jump ball to set up Tom Owens for the winning basket.

Good thing I didn't know then what I was to learn 40 years later while reading *The Dean's List* by Art Chansky. When Roche approached Dean Smith afterward, a net draped around his neck, Smith extended his hand. Roche was having none of it.

"Fuck you," he snapped. "We won."

By then, no behavior was too brazen or boorish for the son of an examiner for the Chase Manhattan Bank who grew up on the mean streets of Manhattan's East Side.

John Roche

While playing with Owens at La Salle Academy, Roche was considered a defensive specialist who might be a mite slow. He won over Frank McGuire as much for his pugnacity and courage as his ability to run a team and hit clutch shots. It proved one of the most famous—or infamous—coach-player relationships in league history.

"I wouldn't trade the dirt under his fingernails for anyone else's soul," McGuire told Curry Kirkpatrick of *Sports Illustrated*.

McGuire was never known as a brilliant tactician, nor did he have to be with Roche at point guard.

"There's no secret about our strategy," he explained. "It's what it has always been—when in trouble, go to Roche."

Roche was loathed for two reasons, the first being he was great. Bile never flows swiftly when it's pumped by mediocrity. The second was his readiness to mix it up at the drop of a hat. Over his career, he took a swing at Auburn's John Mengelt, kicked a fallen Dick DeVenzio of Duke (for which he drew a technical), and kneed Steve Previs of North Carolina.

"He goes crazy sometimes," teammate Owens said. "He's so intense, wants to win so badly. He has that look, like he's asking for trouble—an amazing hothead. Ask him."

We fans of the time responded like we were watching championship wrestling and Roche was the Iron Sheik. At Wake Forest, students staged a mock ritual of flushing an effigy of Roche down a commode. When Roche sprained his ankle during the 1970 ACC Tournament, cheers issued forth at the Charlotte Coliseum. He received bagfuls of mail, little of it inviting him to dinner.

By the end of his career, he admitted to being worn down by the spite, rancor, and animosity.

"Yes, I am glad to leave," Roche said after his final ACC Tournament. "It has been hard to play in this league under the circumstances. . . . There is so much hate throughout the ACC, especially among the fans."

He went on to establish a solid professional career (averaging 11.2 points over eight ABA and NBA seasons), to graduate from the University of Denver College of Law, and to establish a law practice in Denver.

With the luxury of hindsight, he acknowledged he might have asked for at least a little of the trouble he spent three tumultuous years stirring up.

"By the time our team was seniors, I don't think I was alone in feeling that we had had about enough of playing in the ACC," Roche told Ron Morris in *ACC Basketball*. "Some of that frustration and feeling showed in our performance as players and as people. So we contributed to those feelings against us."

TOM OWENS

6-10 Center | South Carolina | 1968–71 | No. 24

1969	Second-team All-ACC, seventh-most votes	250
1970	First-team All-ACC, fifth-most votes	300
	First-team All-Tournament	75
1971	First-team All-ACC, fifth-most votes	300
	First-team All-Tournament	75
Awards Points		**1,000**

The day was March 13, 1971. I remember it like it was last week.

If only I could forget.

It was the spring before I took up sportswriting in earnest. I was a freshman at North Carolina, so I had more reasons than most to be screaming for

Tom Owens
ACC Media Relations

the Tar Heels as they played South Carolina's despised Gamecocks for the championship of the ACC Tournament in Greensboro.

And we had 'em dead to rights, leading 51–50 with only six seconds remaining. A jump ball was contested in front of the South Carolina basket, and all 6-10 Lee Dedmon had to do was what Dean Smith had told him to—out-jump six-three Kevin Joyce, tap the ball to George Karl, and pop the champagne corks to let the partying begin.

Only everything went tragically wrong. Joyce—entreated by his coach, Frank McGuire, to "jump to the moon"—outskied Dedmon and tapped the ball to an open Tom Owens, who simply turned and laid the winning basket through the net.

In my 40 years of writing sports since, whenever I wonder how anybody could get ridiculously bent out of shape over the outcome of a game, all I have to do is think back to March 13, 1971, to understand.

Of the many pleasures I had in putting this project together, one of the best was talking with Bobby Cremins and getting the other side of the story. I called Cremins, as beloved by the media as any man to ever coach (and play) in the ACC, to find out more about Tom Owens. Who was he? What was he like?

My research had yielded little. I'd dug out how Owens grew up in the Bronx and played high-school basketball with John Roche at LaSalle Academy. The two became fast friends, even though Owens was known to torment his smaller sidekick by blocking Roche's exit off the train at the right stop until just before the doors closed, causing Roche to get trampled by the rush. They had a good team at LaSalle, which they proved by beating Dean Meminger's Rice High School three times their senior season, once in the New York City championship. According to Roche, Owens was the one McGuire really wanted in the package deal that brought them south.

And no one can forget the turmoil and acrimony of their three seasons in Columbia, when the rough-and-tumble Gamecocks, playing the role of conference outsider to the hilt, gave as good as they got in front of wild-eyed, bile-consumed fans throughout the league—of whom I was one. J. Samuel Walker wrote in *ACC Basketball* how a fan in Chapel Hill once slipped up behind the visitors' bench and stuck gum in Owens's hair. I swear it wasn't me—but only because I wasn't sitting close enough.

Brawls of the knock-down, drag-out variety erupted all over the league whenever the big, bad Gamecocks came to town. But maybe the most outrageous moment in conference history occurred in Columbia on December 16, 1970. During one of many melees, Jimmy Powell bear-hugged Maryland coach Lefty Driesell from behind as six-eight enforcer *extraordinaire* John Ribock hauled off and punched Driesell right smack in the face. Officials George Conley and Joe Agee called the game off with 4:52 remaining and declared the Gamecocks, who were leading 96–70, the winners.

"I shook hands with Driesell," McGuire said after order was finally restored. "But he was very mad."

And as unbelievable as it seems today, Ribock got away with it. Driesell, of course, screamed bloody murder, but McGuire sloughed off the whole donnybrook like it was another day at the office.

"The best we can find out from looking at the film is that Lefty was swinging and hit himself in the mouth," McGuire reported in Ron Morris's *ACC Basketball*. "That's what it looked like."

"That's ridiculous," Driesell sputtered. "The films have been on TV. I know

I've got a split lip, and I know I didn't swing at anyone. That's a lie."

Owens wasn't as much a brawler as frontcourt mates Ribock and Tom Riker, perhaps because he was so skinny. Though Owens was listed at 223 pounds, the irrepressible Curry Kirkpatrick of *Sports Illustrated* reported that he had been called "the advance man for a famine."

Nobody on the South Carolina team escaped the vitriol and rancor.

"We're tired of all the hatred," Owens told *SI*. "I came here to play basketball, not to grow to hate people.

"If we win the national championship, I just want to ride around the state of North Carolina with a megaphone, yelling at everybody, 'Drop dead.' Among other things."

I read that Frank McGuire called Owens "the smartest big man in college basketball." That quality stood him in good stead during the 12 seasons he played for 11 different teams in the ABA and NBA. He was a solid player, averaging 11.3 points and 6.8 rebounds in his 877 games. Lenox Rawlings, my former compadre with the *Winston-Salem Journal*, covered Owens with the Carolina Cougars and remembers him as a good guy and one of the few he saw in pro ball who actually read books.

It's unfortunate that fans of the Indiana Pacers blame a down period in franchise history on "the curse of Tom Owens," in honor of the team's move in 1981 to trade its number-one pick for Owens, thus missing a crack at drafting Michael Jordan.

And I came across a campaign Ron Morris covered for Columbia's *The State* in which Dave Odom, then the coach of South Carolina, and Eric Hyman, the director of athletics, tried to convince Owens to return from Portland, where he lives today, to have his jersey retired by the school. But Owens was said to be sore from not having his number retired at the end of his career, as Roche's was. Odom said his calls to Owens went unanswered.

And there the trail went dead until I called Cremins and asked him to tell me about Owens.

"Sure," Cremins said. "Are you ready?"

Was I ever.

"My parents moved me to a neighborhood when I was going into high school, and we moved from one part of the Bronx to another," Cremins said. "When I got there, I played in the schoolyard, and in my new neighborhood the word got out that I was a pretty good player. And they all told me that there was a big kid in the neighborhood who was pretty good, and they wanted me to play him one-on-one. That was Tommy Owens. Tommy and I became best friends."

Cremins was a year older than Owens

"Tommy and John [Roche] were best friends, and they wanted to go to school together," Cremins said. "So Coach McGuire had me working over Owens really hard, because he was my best friend. And Coach McGuire ended up getting both of them, and that turned everything around at South Carolina. They'd put South Carolina on probation because of [the recruitment of] Mike Grosso, and Coach McGuire's wife had died, and things were looking like gloom and doom for South Carolina and Coach McGuire. And the signing of Roche and Owens turned everything around."

Cremins was playing professionally in, of all places, Ecuador the day the Gamecocks beat North Carolina for the ACC title. But he still carried the scars from the previous season, when Roche sprained his ankle in the ACC Tournament and the Gamecocks were upended in double overtime by N.C. State. So nobody knew better what Joyce's tap to Owens meant to South Carolina.

"What I get upset about is when they talk about the greatest plays in ACC Tournament history, they forget the jump ball," Cremins said.

"How could that be?" I asked.

"Because South Carolina left the ACC."

Of course.

"But people understood the circumstances involved, what happened the year before when I was a senior, Roche got hurt, and we lost in double overtime," Cremins continued. "We were undefeated in the league, and the regional was back in Columbia, and it had torn my heart out and Coach McGuire's heart out.

"And then the next year, they're going to lose again with this jump ball with four or five seconds left, Kevin Joyce against Lee Dedmon. And Dean Smith rotates his guys, and Kevin outjumps Lee and taps the ball to Owens, who turns around and lays it in.

"It was one of the most remarkable plays in the history of ACC basketball."

So who, I asked, was Tom Owens?

"He was intelligent, very intelligent," Cremins said. "He was always shy because of his complexion. He was tall, skinny, and had a bad complexion. For that reason, he was always very, very shy."

And whatever became of him?

"He went to Portland, Oregon, and went through kind of a bitter divorce," Cremins said. "And then he just kind of disappeared. I had to track him down about 15 years ago. I just got tired of never talking to him, never seeing him. I was out in the Portland area, and I met him for about a half-hour. I just wanted to see his face. But he just decided that was it. He just kind of wanted to be away from everything."

Cremins was aware of South Carolina's efforts to lure Owens back.

"A part of that was the divorce he went through," Cremins said. "He just didn't want to come back to South Carolina.

"But he was a great person. He loved Columbia, he loved South Carolina, he loved Frank McGuire. He was a wonderful young man—wonderful, bright, great kid, and one of my dearest friends of my life."

CHARLIE DAVIS

6-1 Guard | Wake Forest | 1968–71 | No. 12

1969	First-team All-ACC, fifth-most votes	300
	First-team All-Tournament	75
1970	First-team All-ACC, fourth-most votes	325
	First-team All-Tournament	75
1971	First-team All-ACC, unanimous	425
	Second-team All-Tournament	50
	ACC POY	200
Awards Points		**1,450**

By pretty much every account, including his own, Charlie Davis wasn't much to look at stepping off the team bus. He stood six-one, if that, weighed 145 after a heavy meal, and walked with a decidedly pigeon-toed gait.

"When I came on the court, I wore a size 12, was awfully thin and I didn't look like a player," Davis told Ron Morris in *ACC Basketball*. "I don't know if it's true or not, but I think I got 8 or 10 points before people realized, 'Hey, he can really play.'"

Could he ever. A fierce competitor with a deadly stroke, Davis averaged 24.9 points and 4.8 rebounds over his career while shooting 46 percent from the floor. An emphasis of every scouting report against Wake Forest was to not foul Davis. His free-throw percentage of .873 was the ACC standard from the last game he played in 1971 until J. J. Redick of Duke broke it 35 seasons later.

Davis always seemed to save his best for the Deacons' biggest rival, averaging 30.6 points over the seven games he played against North Carolina. His junior year, he scored 34 in the first game and 41 in the next as the Deacons

Charlie Davis
COURTESY OF JOHN PAGE

swept Dean Smith's Tar Heels, led by Charlie Scott.

"The way Dean's teams play defense, it was made for me," Davis explained in *ACC Basketball*. "His teams don't play a trap unless you pick up the ball. If you just take a step backwards, it will always break their pressure.

"We also took the first open jump shot instead of driving to the basket."

His father, Charles Davis Sr., was a left-hander who played for the Harlem Yankees, a local knockoff of the Harlem Globetrotters. He grew up across the street from another skilled basketball player, Norwood Todmann, who, as fate would have it, became the first black player at Wake Forest. He excelled on the court at Brooklyn Tech, a mostly white high school of 6,000 students. Stung by defeat in a game in which he was held to 16 points, Davis made some serious amends by pouring in 57 of Brooklyn Tech's 72 points in the rematch.

Davis's work in the classroom left something to be desired, however, so Billy Packer, then a Wake Forest assistant coach, convinced him to transfer to Laurinburg Institute, a prep school in North Carolina, for the spring semester of his senior season to improve his academic standing. When Todmann, a year ahead of him, convinced him that Wake was a cool-enough place for a young black from New York to spend four years, Davis cast his lot with Coach Jack McCloskey of the Deacons.

He was extremely popular at Wake Forest, not just for sticking it to North

Carolina but for his warm, engaging personality as well.

Gene Hooks, the director of athletics at Wake from 1964 until 1992, said Davis was something to see on the basketball floor.

"It was because he could shoot so well and because he was good with the ball," Hooks recalled. "He didn't turn it over. And of course, he got fouled a lot, and he could make all the free throws. So he was money in the bank when it was a close game down to the wire, because when they'd put the ball in his hands, he would either get fouled or he would make a shot or something.

"He wasn't very fast, and he wasn't a very good defensive player, but he was really a good offensive player and had enough showmanship—not an in-your-face-type thing, just sort of a magical presence, as far as operating with class and doing a really good job."

In his 20th varsity game at Wake Forest, Davis took umbrage at a hard foul committed by Gordon Stiles of American University in a non-conference game at Memorial Coliseum in Winston-Salem. He got even by scoring 16 points in the first half, and he kept getting even until he had poured in 51 and broken the school record of 50 Len Chappell had set seven seasons earlier. Over one particularly torrid span of four minutes and 54 seconds, Davis scored 15 straight Wake Forest points.

"Today, they call it 'being in another zone,' but back then you were 'unconscious,' and I was," Davis recalled 25 years later. "It's easy to look back on that night in retrospect and try to figure out why or how it happened, but all I know is I was playing awfully well."

Life wasn't always easy for a young black playing basketball in the South, and Davis remembered some unsavory times. But Winston-Salem, thanks in large part to another legend, Big House Gaines from across town, was a haven.

"Winston-Salem was a great place back then," Davis told Charlie Atkinson of the *Greensboro News and Record*. "The black community opened up their arms to us. I remember going over to Winston-Salem State, and Coach Gaines put that big paw on me and said, 'If you have any problems, you can always come over here.' He wasn't talking about playing basketball. He was saying to come see him for anything."

His slender build wasn't exactly conducive to the physical world of NBA basketball. Davis played only 144 games over three seasons with the Cleveland Cavaliers and Portland Trailblazers.

He made news of a more heartwarming variety when he graduated from Wake Forest 19 years after playing his final game for the Deacons. Down on himself because he hadn't completed his studies, Davis took three classes in the spring of 1990 to earn his bachelor's degree in English.

"I am ecstatic," Davis said. "I am absolutely as proud of myself as I can be without being egotistical.

"I struggled. There were some nights when I was sitting in the basement at one and two in the morning studying and I'd ask myself, 'Charles, is it worth it?' Sure, I said that a couple of times. But every time, the answer was, 'You're damn right it's worth it.'"

Davis added a master's in liberal studies in 1997 and has since put both degrees to use as the director of athletics at Bowie State and North Carolina A&T.

CHARLIE SCOTT

6-6 Guard | North Carolina | 1967–70 | No. 33

1968	First-team All-ACC, third-most votes	350
	Second-team All-Tournament	50
1969	First-team All-ACC, second-most votes	375
	Everett Case Award	100
	ACC POY runner-up, heavily contested	125
	Second-team All-American	150
1970	First-team All-ACC, unanimous	425
	Second-team All-Tournament	50
	ACC POY runner-up, heavily contested	125
	Second-team All-American	150
Awards Points		**1,900**

Understanding Charlie Scott—or Charles Scott, as Coach Dean Smith religiously called him—was never easy. An intelligent, sensitive, and intensely proud black man who could detect the merest semblance of an affront a mile away, he wore his complexity like a badge.

To know Scott, one had to know—perhaps more so than with any other player in this book—the times in which he played.

Here was a young African-American from the cosmopolitan confines of New York City who was valedictorian of Stuyvesant High School, valedictorian of Laurinburg Institute, an Academic All-American in college, the first black member of a fraternity (St. Anthony Hall) at North Carolina, and a star for his country in the 1968 Olympics in Mexico City.

Yet none of that mattered a hill of pole beans to many in the Jim Crow South of the 1960s.

Charlie Scott

It didn't mean anything to the man in the vigilante mob who pointed his shotgun at Scott in Laurinburg, North Carolina. Nor did it impress the fan in Columbia, South Carolina, who called him a baboon.

The incident with the shotgun resulted from mistaken identity following the gang rape of a white woman by three black men. Scott happened to be walking down the street with two other blacks. The altercation in Columbia was one that, according to Smith, the offending University of South Carolina Gamecocks fan apologized for years later.

Race was woven throughout Scott's career at North Carolina. In fact, it played a part before he ever wore Carolina blue in the first place.

Scott originally committed to Davidson and the Wildcats' firebrand coach, Lefty Driesell. His recruiting trip to the campus 20 minutes north of Charlotte went well. But when Scott returned later with headmaster Frank Duffie of Laurinburg and Duffie's wife, he was denied service while sitting in a whites-only section of a local restaurant. Incensed, Scott reopened his recruitment. Smith swooped in and outmaneuvered Duke, West Virginia, and Princeton to sign North Carolina's first black scholarship athlete.

Scott said later he felt his high-school coach secretly wished he would pick North Carolina. But what sealed the deal was the tolerance he found on the streets of Chapel Hill after he slipped away alone on his recruiting trip.

"He told me he took off by himself and walked into town," Smith recalled. "He wasn't with the coaches, you know, and everybody was nice to him. He said he felt like he belonged. He said he saw a couple of hippies down on Main Street, and then he really felt better."

Nor did it hurt that the Temptations and Smokey Robinson and the Miracles happened to be playing the Jubilee Festival on campus the weekend Scott visited.

One of the most overlooked chapters of Scott's pre-NBA career was his performance in the 1968 Olympics. That was the year Lew Alcindor, Elvin Hayes, Wes Unseld, Pete Maravich, Dan Issell, and Calvin Murphy all, for various reasons, declined invitations to try out. So it was left for coaching legend Hank Iba to fashion a team out of Scott, Jo Jo White of Kansas, Bill Hosket of Ohio State, and a largely unknown junior-college standout named Spencer Haywood. Iba did his job well enough for the upstart United States team to knock off Balkan power Yugoslavia for the championship. Scott returned to Chapel Hill for his junior season sporting a gold medal.

All of which made it hard for him to swallow when John Roche was named ACC Player of the Year the following season, even after Scott scored 40 points against Duke in the ACC Tournament championship game while leading the Tar Heels to the crown.

Smith originally said the decision was based on ignorance of basketball. But he changed his mind by the time he wrote his biography.

"It was transparently racist," Smith charged in *A Coach's Life.* "The real telltale sign of what happened was that five voters did not put Charles on their all-conference team—despite the fact that he was an Olympian and [an] . . . All-American. It was a clear insult."

Scott was so put off he considered not playing in the NCAA Regional. But he and Assistant Coach John Lotz drove around Washington, D.C., long enough for Scott to realize he needed to play—if not for himself, then for his school.

That didn't keep him from hinting he might not be back for his senior season.

"I just want to win no matter who we are playing because this might be my last time around," he said.

That proved to be bad news for Davidson and the man who lost the recruiting battle. In the East Regional final, in the last game Driesell coached at Davidson before leaving for Maryland, Scott capped a 32-point performance with the game-winning 20-footer at the buzzer.

Scott indeed returned for his senior season, which proved something of a disappointment when the Tar Heels, at 18–9, failed to win 20 games for the first time since 1966, lost to Virginia in the first round of the ACC Tournament (despite Scott's 41 points), and fell to Manhattan in the first round of the

NIT. Further, Scott lost the vote for Player of the Year to Roche for a second-straight season.

There was no Jackie Robinson in ACC basketball. The man who broke the color barrier, Billy Jones of Maryland, could play, but he wasn't of that stature. The real pioneer was Scott, the league's first black superstar, who paved the way for the multitude of great black players to follow.

"When blacks turned on their TV at that point and time, they only had one person to cheer for," Scott told Anthony Jeffries of the *Chapel Hill News* in 2001. "So I had to really stand up for a lot of people.

"I was really grateful to hold a torch that they were able to associate with."

Scott, to no one's surprise, was a superstar in the ABA—setting a single-season record by scoring 34.6 points a game for the Virginia Squires—and a solid star in the NBA for the Phoenix Suns. When he helped lead the Boston Celtics to the 1976 title, he also proved he could play a role.

In 10 professional seasons, which included stops with the Los Angeles Lakers and Denver Nuggets, he averaged 20.7 points, four rebounds, and 4.9 assists.

LARRY MILLER

6-4 Guard | North Carolina | 1965–68 | No. 44

1966	Second-team All-ACC, sixth-most votes	275
	Second-team All-Tournament	50
1967	First-team All-ACC, second-most votes	375
	ACC POY, heavily contested	150
	Everett Case Award	100
	Second-team All-American	150
1968	First-team All-ACC, unanimous	425
	Everett Case Award	100
	ACC POY	200
	First-team All-American (with Lew Alcindor of UCLA, Elvin Hayes of Houston, Pete Maravich of LSU, and Wes Unseld of Louisville)	200
Awards Points		**2,025**

Larry Miller

Only with the ink dry on Larry Miller's signed letter of intent could Dean Smith reveal the sacrifice made by Ken Rosemond, a faithful assistant coach who did much of the heavy lifting in the recruiting process.

"Never once did they suspect the truth," Smith wrote of the Miller family in his autobiography, *A Coach's Life*. "That Ken Rosemond hated beer."

Rosemond, Smith explained, visited the Miller family on three occasions and each time drank Pabst Blue Ribbon. Julius Miller, Larry's father, was an employee of Mack Trucks in Catasauqua, Pennsylvania, who liked his PBR.

The Tar Heels were playing catch-up to Vic Bubas of Duke, who got into the hunt when Miller was a sophomore—a 214-pound, left-handed guard with the strength and power to stir things up inside and the stroke to punish from outside.

"It was usually late in your junior year when the recruiting started," Miller told Joe Menzer in *Four Corners*. "But Vic and his wife came up to visit me in the Poconos when I was in high school, and I liked him very much.

"Vic and his wife and I became good friends during the recruiting process. We were real tight."

Catasauqua was a rough-and-tumble suburb of Allentown. Seeing athletics as a way of keeping his son out of trouble, Julius Miller built Larry an isometrics rack and encouraged him to run in lead boots.

"You know, when I was a kid, I was really on the wrong side of the fence," Miller said in *Four Corners*. "I was in a gang. We'd steal a few things, wreck a few things. We were picked up by the cops a lot of times. I was near real trouble. I was getting very good training to be a gangster.

"I don't know what would have happened, but one day my father—I admire that man more than anyone in the world—he gave me a real licking. I was about 11, I guess. And then, about that time, I found basketball. That helped too."

By the eighth grade, Miller was playing for the Allentown Jets of the Eastern Basketball League. By his senior year, he was averaging 30 points and 30 rebounds and getting offers from UCLA and Michigan. Two brothers from Massachusetts wrote entreating him to attend their alma mater, Harvard. Their names were Bobby and Teddy Kennedy.

Rosemond finally convinced Miller to at least visit Chapel Hill.

"You know, Larry, the saddest thing is, if you went from here to Duke, you'd be going all that way and you'd still be five minutes from heaven," Rosemond said.

The visit sealed the deal.

"I think what made me go to Carolina was that I just fell in love with Chapel Hill," Miller said in *Four Corners*. "I really did. There's no doubt about it.

"I think that's what drew me there more than anything."

North Carolina's gain might have been the greatest loss ever for Bubas, whose Blue Devils had taken three of four ACC titles from 1963 to 1966 before Miller's Tar Heels won his junior and senior years.

"Miller was the first guy we got that Duke wanted," Smith said.

Miller's popularity back home was such that 14 buses loaded with friends and family made the trip down to watch him play not for the varsity but for the freshman team. That's loyalty. When Miller graduated to the varsity for the 1965–66 season, the good folks of Catasauqua footed $4,000 worth of advertising—serious coin in that day—to have Tar Heels games broadcast on an Allentown station.

He was the big man on campus, party-hopping on fraternity row with a six-pack under one arm and a stunning blond under the other. The fantasy of every Tar Heel coed was to tool up and down Franklin Street in Miller's fire-engine-red Corvette.

Miller was a hunk (or so I've been told by those who know such matters better than I) who once made an appearance on *The Dating Game*. He also played basketball with an irrepressible flair. Tar Heel fans old enough to remember still chuckle into their cocktails about the night in Wake Forest's dank, smoky, pulsating Memorial Coliseum when Miller pulled a Forrest Gump. Sweeping up a loose ball, he scored the winning layup and kept right on running—past the baseline, through a corridor of fans, and right over Jack Williams, North Carolina's sports information director, who wanted to shake his hand.

"I didn't even watch it go in," Miller told Ron Morris in *ACC Basketball*. "I just darted straight for the door.

"When it wasn't open, I broke it down."

His adoring fans called him "Captain Clutch."

"He was a lot like Joe Namath," Smith said. "When he made up his mind to do it, he would do it and do it well."

Morris wrote in *ACC Basketball* the reaction from Coach Paul Valenti of Oregon State after Miller scored 27 points in the second half of a 68–61 victory over the Beavers.

"I've seen a lot of college teams that couldn't beat Larry Miller and four girls," Valenti observed.

Miller had a hard-headedness about him and didn't mind who knew it, be it the media or his coach.

Before the ACC Tournament Miller's junior year, Smith Barrier wrote a column for the *Greensboro Daily News* predicting Duke would win. Miller clipped the column and kept it in his locker through the first two rounds. Before the championship game, he folded the clipping and put it in his shoe. Properly motivated, Miller made 13 of 14 field-goal attempts in a vintage 32-point, 11-rebound performance. When the media flocked to his locker after the Tar Heels' 82–73 victory clinched North Carolina's first ACC title since 1957, Miller proudly showed them Barrier's column.

At the time, Smith had a rule that all his players attend the church of their choosing on Sunday and bring him bulletins as proof. Miller balked, saying he had been raised a Catholic but didn't believe in the hypocrisy of organized religion. He told Smith it wasn't that he didn't believe in God, it was just a personal issue. He also said that if he were back home in Catasauqua, his parents wouldn't insist he attend.

Smith relented.

NBA coaches and general managers apparently didn't think Miller's game would translate well to the pros, so he went undrafted until the 62nd-overall pick, when he was finally selected in the fifth round by the Philadelphia 76ers. So he took the other option of the time and played in the ABA, where he averaged 13.6 points and five rebounds over seven seasons with the Los Angeles Stars, Carolina Cougars, San Diego Conquistadors, and Utah Stars. His peak season was 1971–72, when he averaged 18.4 points and 4.8 rebounds for the Cougars. That year, he set the ABA single-game scoring record of 67 points.

BOB VERGA

6-0 Guard | Duke | 1964–67 | No. 11

1965	First-team All-ACC, fifth-most votes	300
	First-team All-Tournament	75
1966	First-team All-ACC, third-most votes	350
	First-team All-Tournament	75
	Second-team All-American	150
1967	First-team All-ACC, unanimous	425
	First-team All-Tournament	75
	ACC POY runner-up, heavily contested	125
	First-team All-American (with Lew Alcindor of UCLA,	200
	Clem Haskins of Western Kentucky, Bob Lloyd of Rutgers,	
	Elvin Hayes of Houston, Wes Unseld of Louisville, and	
	Jimmy Walker of Providence)	
Awards Points		**1,775**

Sports Illustrated made a trip to Durham in the fall of 1966 to feature Bob Verga for its annual basketball issue. *SI* profiled an All-American who was the son of an affluent doctor from Sea Girt, New Jersey, drove a burgundy Corvette, dated a model working in New York City, studied three or four hours nightly in his pursuit of a psychology major, played pool well enough to finish runner-up in a campus tournament, and still found time to bond with his brothers in the Kappa Alpha fraternity.

The title was "Lonely and Lively Hours of a Star."

What the article didn't mention was where Verga might be found on nights he wasn't studying, hustling his classmates in pool, or launching his deadly, if unorthodox, jumper off the top of his head. He was known to hop in his Corvette and point it south down Cornwallis Road to an infamous all-night establishment called the Stallion Club, where on any given night the almost exclusively black clientele could hear the righteous riffs of Ike and Tina Turner, Maurice Williams and the Zodiacs, the Tams, Doug Clark and the Hot Nuts, or Joe Tex. The Stallion Club was about as far away culturally and architecturally from the leafy, gray stone campus of Duke University as a man could get in the mid-1960s. But that's where Verga got whenever the getting was good.

Bob Verga
Duke Sports Information

Which was why those in the know couldn't help laughing when Verga slipped through the dragnet that landed most of his teammates a one-game suspension. Nine Blue Devils, including center Mike Lewis and three other starters, were busted by the coaching staff for attending a bash on New Year's Eve in 1966 that raged way too long into 1967. Their sentence was to sit out the next game, scheduled for January 3 against Penn State. So the amateurs had to watch while the real party pro—who, according to rumors, had done his New Year's Eve reveling down at the Stallion Club—took the floor with a ragtag lineup and scored 38 points in an 89–84 Duke victory.

Barry Jacobs, an author and fast friend who knows as much about ACC basketball as there is to know, added an asterisk to the episode by noting that was the game C. D. Claiborne, Duke's inaugural black player, first took the floor for the Blue Devils.

Verga, who did serve two suspensions at Duke for curfew violations, was hot stuff before he ever played a varsity game. As a freshman for the Blue Imps, Verga buried the Virginia Tech freshmen by scoring 51 points—the most ever in the arena today known as Cameron Indoor Stadium.

The 21 he scored against Syracuse in the East Regional final of 1966—when he made 10 field goals on 13 attempts—carried the Blue Devils into their third Final Four in four seasons. Verga was named Most Valuable Player of the regional.

But his college career may be best remembered for the bout with strep throat that hospitalized him in the days leading up to the Blue Devils' showdown against Kentucky in the epic 1966 Final Four in College Park, Maryland. Verga climbed out of bed with a temperature topping 100 degrees to play 28 minutes. But he didn't play them very well, making one of seven shots from the floor to score four points, while Louie Dampier, the Wildcats' star guard, went off for 23.

As it turned out, the game might have saved Duke from ending up as the foil in Texas Western's iconic run past UK to the national title.

Some have said Verga got along better with his Kappa Alpha brothers, models working in New York, and patrons of the Stallion Club than he did with other Blue Devils. Art Chansky wrote in *Blue Blood* that "the moody Verga didn't talk to some of his teammates, and had a two-year personality clash with [Jack] Marin, who was more outgoing."

Picked in the third round by the NBA's St. Louis Hawks, Verga had a nice pro career, averaging 21 points over more than 300 games for several ABA teams and a smattering of contests for Portland of the NBA.

He must have been on the outs with his coach the evening I drove over from Chapel Hill to see him eating popcorn on the Carolina Cougars' bench. I figured his night was done, at least in Greensboro.

But the Stallion Club was only an hour's drive away.

BOB LEWIS

6-3 Guard/Forward | North Carolina | 1964–67 | No. 22

1965	Second-team All-ACC, seventh-most votes	250
1966	First-team All-ACC, most votes	400
	Second-team All-Tournament	50
1967	First-team All-ACC, third-most votes	350
	First-team All-Tournament	75
Awards Points		1,125

Bob Lewis

Back before the coaches of championship basketball teams lived in gated communities, sequestered from the great unwashed, they might be seen in neighborhoods buying groceries, jogging around the block, or maybe even eating in restaurants.

Red Auerbach, who coached the dynasty in green known as the Boston Celtics, lived part of his life in the Georgetown neighborhood in Washington, not far from an electrical engineer named John Lewis. I've seen no references to suggest Auerbach and Lewis were tight, but residing in the same neighborhood as a basketball great had to be pretty cool for Lewis's son, Bob, who turned 12 in March 1957, about the time Auerbach won the first of his nine NBA titles.

So it was with great interest that young Bob picked up a book written by Auerbach that, on its very first page, revealed that "to become a good basketball player, you have to play basketball all the time."

Marching orders received, Lewis, according to a story by George Cunningham in the *Charlotte Observer*, stopped playing baseball and football to pursue hard-court greatness. So serious was Lewis that, according to the story, he didn't date until his junior year of high school. But once he picked out a girlfriend, Bettejane Burrows, he wasn't one to play the field. He dated Bettejane right through his college days and in fact declined to have his photograph taken with the comely coeds of Carolina, lest Bettejane back home get the wrong idea.

Lewis was good enough by his senior season to make high-school All-American, playing for the scarlet and gray of St. John's Academy in D.C. His stiffest competition came at the Chevy Chase Center, where the likes of Dave Bing (Syracuse), Fred Hetzel (Davidson), Ronnie Watts (Wake Forest), Tom Hoover (Villanova), and John Austin (Boston College) were known to come around. An article by Frank Deford for *Sports Illustrated* mentioned another regular, John Thompson, who played at Providence before becoming a coaching legend at Georgetown. Thompson must have been a tough match-up for Lewis; in addition to being 6-10 and powerful, Thompson was three and a half years older.

Lewis's special talent was his leaping ability, described by Dean Smith as "gazellelike." Deford's article mentioned that Lewis tied the 6-10 Hoover in a dunking contest, each slamming two basketballs—one with the left hand, one with the right—on the same bound.

College coaches began frequenting Lewis's home in Georgetown. Adolph Rupp of Kentucky once made himself so much at home that he became a prototype for John Belushi's infamous "Thing That Wouldn't Leave." According to Ken Rappoport in *Tar Heel: North Carolina Basketball*, Lewis at long last excused himself to go to bed while "the Baron" sat there and leafed through his recruit's scrapbook.

Luckily for North Carolina, but not so much for the other 150 schools pursuing Lewis, the Tar Heels' game against Notre Dame in 1963 was one of the rare ones of the day to be televised. Lewis, 17, watched transfixed as Billy Cunningham nailed a long jumper to force overtime, allowing the Tar Heels to pull out a 76–68 victory in South Bend.

When Smith got Lewis on campus a few months later, Cunningham showed him around. That's how Lewis became what Smith described as his first "name" recruit, which makes one wonder if he addressed those who came earlier by their numbers.

The campus was abuzz over Lewis's exploits on the freshman team. Smith did little to tamp down the expectations, for which he later expressed regret when Lewis didn't set the ACC on fire as a sophomore.

I have to believe that Smith's penchant for mother-henning newcomers came from his experience with Lewis. By the time I arrived on the scene in 1971, freshmen were never allowed to talk with the media until their first game, and were consistently passed over for postgame praise.

"That was the year for too much emphasis on sophomores coming up to the varsity," Smith said in Art Chansky's *The Dean's List*. "Since then we have never oversold a player before he proves himself on the college level. Bobby averaged over 35 points as a freshman, but he was a post man against teams he could jump over. I knew he'd have trouble at 6-3 and very thin, scoring like that on the varsity.

"I pushed him, because I thought it would be great for Bobby. I was wrong."

Lewis was so wraithlike his father called him "poor old skinny Bob." He struggled to get his weight above 175 pounds. "The nervous energy just sort of runs out of me," he told Deford, who observed in his *SI* article that Lewis had hollow cheeks, sported dark rings around his blue eyes, and talked with a bit of a stammer.

But he wanted to be good badly enough that he was the first on the court for practice and the last to leave. According to Rappoport, when Smith or one of his assistants tore into the team, Lewis would sit there bobbing his head.

Smith was apologetic about having to play Lewis inside as a sophomore and junior, because that's where he was needed. But he was a tough match-up for bigger, less mobile forwards.

His senior season, after 6-10 Rusty Clark and six-eight Bill Bunting moved up from the freshman team, Lewis was finally moved to the backcourt to play alongside yet a third sophomore to crack the starting lineup, Dick Grubar. That was the team that broke the hegemony Vic Bubas and his powerful Duke program held over the conference. The Tar Heels, with Larry Miller pouring in 32 points and Lewis contributing 26, knocked off the Blue Devils 82–73 for the conference championship and kept rolling until they had made their first of three straight trips to the Final Four.

Sportswriters, always looking for a hook, nicknamed Lewis and Miller "the L&M Boys." It didn't matter that the moniker wasn't exactly original, York Larese and Doug Moe having been given it a half-dozen seasons earlier. What did matter was that L&M was popular shorthand for Liggett & Myers Tobacco. The free advertising did not please other tobacco companies that called North Carolina home. Ultimately, the university had to scrub the references off promotions and releases. According to Deford in *SI*, university officials denied knuckling under to deep-pocketed donors but had trouble finding anyone who believed them.

For all the Tar Heels' success of 1966–67, when they went 26–6 overall and 12–2 in conference play, it wasn't Lewis's easiest year. With Miller emerging as the go-to guy and Clark and Bunting providing balance inside, Lewis's scoring average plummeted from 27.4 points a game to 18.5.

He told Deford for *SI* that he had no qualms about his new role.

"I'm really enjoying this season," Lewis said. "It's so different. You know, before this year, I never went into a game when I didn't just assume that I would score 25 points. I expected that of myself. If I only got something like 14 points, I'd go crazy. I'd start worrying what was wrong. I'd even stay afterwards and practice.

"Now, listen, I've always wanted to win, but I've always wanted to win and score points. I was always thinking about that. But I wanted to prove something this year. Look, I've scored. . . . I scored 27 points [per] game, and that's a lot of points. Now I want to show I can do everything else."

Lewis, showing the same loyalty toward roommates as he did girlfriends, roomed with Tom Gauntlett of Dallas, Pennsylvania, all four years at North Carolina.

After graduating with a degree in sociology, Lewis was drafted in the fourth round by the San Francisco Warriors. Though his slender frame wasn't exactly suited to the NBA, he played 255 games over four seasons with the Warriors and Cleveland Cavaliers, averaging 5.8 points, 2.1 rebounds, and 2.2 assists a game.

JACK MARIN

6-6 Guard/Forward | Duke | 1963–66 | No. 24

1965	First-team All-ACC, third-most votes	350
	Second-team All-Tournament	50
1966	First-team All-ACC, second-most votes	375
	Second-team All-Tournament	50
	ACC POY runner-up, contested	100
	Second-team All-American	150
Awards Points		**1,075**

Of all the players I researched for this labor of love, I found few, if any, more fascinating than Jack Marin.

He was a native of the coal and steel country of western Pennsylvania whose father played for Duquesne in the Orange Bowl. He was a star basketball player for the legendary Ed McCluskey at Farrell High School, as well as valedictorian of his class.

At Duke, besides being what Vic Bubas described as "the most fundamentally sound player I ever coached," he was a Dean's List student in premed

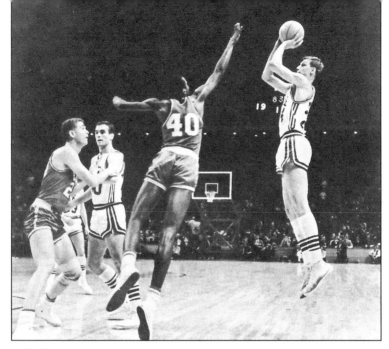

Jack Marin

and president of his junior and senior classes. He was known on campus for getting along with pretty much everybody except teammate Bob Verga, who, if accounts of the time are accurate, got along with hardly anybody.

He had already been accepted to Duke's medical school and told the administration to save him a spot when he was selected by the Baltimore Bullets with the fifth pick of the 1966 draft. Once he heard what the Bullets were offering—$18,500, the third-highest rookie salary in the NBA—he decided his career as a doctor could wait.

"I thought I'd play for a few years, then go to medical school," Marin said.

The Bullets got their money's worth. Marin registered 16.7 points and 6.2 rebounds a game for six seasons before they traded him to Houston for Hall of Famer Elvin Hayes.

He was still with the Bullets when he rethought his plans and started taking classes at the University of Maryland's law school in Baltimore. Then, after wrapping up one of the most distinguished NBA careers any Duke player ever enjoyed (he competed 11 seasons for the Bullets, Rockets, Buffalo Braves, and Chicago Bulls), he applied to Duke's law school and was admitted.

He subsequently dabbled in politics, running an unsuccessful campaign for the United States House of Representatives, practiced real-estate law, and returned to athletics to represent ACC players Delaney Rudd, Vinny Del Negro, Dante Calabria, and Brian Howard in their professional contract negotiations. Along the way, he found time to represent the National Basketball

Retired Players Association and to keep his game on the links sharp enough to win a number of tournaments on the Celebrity Players Golf Tour.

But my favorite Marin tidbit was how he dealt with the red birthmark that stretches from shoulder to elbow on his left, or shooting, arm. To some, it might be a sensitive subject. But Marin was above all that.

"I told people that one night my shooting was so hot that I set my arm on fire," he joked to the *Baltimore Sun*.

And as the husband of a wife who can take or leave sports, I also appreciate Robin Marin, Jack's wife of almost 40 years.

"I met my wife in Houston," he told the *Sun*. "She wasn't into basketball.

"I told her I was with the Rockets. She thought I worked at the space center."

Look deeply enough into the background of any great player and you'll find a figure who was there when needed most. For Marin, that was McCluskey.

"I played for the greatest coach in Pennsylvania history," Marin told Al Featherston in *Game of My Life*. "His program made basketball *the* thing to do in my hometown."

If not for McCluskey, Marin would have probably stuck with football, played not only by his father but his two brothers, one at Ohio State, the other at Louisville.

After rarely getting off the bench as a sophomore on a Farrell High team that McCluskey coached to a 30–1 record and a state championship, he spent the following summer playing for three off-season leagues the coach organized. Though Marin was six-five as a senior, McCluskey put him at guard and played a 5-10 son of a mill worker at center.

The 5-10 kid must have had some grit. The team went 23–3.

"He was tough and made us tough," Marin remembered of McCluskey in *Game of My Life*. "He routinely embarrassed us in practice, so that we routinely embarrassed the other teams in games. Athletes learn to take derision. Watch Mike [Krzyzewski]—he'll call you every name in the book. He knows that most guys will respond to that.

"You're never going to get out of yourself what a great coach will get out of you. You just won't do it."

Recruited by more than 80 schools (none with greater fervor than Lefty Driesell's Davidson), Marin considered attending Michigan—until he showed up there for a visit on a cold, drizzly weekend. The weather was much nicer on his trip to Durham—70 degrees, blue skies—so Marin headed south.

Having learned from McCluskey how much work it took to be good, he was determined to be great. Luckily for Duke and Coach Vic Bubas, so were Steve Vacendak and Bob Verga.

"We were the last people on the floor at practice," Marin told Jim Sumner for theACC.com. "I think it was because we didn't want the other guy to get ahead, and it certainly didn't hurt us when we played other people."

He shot 50 percent for his career and averaged 10.3 rebounds as a junior and 9.7 as a senior. Once he found his range, he poured in 20-footers like they were snowbird layups.

One would have to look through the back pages of ACC history to find a player ever hotter than Marin was midway through his junior season, when, over a torrid seven-game stretch, he averaged 27.4 points (and 12.4 rebounds) while making an incredible 80 of 117 shots (69 percent) from the floor.

And it wasn't against N.C. Central or Campbell. The opponents were West Virginia, South Carolina, Notre Dame, Wake Forest, Virginia, and N.C. State (twice).

"I was making three of every four shots for awhile there," Marin told John Roth for *Encyclopedia of Duke Basketball*. "It was really wild, especially for an outside player. We averaged 90 points a game that year, and we'd have averaged 105 a game with the 3-pointer.

"We just ran people out of the gym."

Though it wasn't renamed Cameron Indoor Stadium for another seven seasons, the Blue Devils' home arena apparently got as wild and cacophonous back then as today. Having seen many games in the building, I certainly recognized the place from the description Marin gave to Smith Barrier for the book *Tobacco Road*.

"It was a real experience to play in Duke Indoor Stadium," Marin said. "Almost indescribable.

"One night I heard the loudest noise I've ever heard in my life. We were playing Michigan and we were behind and starting catching up. The fans got behind us and began roaring and the noise was incredible. It was like a jet engine."

BILLY CUNNINGHAM

6-6 Center | North Carolina | 1962–65 | No. 32

When Frank McGuire departed North Carolina in a huff, he left behind the one thing his successor, Dean Smith, needed to survive three turbulent seasons and turn the program into one so many others judge themselves by.

Billy Cunningham

1963	First-team All-ACC, unanimous	425
	First-team All-Tournament	75
1964	First-team All-ACC, unanimous	425
	First-team All-Tournament	75
1965	First-team All-ACC, most votes	400
	ACC POY	200
Awards Points		**1,600**

McGuire left behind Billy Cunningham.

McGuire never coached Cunningham at North Carolina. He headed north to coach Wilt Chamberlain and the Philadelphia Warriors in the spring of 1961, and Cunningham didn't arrive in Chapel Hill until that fall. But Smith needed to make only one recruiting trip to New York City as an assistant under McGuire to know who was responsible for Cunningham's wearing Carolina blue. As Smith learned the day he arrived there, McGuire was great friends with an assistant chief of the New York City Fire Department who just happened to be Cunningham's father.

"My father told me I could go to any college where Frank McGuire was the coach," Cunningham famously said.

McGuire's ties with the Cunningham family didn't end there.

"Frank was wired in New York City," Cunningham said in Scott Fowler's

North Carolina Tar Heels: Where Have You Gone? "His sister lived right around the block from me.

"To this day, one of my sister's best friends is Frank McGuire's niece."

Cunningham knew what he wanted to do with his life from his fifth birthday, when his present was a basketball. His father stressed education—so much so that he himself returned to college at age 57 to receive his degree—but Cunningham was enthralled enough with basketball that he played it whenever he got the opportunity. And in New York City, there was no shortage of opportunities to play "the City Game."

He did have to watch for two years, when he was 10 and 11, while his broken arm healed. He later said the experience was almost too much to bear. But by his junior-high days, he was riding the subway from one borough to the next in his never-ending search for games. Summertime, he would play as many as five a day.

"We'd go from Eighth Street to the Village to Coney Island and on to Manhattan Beach," Cunningham said. "It was tough at the beach. Everybody from the city would come just to play three-on-three half-court."

Early on, McGuire saw through Cunningham's innocent-looking face and pipestem body.

"He's a New Yorker," McGuire pronounced. "He looks young and soft, but he always got a seat on the subway. That's a sign of aggressiveness."

And nobody could miss the way Cunningham got off the ground. He didn't receive the nickname "Kangaroo Kid" because he could box.

"I could always jump," he recalled. "I never worried about my scoring. Scoring was always something that seemed to go with my game."

His aggressiveness and spring made him one of the city's best players during his career at Erasmus High School, a venerable institution that also claims as alumni such luminaries as Bernard Malamud, Beverly Sills, Mickey Spillane, Mae West, Neil Diamond, Al Davis, Sid Luckman, and Doug Moe. Around 50 schools recruited Cunningham, but his destination was ordained.

As the last cargo to arrive on North Carolina's famed basketball "Underground Railroad," Cunningham quickly recognized that his reputation preceded him. Sportswriter Dick Herbert of the Raleigh *News & Observer* noted how some were predicting Cunningham would be the greatest player in Tar Heel history.

His debut as a sophomore was inauspicious. He scored just two baskets against a nondescript University of Georgia team. But he warmed up to pour in 32 against Wake Forest, 31 against Duke, 33 against Virginia, and 28 against Indiana.

Opponents such as Wake Forest's Frank Christie were suitably impressed.

"I've guarded Art Heyman of Duke, Jerry Lucas of Ohio State, and Fred

Hetzel of Davidson, but Cunningham is the best of the bunch," Christie said.

Smith has mentioned he regrets having to play Cunningham—who was six-four as a freshman and grew to six-six by his senior year—out of position at center all three seasons. Yet that didn't stop Cunningham from ranking first in the ACC in rebounding and second in scoring (to Heyman) as a sophomore and first in both categories as a junior and senior.

"Billy never really got his full opportunity in college," Smith said. "I played him out of position because we needed him at center.

"He never complained. He was always serious about practice sessions. He had savvy. A player develops savvy at an early age. You don't teach it. A player with savvy knows instinctively what is required in a situation.

"Billy always knew."

Cunningham probably saved Smith at North Carolina literally. He certainly did metaphorically.

Who hasn't heard the tale of the midwinter night in 1965 when the North Carolina team bus limped back into Chapel Hill from a 107–85 thrashing by Wake Forest in Winston-Salem? Around a hundred students had gathered across the street from Woollen Gym, and Assistant Coach Ken Rosemond noticed they were burning an effigy.

Smith, taking note of the long nose, saw the effigy was of him.

Two players, Cunningham and Bill Galantai, would have none of it. They bounded off the bus and tore down the flaming figure.

Smith made light of the incident, saying it wasn't a big deal, but he did note that his team won nine of its remaining 12 games to finish 15–9 overall and 10–4 in ACC play.

Cunningham left after that season to become one of the greatest sixth men in NBA history on one of the greatest (if not *the* greatest) teams of all time—the 1966–67 Philadelphia 76ers, who won 68 (of 81) games and a championship.

But as good as he was with the 76ers and the Carolina Cougars of the ABA, Cunningham was an even better coach.

Named head coach of the 76ers in 1977 despite not having any coaching experience, Cunningham compiled a winning percentage of .698 over eight highly successful seasons. The 76ers won the Eastern Conference three times. And in 1983, led by Moses Malone, Julius Erving, and another high-flier from North Carolina, Bobby Jones, they won it all.

By the end of the 1984–85 season, Cunningham was tired of travel and of being away from daughters Stephanie and Heather. He quit coaching, never to return.

He was 42.

JEFF MULLINS

6-4 Guard/Forward | Duke | 1961–64 | No. 44

1962	First-team All-ACC, third-most votes	350
	First-team All-Tournament	75
1963	First-team All-ACC, third-most votes	350
	First-team All-Tournament	75
1964	First-team All-ACC, unanimous	425
	ACC Tournament MVP	100
	ACC POY	200
	Second-team All-American	150
Awards Points		1,725

His coach, Vic Bubas, knew one simple reason Jeff Mullins got along so well with cantankerous teammate Art Heyman.

"Jeff got along with everybody," Bubas said. "He was just that kind of person."

On the court, they complemented each other like lyric and melody. Heyman, Bubas pointed out, was a far better passer than he was given credit for, and Mullins knew if he kept on the move then Heyman would find him open.

Recruiting Mullins out of Lexington at a time Coach Adolph Rupp of Kentucky was such a force in the Bluegrass State wasn't the miracle many assumed.

"Mullins, he was the golden boy," Bucky Waters, then an assistant at Duke, said in Joe Menzer's *Four Corners.* "The thing that made it possible for us to get him is he didn't grow up in Kentucky listening to Cawood Ledford. His dad was with IBM and he only moved to Lexington when Jeff was a sophomore. His roots weren't there."

Mullins also didn't take kindly to the way the Baron treated Jon Speaks, a high-school teammate.

"He had not recruited Jon all year, but that spring, Rupp was the speaker at our athletic banquet," Mullins said in Al Featherston's unpublished history of the ACC Tournament, "Every Game a Feast." "Jon and I were together before the banquet when Coach Rupp came up to us. I started to walk away, but

Jeff Mullins

he told me to stay. Then he turned to Jon and said, 'Son, I want to offer you a scholarship.'

"Jon was very interested, but he told Coach Rupp he needed to talk to his parents about it. Rupp said, 'No, I want to announce it tonight. If you don't accept tonight, I'll give it to somebody else.' He got pretty mad—his face turned red. It really turned me off."

Bubas, an assistant to Everett Case at N.C. State just before becoming head coach at Duke, whisked Speaks away to Raleigh and thereby made a connection with Ralph Carlisle, the legend who coached Speaks and Mullins at Lexington's Lafayette High School. Before he headed to Duke, though, Mullins swung by the Governor's Mansion, where Edward Breathitt, a UK grad, tried in vain to talk him into becoming a Wildcat. Not even the fact that Mullins's girlfriend and wife-to-be, Candy, was headed to UK (where she would become a cheerleader) could dissuade Mullins from picking the Blue Devils.

Nor could all the warnings he received from other coaches about playing with the hell-raiser named Heyman.

"Between Thanksgiving and spring, every other coach had stories about Art Heyman," Mullins said. "That's one of the main reasons why I made another visit to Durham in the spring. I didn't meet Art on my first visit, and I wanted to see what he was like. From day one, we hit it off."

According to *Sports Illustrated*, Mullins was "not as exciting as Heyman—which is probably just as well."

But as Waters said in Menzer's *Four Corners* and Bubas reiterated years later, the odd couple of the pugnaciously flamboyant Heyman and the unflappable All-American boy Mullins not only coexisted but brought out the best in one another.

"Jeff was Mr. Basketball in Kentucky and could have played anywhere he wanted," Waters said. "Lots of times big stars like that choose schools where they know they will be the big man on the team, but Jeff knew we already had Art Heyman, one of the best players in the country.

"But Jeff didn't care who would get top billing, he didn't have that kind of ego. He was the epitome of a team player, and he wanted to make everyone else on the team better.

"Jeff Mullins was all about winning games. In fact, he was a winner in life as well. It was a privilege to coach such a fine human being."

Mullins had the quirky routine of bouncing the ball 13 times before each foul shot. Although Duke Indoor Stadium would not be renamed Cameron Indoor Stadium until 1972, the Crazies of the day counted each bounce in unison.

Though he played mostly on the perimeter, Mullins was hard to keep off the boards, as his career average of nine rebounds a game attests.

"Seldom have I seen a forward of his size get as many tap-ins and offensive rebounds and he also is a fine team player and defender," wrote Bill Brill, sports editor of the *Roanoke Times*.

Irwin Smallwood of the *Greensboro Daily News* was similarly impressed: "Jeff Mullins reminds me of a cat. His moves on the basketball floor, if transferred to written words, would be classified as poetry. He is never bad. Only good and better."

It's worth noting that Duke didn't reach the NCAA championship game until 1964, after Heyman departed. The Blue Devils were knocked out by Loyola of Chicago in the semifinals in 1963 but made it back to the Final Four the next season by rolling past Villanova 87–73 and Connecticut 101–54 in the regionals.

Mullins was at his most magnificent in the regional semifinal against Villanova. He drained 19 of 28 shots from the floor for a career-high 43 points to go with 12 rebounds, while making life miserable for Richie Moore, the Wildcats' leading scorer, who managed only four field goals on 12 tries for eight points.

The Final Four was in Kansas City, at a time when the Leiber and Stoller song of the same name was all the rage. On to Kansas City Mullins and the Blue Devils did go, where they brushed past Michigan 91–80 in the national semifinal before losing to UCLA 98–83 in the championship game. The Bruins of Gail Goodrich and Walt Hazzard were the first of

John Wooden's 10 national champions over the next 11 seasons.

"I can live with defeat," Bubas said. "We lost to a great UCLA team, and it's no disgrace to lose to the nation's number-one team. But I had hoped we would give them a better game.

"I didn't want to lose the way we did. We lost our poise against their pressure defense and went to pieces."

Mullins played for the gold-medal United States team in the 1964 Olympics in Tokyo and embarked on a 12-year NBA career. The fifth pick of the draft by the St. Louis Hawks, he flourished as a five-time All-Star for the Golden State Warriors, averaging 16.2 points, 4.3 rebounds, and 3.8 assists for his career.

He settled in Charlotte, where he was coach and director of athletics at UNC-Charlotte.

ART HEYMAN

6-5 Guard | Duke | 1960–63 | No. 25

Year	Award	Points
1961	First-team All-ACC, unanimous	425
	First-team All-Tournament	75
1962	First-team All-ACC, unanimous	425
	First-team All-Tournament	75
	Second-team All-American	150
1963	First-team All-ACC, unanimous	425
	ACC Tournament MVP	100
	ACC POY	200
	Final Four MVP	150
	National POY (with fellow first-team All-Americans Barry Kramer of NYU, Jerry Harkness of Loyola, and Ron Bonham and Tom Thacker of Cincinnati)	250
Awards Points		**2,275**

Art Heyman was a force of nature who stirred up a commotion the likes of which the ACC had never known, and may never know again.

My sense of who Heyman was and what he was all about comes from a photograph and two quotes.

Art Heyman
<small>Duke Sports Information</small>

The photo can be found on page 85 of Ron Morris's treasure of a book, *ACC Basketball*. It shows Heyman driving to the basket against St. Joe's in the 1963 East Regional final. Thick-legged, broad-shouldered, and hell-bent, he's a rampaging bull ready to run over anyone on his way to the basket.

The first quote is from one of my favorite authors, Pat Conroy, in *My Losing Season*, a book recommended by Skip Prosser, the late coach at Wake Forest. Conroy, a walk-on at the Citadel who first confronted Heyman in basketball camps, described our hero thusly: "Art's game was urban, black, big-city, kiss my ass and hold the mayo, in your face, wiseass Jewish, no-holds barred and a hot dog at Nathan's after the game."

The other quote is from his coach at Duke, Vic Bubas, who took exception to those who compared Heyman to Dick Groat, a Blue Devils legend from the previous decade: "Everybody talks about how great Dick Groat was. Groat was a great player. I guarded him. But Heyman is bigger and stronger. He's got to be the best player to ever put on a Duke uniform."

Coach Butch van Breda Kolff of Princeton once said of Heyman, "If there are two points on the other side of a brick wall, he'd go through it to get them."

Billy Packer, then a guard for Wake Forest, said Heyman was a load for any player not as powerful or mobile as he was. And players like that were few and far between in the ACC of the early 1960s.

"In the modern game, you talk about match-ups," Packer said. "And Art was too big for guards, and he was too quick for front-line people. He was capable of overpowering a guard, and he was obviously capable of outmaneuvering a front-line player. And he was very tough, tough and aggressive."

Bubas gave his initial impression of Heyman, who walked with a shuffle and a pronounced forward lean: "The first time I saw him, I wasn't so much concerned over his basketball ability as whether or not he was going to fall down."

The mayhem Heyman created preceded him to the ACC.

He originally committed to North Carolina and was set to room with Larry Brown. That was before his stepfather, Bill Heyman, got into a spat with the Tar Heels' combustible coach, Frank McGuire. The elder Heyman said something about McGuire's focus on academics, or lack thereof. McGuire took offense, and boom, the two were near blows.

"I had to step between them," Heyman recalled. "My stepfather called Carolina a basketball factory, and McGuire didn't like that. They were about to start swinging at each other."

Vic Bubas swooped in and promenaded Heyman over to Duke, and the rest is indeed some of the most spirited, controversial, and brawling history of ACC basketball.

The first sparks flew even before Heyman was eligible for varsity competition. The Duke and Carolina freshman teams, the Blue Imps and the Tar Babies, played three times in 1960. Their game in Siler City could not have been uglier. The Tar Babies taunted Heyman with ethnic slurs ("Jew bastard," "Christ killer"). Bucky Waters, Duke's freshman coach, kept Heyman in check by promising that if the Blue Imps won, Heyman could respond to the abuse he'd been taking. After leading Duke to victory with 34 points, Heyman pointed to the scoreboard on his way off the court. Incensed, Dieter Krause of Carolina reacted with a punch to Heyman's head that caused a gash deep enough to need six stitches. In the ensuing chaos, Waters grabbed Coach Ken Rosemond of Carolina by the lapels and shoved him into the scorer's table.

"Here I had worked so hard to convince Art to keep his cool, and I lost mine," Waters told Al Featherston of GoDuke.com.

That was a mere warmup for 1960–61, Heyman's first year on the varsity.

Held in check by North Carolina's Doug Moe in the Dixie Classic, Heyman ripped a photo of Moe from a Durham newspaper and pasted it on his dorm-room wall. The rematch was bathed in the national spotlight when an ice storm blanketed the Triangle and shot the TV ratings for the showdown between the number-four Blue Devils and the number-five Tar Heels through the roof of Duke Indoor Stadium.

Heyman got rolling early despite the concentrated, if unsanitary, efforts of Moe.

"He spit on me," Heyman told Al Featherston in *Tobacco Road*. "Every time I took a shot he spit on me. I was not going to take that."

The brawl that earns my vote for the most memorable in ACC history ensued late in the game when Heyman grabbed Larry Brown by the shoulders on Brown's drive to the goal. Brown wheeled and threw the ball, then a punch. About that time, Donnie Walsh arrived off the Tar Heel bench to cold-cock Heyman. In the 10-minute donnybrook that followed, which raged so out of control that it took 10 Durham policemen to restore some semblance of order, Heyman was buried beneath a North Carolina dog pile, as fans streamed out of the seats to join the fray.

Heyman was blamed by the media, as well as by official Charlie Eckman. The rush to judgment prompted Bubas to hold a press conference the next day, at which he showed films revealing that Brown had thrown the first punch.

Commissioner James Weaver, pushed to his limit and beyond, ruled a pox on both houses by suspending Heyman, Brown, and Walsh for the rest of the regular season.

And who can forget the time 300 spectators jammed a courtroom to see Heyman face a charge of assault on a male North Carolina cheerleader, who had made the mistake of patting Heyman on the back of the head on the player's way to the locker room? Heyman swung at the cheerleader, prompting Blackwell M. Brogden, a Durham attorney and North Carolina alum, to swear out a warrant. The cheerleader declined to testify on his own accord but was subpoenaed.

The Tar Heels lost that one, too, as the case was dismissed.

I laugh every time I hear the story how Heyman, during his sophomore season, was arrested for taking an underage girlfriend across the state line to Myrtle Beach. The funny part isn't the indiscretion, but rather Heyman's inspiration in registering into a motel as Mr. and Mrs. Oscar Robertson.

Heyman told Ron Morris that Bubas paid the bill and handled the charges.

Unless riled, Heyman was one of the most obliging greats to ever play in the ACC. He was known for volunteering at local hospitals and for spending interminable sessions signing whatever anyone wanted him to sign. He once, in a legendary gesture of generosity, stripped off his warmup suit and tossed it to a lucky fan.

And for all the uproar he caused on the court, he studied hard in the classroom and graduated in four years.

"I wasn't a Boy Scout," Heyman told Morris. "But I never drank, never smoked and always took care of myself. I went down there as a kid and came out as a man. You had to be a man to survive all the crap I went through there."

The first pick of the 1963 draft by the New York Knicks, Heyman had an immediate impact by averaging 15.4 points a game and making the NBA All-Rookie team. But being the pain in the ass he was, he wore out his welcome by his second season and was out of the league after briefs stays with the Cincinnati Royals and Philadelphia 76ers.

He landed in the ABA, where he played for the New Jersey Americans, Pittsburgh Pipers, and Miami Floridians over three years. He caught fire to average 20.1 points a game for the Pipers in 1968 but retired in 1970 after averaging 7.8 for the Floridians.

ART WHISNANT

6-4 Center | South Carolina | 1959–62 | No. 44

1960	Second-team All-ACC, sixth-most votes	275
1961	Second-team All-ACC, sixth-most votes	275
	First-team All-Tournament	75
1962	First-team All-ACC, fourth-most votes	325
	Second-team All-Tournament	50
Awards Points		1,000

Art Whisnant is the one player in this book better known for his progeny than for what he did on the court.

Of course, his progeny—grandson Dustin Johnson, a star of the PGA Tour—is really good, whereas the team for which Whisnant played really wasn't.

All it took was one stray drive for Whisnant to receive more national publicity than he did his whole time at the University of South Carolina, where he averaged 19.1 points and 9.2 rebounds for teams that finished fifth (6–8), seventh (2–12), and fourth (7–7) in the conference. It was at the Doral Open in 2011 that Johnson beaned his grandfather with a drive off the first tee.

"He said it hit him on the fly," Johnson recalled. "I walked up there and he was standing next to the ball and said, 'You hit me in the head.'"

Those who know pro golf go gaga over Johnson's athleticism. He's the same height as his grandfather, but six-four is sizable for a pro golfer and rather diminutive for a major-college center. Johnson's drives come off the

Art Whisnant

club head at close to 190 miles an hour (compared to the tour average of 165), and he can spring flat-footed and dunk a basketball. But he has yet to prove himself the scrapper his grandfather was while going up against the likes of Len Chappell, Art Heyman, and Doug Moe.

"He was mean," Johnson said to Rich Lerner of the Golf Channel. "And he could jump out of the gym."

Whisnant had to be mean to take care of himself in the wars underneath the basket. At times, his coaches wondered if he would survive. Tom Price wrote in *Tales from the Gamecock Roost* how in one game Whisnant got such a gash that trainer Jim Price wrapped a bandage around his head that made him appear as though he were playing the second half wearing a turban. He wasn't stitched up until after the game.

"I've never seen a kid take the beating Whisnant takes and still come back for more and do a great job," Gamecocks assistant Gordie Stauffer told Warren Koon of the *Charleston News and Courier*.

But Whisnant, recruited out of the hardscrabble foothills of Burke County, North Carolina, gave as good as he got.

"He's an amazing kid," Coach Bobby Stevens told Koon. "I honestly don't see how he does what he does."

Koon described Whisnant as an unorthodox player known to dribble right-handed to his left, then pull back and shoot right-handed over his defender.

"The reason he can get away with that, instead of using his left as fancier players would, is that he's so strong," Stevens explained. "When you're strong you can get away with a lot of things.

"Thank heavens for him."

Whisnant made only 40.5 percent of his field-goal attempts but did prodigious damage at the free-throw line, where he shot a more respectable 64 percent. He had plenty of practice, hitting 567 of 880 free throws over his career. He ranks third all-time in the ACC with 11.1 free throws per game, trailing only Dickie Hemric (13) and Buzz Wilkinson (12.2).

"He will not only stick the ball up in the basket, if you hang on, he'll take you and put you right in the basket, too," Stevens said.

The sharpest picture of Whisnant and the wild times he had at South Carolina comes from *Tales from the Gamecock Roost*. In it, Price, the university's longtime sports information director, described a hell-raiser who cut a wide swath through Columbia in the early 1960s.

Whisnant once "borrowed" a mule from a man living in a decrepit nearby neighborhood and drove it around Davis Field, where the Gamecocks played baseball. For a mere pittance, he would let his classmates ride.

"We took up a collection and raised about $50 and gave it to the old guy who owned the mule," Whisnant said. "That mule wasn't worth half that."

Trainer Jim Price once had to rush to Whisnant's room when the Gamecocks were staying at the Dupont Plaza Hotel in D.C. Word got out that Whisnant and teammate Joe Laird were standing on the balcony dropping water balloons on pedestrians and cars. It was left to Price to confiscate the payload.

Whisnant once whacked Coley Brundrick, the campus police chief, in the head with a snowball and had to vacate the premises on the fly to escape apprehension.

It wasn't his only brush with campus authorities.

"I had accumulated about 60 or 70 parking tickets, and the police came knocking on my door," Whisnant recalled. "They said I owed them several hundred dollars. I told them I didn't have but $20 or $30. They took my $20 or $30 and let me go."

That being the early 1960s, and boys being boys, the obligatory panty raids took place. Whisnant said he was climbing through the window of a women's dorm when he was doused by a bucket of hot water thrown by the housemother.

"A cop grabbed me, but I pointed to a guy holding a laundry bag who was watching and told the cop the guy had a bag full of panties," Whisnant said.

"And he turned me loose and grabbed that guy. The bag was full of his dirty laundry."

But once Whisnant stepped onto the basketball court, he was serious about his business.

"Whisnant doesn't give one much of an impression of being a basketball player," Koon wrote. "He isn't fast, his expression remains so constant you don't see any grins or frowns, he makes moves which would drive a coach crazy, and he's only 6-4, so he gives away height to almost every opponent.

"All Whisnant can do is play basketball. All he can do is lead the Gamecocks in points and rebounds, play defense and fight off bigger men with ease."

He was a fifth-round pick of the Los Angeles Lakers but never played in the NBA. He settled in the Columbia area and became a businessman, eventually founding a realty investment company, Art Whisnant Enterprises, in Chapin.

LEN CHAPPELL

6-8 Center | Wake Forest | 1959–62 | No. 50/51

1960	First-team All-ACC, most votes	400
	First-team All-Tournament	75
1961	First-team All-ACC, unanimous	425
	ACC Tournament MVP	100
	ACC POY	200
1962	First-team All-ACC, unanimous	425
	ACC Tournament MVP	100
	ACC POY	200
	First-team All-American (with Terry Dischinger of Purdue, Jerry Lucas of Ohio State, Billy McGill of Utah, and Chet Walker of Bradley)	200
Awards Points		**2,125**

Off the court, Len Chappell was a go-along kind of guy—especially when his more extroverted, forever calculating Wake Forest teammate, Billy Packer, had his hand in the small of Chappell's back.

"Packer was the ringleader of that bunch," Charlie Bryant, an assistant

Len Chappell

at the time, recalled. "He led them around. If Packer wanted something, he always had Len up front to do the dirty work."

Chappell was also easy to underestimate—again, off the court only.

"Len was a sharp guy," Bryant maintained. "Everybody thought Len was a dummy. He wasn't. He was very sharp.

"But Len was just a dynamite player. He had the best touch for a big, husky guy I've ever seen."

Needing to restock the cupboard when he became head coach in 1957, Bones McKinney of the Deacons happened to be visiting Duke coach Harold Bradley when he noticed the names of two recruits on Bradley's blackboard. One was Len Chappell, the other Billy Packer.

"That was his story," Packer said years later. "He always said that's how he got our names."

Inspired, McKinney made enough 11-hour jaunts from Winston-Salem to Portage, Pennsylvania, to convince Chappell to help lead the revival of Wake Forest basketball. The key was selling Chappell's recently wid-owed mother, who happened to mention on one visit that another school had offered a scholarship plus $100 a month for Chappell to sign. McKinney pointed out that if a school broke the rules, it would continue to do so after Chappell arrived. Duly won over, Chappell signed with the Deacons, who became a force in the ACC the day he became eligible as a sophomore.

"Chop him off at the knees," Coach Bud Millikan of Maryland said. "That's the only way you'll stop him."

"If you let him get his hands on the ball," Coach Everett Case of N.C. State cautioned, "he'll put it in the basket—and you along with it."

Nobody knew better than Packer what Chappell could and couldn't do.

"In those days, six-eight was pretty tall for a center," Packer said. "But he weighed 255 pounds, and it was all solid, and he was an incredible shooter. And he had really good speed, and he was a great rebounder, although he was not a great jumper. He had terrific hands.

"He was not a playmaker, and he was not a finesse player, but he could shoot and he could rebound and he could score and he could shoot from inside and outside. And he more than held his own defensively. He was by far and away the best big man in the league."

He must have been, considering he averaged 17.4 points and 12.5 rebounds as a sophomore, 26.6 points and 14 rebounds as a junior, and 30.1 points and 15.2 rebounds as a senior. No ACC player has averaged 30 points in a season since. It's a record akin to batting .400 in the Major Leagues, which hasn't been done since Ted Williams posted a .406 average in 1941. It will be interesting to see which mark falls first, if either ever does.

Chappell's impact on the Wake Forest program, and on the ACC at large, was immense. The Deacons were 15–27 in conference play the three seasons before he became eligible and 35–7 the three he was on the floor. Coached by the tightly wound McKinney, they careened through a rough patch every season in January and/or February before finding their traction by the time the ACC Tournament cranked up. Among the reasons the Deacons enjoyed postseason success (13–3) they have not matched since, the biggest was Chappell, who averaged 27.5 points and 12 rebounds over eight ACC Tournament games and 17.6 points and 17.1 rebounds over eight NCAA Tournament games.

"Every year, he would start out in December and he would average about 17 or 18 points," Bryant said. "And then in January, he would be at about 20, 22, or 25. Then by February and March, he was in the 30s. He would get better each year from December to January to February to March."

The fourth-overall pick of the 1962 draft by the Syracuse Nationals, Chappell had a better (or at least longer) pro career than many people remember. He played 10 seasons for nine NBA teams before closing it out with the ABA's Dallas Chaparrals in 1972. He had a standout season in 1963–64, when he made the All-Star team while averaging 17.3 points and 9.8 rebounds for the New York Knicks. Three seasons later, he was picked by the Chicago Bulls in the NBA expansion draft.

YORK LARESE

6-4 Guard | North Carolina | 1958–61 | No. 22

1959	First-team All-ACC, most votes	400
	Second-team All-Tournament	50
1960	First-team All-ACC, fourth-most votes	325
	First-team All-Tournament	75
1961	First-team All-ACC, unanimous	425
Awards Points		**1,275**

During his rough-and-tumble days playing for St. John's, Frank McGuire had a teammate named Dave "Java" Gotkin. It so happened that Gotkin was Jewish, which from time to time made him the object of taunts and slurs from opponents who had yet to attain a high-enough state of consciousness to know better.

Well, McGuire, ever the pugnacious Irishman, took up for his teammate, telling the ill-mannered ruffians that if they had anything to say to Gotkin, they should go ahead and say it to him first and let the fisticuffs begin.

It also so happened that Java Gotkin had a brother named Harry, who, in addition to manufacturing baby bonnets for the family business in the Garment District, honed his keen eye for basketball talent by watching more than 20,000 games over 30 or so years. Harry Gotkin—or "Uncle Harry," as he came to be known—was the most famous of the many scouts (a more respectable word than *runner* or *street agent*) who tipped off college basketball recruiters to players worth pursuing. In exchange for services rendered, the "scouts" received recompense ranging from tickets and train fares to walking-around money.

Everyone knew what Gotkin was up to, but he was never caught with his hand in the till.

"The NCAA once came in and investigated the books in my factory because they thought I was taking payoffs," Gotkin said. "Of course, they found nothing. But even if I was taking money for players, did they think I would

York Larese
UNC ATHLETIC
COMMUNICATIONS

have been stupid enough to put it in my books?"

So why did he spent all his free time supplying players to colleges?

"I did it because I enjoyed helping kids," Gotkin explained.

For a while, Gotkin rendered most of his selfless service to Everett Case of N.C. State. But then he sent Case his nephew, another Dave Gotkin, and that's when the bond started to crack. Case, in Uncle Harry's considered view, didn't give nephew Dave enough PT. And on top of that, Case had the temerity to pass on Lennie Rosenbluth, another of Gotkin's finds, who went on to lead undefeated North Carolina to the 1957 national title.

So by 1957, when York Larese was wearing out the nets at St. Ann's Academy (now known as Archbishop Molloy), Gotkin had burned his bridge at N.C. State and had taken up with old family friend McGuire over in Chapel Hill.

Howard Garfinkel, in an attempt to fill the void at N.C. State left by Gotkin's defection, actually talked Larese into committing to Case and the Wolfpack. Then Gotkin stepped in and convinced Larese he would be better off 30 miles west.

By then, Uncle Harry had another nickname. He was known as "the North Carolina Man" for his role as conductor of the infamous "Underground Railroad" from New York to Chapel Hill.

"Look, I just speak to the kid," Gotkin said in *Tales from the North Carolina Tar Heels Locker Room* by Ken Rappoport. "I talk North Carolina to him. I arrange for the kid to see Carolina's campus in Chapel Hill. I see that he meets some players.

"Somebody takes him over to Raleigh to see North Carolina State's campus with the railroad running through it. That makes up the kid's mind. He sticks with us."

Seven guards from New York City are honored in this book—nine, if you count Jim Spanarkel and Bobby Hurley from just across the Hudson River in Jersey City. Back before Julius Hodge, Kenny Anderson, Kenny Smith, Charlie Davis, Charlie Scott, and John Roche, there was York Larese.

Larese got to campus in time to watch the varsity win the national championship in 1957 but sat out the 1957–58 season recovering from a knee operation. That's how he was able to play with Doug Moe for three years, forming the first "L&M Boys" a half-decade or so before Bob Lewis and Larry Miller came along.

Larese sharpened his eye working out night after night with Buck Freeman, McGuire's trusted right-hand man.

"Many times, we would work on shooting, just the two of us, for several hours," Larese recalled. "A couple of times, we were surprised to see the sun coming up."

A confirmed bachelor known for loving his bonded libations, Freeman kept his quarters in a cramped apartment attached to Woollen Gym. But he knew his basketball, and the results of his nocturnal sessions with Larese were impressive.

"I can't ever remember a better shooter in the league," Coach Vic Bubas of Duke said.

"I'll tell you one thing," piped in Charlie Bryant, then an assistant at Wake Forest. "He could shoot the living eyes out of it."

Larese's deadly eye made him the bane of carnival barkers everywhere. One story had him being turned away from a booth after swishing so many shots that he walked off with six large teddy bears. No doubt, he gave them to Vivian Churico, whom he married before his senior season and who provided the family income by teaching third grade in Durham.

Named for the city he grew up in and the northern Italian town where his parents met, York Bruno Larese spoke Italian in the family's Greenwich Village home before entering grade school. In college, he fortified his vocabulary by engaging in word games he organized (and usually won) on road trips.

His nickname was "the Cobra," derived from his singular style of shooting free throws. Larese didn't bear down and concentrate. He took no set number of dribbles, followed by a deep breath and a clearing of the mind. Instead, he shot the ball as soon as the official handed it to him. He was timed taking anywhere from 0.8 second to 1.1 seconds to let it fly.

McGuire and Freeman saw no need to intervene. Larese still holds the ACC record for making 21 of 21 free throws in a game, a feat that came in a 75–53 victory over Duke on December 29, 1959. For his career, he shot 79.6 percent from the line. His 86.8 percent accuracy as a junior stood as a school record until eclipsed by Steve Hale in 1985.

Larese was drafted in the second round by the Chicago Packers but was traded early in the 1961–62 season to the Philadelphia Warriors, with whom he became a footnote to one of the most famous feats in basketball history. A reserve, he was sent into a game against the New York Knicks in Hershey, Pennsylvania, with two instructions. The first was to foul as soon as possible, so the Warriors would get the ball back. Having accomplished that, he was to feed center Wilt Chamberlain. It was a good strategy, considering "Wilt the Stilt" had already scored more than 90 points.

Less than 90 seconds remained on the clock when Larese led a three-on-one fast break. But instead of dishing to the wing, he simply threw the ball high into the air as his momentum carried him across the baseline. A trailing Chamberlain soared in from the rafters to catch the lob and slam it through the net.

Chamberlain scored off a feed from another reserve, Joe Ruklick, with 46 seconds remaining to finish with his magic 100 points.

LEE SHAFFER

6-7 Forward │ North Carolina │ 1957–60 │ No. 12

1959	Second-team All-ACC, sixth-most votes	275
	First-team All-Tournament	75
1960	First-team All-ACC, second-most votes	375
	First-team All-Tournament	75
	ACC POY	200
	Second-team All-American	150
Awards Points		1,150

Can you imagine an NBA player good enough to be included in a trade for, say, LeBron James retiring at age 24 not because of any indignity of being

Lee Shaffer
<small>UNC Athletic
Communications</small>

shipped to another franchise but because he could make more money in private business?

If so, that makes one of us.

But that, in a nutshell, is why Lee Shaffer declined to report to the San Francisco Warriors after he was traded—along with Connie Dierking, Paul Neumann, and a $150,000 deal-sweetener—by the Philadelphia 76ers for Wilt Chamberlain. He had been offered a solid, steady job with Kenan Transport—a mover of petroleum and chemical products—in Durham, North Carolina. To the surprise of many, he took it.

"Franklin Mieuli made me a tremendous offer," Shaffer said of the Warriors' owner in a story published by the *Pittsburgh Post-Gazette* in 1986. "They offered me $40,000, a tremendous offer in those days. [Jerry] West and [Elgin] Baylor were only making $20,000 to $25,000.

"I wasn't close to my peak when I quit."

Shaffer wasn't just a throw-in by the 76ers. He was the fifth player chosen in the 1960 draft—after Oscar Robertson, West, Darrell Imhoff, and a player whose name lives in infamy at N.C. State, Jackie Moreland. Violations Everett Case and his staff committed in recruiting Moreland out of Minden, Louisiana, landed the Wolfpack, as repeat offenders, on a crippling four-year probation and denied the 1959 ACC champs a chance of playing for the national title.

Shaffer, a rock-solid 220-pound forward with a sweet shooting stroke, averaged 15.9 points as a rookie for the Syracuse Nationals. The team moved the next season to Philadelphia, where his scoring average climbed to 18.6 points a game. And unlike another, more-heralded forward on the team, Shaffer could be counted on at both ends.

"I always had to guard the other teams' top forwards, players like [Bob] Pettit, [Tom] Heinsohn," Shaffer told the *Post-Gazette*. "Dolph Schayes was our other forward and he couldn't watch them."

Shaffer played in the NBA with the same abandon that had made him so popular with Coach Frank McGuire at North Carolina.

"My nickname was Jimmy Pearsall," Shaffer told the *Post-Gazette*. "I think it's because I played the game so hard. I guess pros aren't supposed to do that."

Instead of ending up at a state mental hospital, where Piersall spent the final seven weeks of his rookie major-league baseball season of 1952 being treated for "nervous exhaustion," Shaffer merely landed himself on the disabled list. But he didn't remain there long enough. He hurt his leg 25 games into the 1963–64 season, but when the team doctors failed to properly diagnose the injury, he returned to compete in the playoffs on a broken leg. The following season brought the trade, along with an offer from Durham he felt he could not refuse.

"I had an unusual business opportunity," Shaffer told the *Post-Gazette*. "In 1965 I received an invitation from Frank Kenan to join his company. Frank told me to get serious about my life. Nobody was making any money in pro ball, including Chamberlain.

"It was a very difficult decision, but it's one I have never regretted."

Shaffer, who would rise to CEO at Kenan Transport, had been playing highly competitive basketball at one level or another for more than 10 years. Like Brad Daugherty three decades later, he was a young senior only 15 years old when he averaged 25 points a game for Baldwin High School in Pittsburgh. He skipped not one but two grades in elementary school.

By the time he prepped a year at Manlius Military School in Upstate New York, he was already on North Carolina's recruiting radar, having attended the All-America Camp conducted by basketball legend Clair Bee at New York Military Academy outside West Point. Buck Freeman, Frank McGuire's coach at St. John's who became his ex-pupil's assistant at North Carolina, coached Shaffer at Bee's camp and came away impressed.

Others were as well. Shaffer visited Ohio State, Duke, and Maryland but had pretty much decided to attend Air Force before going instead to North Carolina. Shaffer, York Larese, and Doug Moe were seen as the influx of talent to make the Tar Heels contenders for the ACC crown.

I came across a story by Gerald Holland for *Sports Illustrated* that told how Shaffer was rushed into the breach when Joe Quigg, a center who had started for the 1957 national champions, suffered a broken leg that cost him his senior season.

Holland was talking with McGuire when Shaffer came running up. Here's how Holland recounted the incident:

> "You've got a chance to be as good as Tom Gola, Lee," said McGuire. He tapped his forehead. "As soon as you get a little more up here."
>
> Shaffer grinned and dribbled away, with astonishing grace for his height and weight (215) at 18 years of age. He took a shot with the lazy-looking ease of perfect coordination. He was the leading scorer of last year's freshman team with an average of 22.1 points per game.
>
> "Shaffer," said McGuire, "is a fine student. I was kidding him about something else. He came to me some time ago and wanted my opinion of a car he was going to buy for $1,400. He claimed he had beaten the price down from $1,900. I took a look at it and told him I'd give him a 100-to-1 if he could go out and find a buyer for the car at $700. I doubt if it was worth that. I finally told him that if he wanted to make this ball club, he'd better wait until spring to get a car.
>
> "He went along with the idea. Lee is very serious about making the team."

In one of the most memorable games of the unforgettable Dixie Classic, North Carolina against Oscar Robertson's Cincinnati Bearcats in December 1958, Shaffer dunked in the final seconds, drew a foul, and hit the free throw to help clinch a 72–68 victory.

The memories of his final college game were less pleasant. The top-seeded Tar Heels of 1960 were upset by Duke 71–69 in the ACC Tournament semifinals.

"The sad part is we beat Duke three times that year," Shaffer recalled to the *Post-Gazette*. "That was my biggest disappointment in college."

Married in 1958, he and his wife, Ruth, had their first son, Lee III, in 1959. That's how Shaffer was barely on the backside of 40 when Lee III made first-team All-ACC playing linebacker for the North Carolina football team in 1981.

Two younger sons, Dean Frank (named, indeed, after two of his father's college coaches) and David, gravitated toward basketball. Dean began his career at North Carolina but transferred with Smith's blessing to Florida State, where he was MVP of the 1982 Metro Conference Tournament. David played at Clemson and ended up transferring to compete at Florida State as well.

LOU PUCILLO

5-9 Guard | N.C. State | 1956–59 | No. 20/21

1958	First-team All-ACC, second-most votes	375
	First-team All-Tournament	75
1959	First-team All-ACC, most votes	400
	ACC POY, contested	175
	ACC Tournament MVP	100
Awards Points		**1,125**

Jim Valvano told a story about the first time he saw Spud Webb. His assistant Tom Abatemarco had convinced Valvano to bring Webb in for a visit. As the two were standing at the airport watching the five-seven, 130-pound Webb disembark, Valvano quipped, "If this is him, you're fired."

Everett Case had a similar reaction about 30 years earlier upon receiving a call from his assistant Vic Bubas, who said he had uncovered a future star who was 5-8½, weighed 150 pounds, and had never started in high school. But he was tearing it up against a team from the Philadelphia School for the Blind and Deaf.

"There's just one thing," Bubas cautioned. "I think you're going to have to change your coaching style."

Case, a staunch believer in big, physical guards who did what the coach told them—not showboating pepper pots who idolized Bob Cousy—wasn't sure of the telephone connection between Philadelphia and Raleigh.

"You're telling me that you saw this kid against a deaf-and-mute team who is 5-8½, 150 pounds, and he throws the ball behind his back, and you want me to take him," Case responded. "Have you been drinking?"

And that was the inauspicious beginning of the college career of Lou Pucillo, the smallest and one of the best-loved players Case ever recruited.

Pucillo didn't make the team at Southeast Catholic High School as a freshman or sophomore and was too discouraged to try as a junior. He earned a spot as a senior, but Coach Jack Kraft, who years later guided Villanova to the NCAA championship game, played him only a few minutes here and there.

"By the time I made it my senior year, most of the guys had been playing together for a couple of years," Pucillo said. "I never scored in double figures. I

Lou Pucillo
N.C. State Athletics

was very frustrated. I just wasn't at the right place at the right time."

He was taking a summer class in Spanish at Temple Prep, where his father taught, when he heard about the school's basketball team. He signed up for classes in the fall and winter, which was how he happened to attract Bubas's attention.

Getting a scholarship offer—his only one—was tough enough. Even tougher was convincing Case he hadn't wasted it.

By his junior season, when he led N.C. State with 15.8 points a game, Pucillo had succeeded beyond his wildest dreams.

Since the Wolfpack was ineligible for the NCAA Tournament because of recurring violations, the only titles within reach were the ACC championship and the (in some ways even more coveted) championship of the Dixie Classic, Case's celebrated creation that was the rave of college basketball from 1949 through 1960. In Pucillo's senior season, the Wolfpack won both in Reynolds Coliseum.

N.C. State rolled to the Dixie Classic crown by beating Louisville in overtime, second-ranked Cincinnati (led by Oscar Robertson), and seventh-ranked Michigan State (led by Jumping Johnny Green). The Wolfpack also captured the school's fourth conference championship by knocking off South Carolina in overtime, Virginia, and North Carolina in the sixth ACC Tournament.

Of the two accomplishments, Pucillo had no doubt which was better remembered.

"To this day, I could be in Asheville or Wilmington or at a new Bible study class and there is still nothing people ask me about more than that 1958 Dixie Classic," Pucillo told Tim Peeler in *Legends of N.C. State Basketball*. "We were fortunate enough to win those games. I think it was the greatest tournament of all time."

Case overcame his aversion to showboating 5-8½ guards.

"Lou is simply amazing," he gushed. "He shows me something different every time I see him play. He's always thinking one step ahead of everyone else on the court."

Wordsmith Bruce Phillips of the *Raleigh Times*, in his inimitable fashion, called Pucillo a "Hardwood Houdini."

But after his college career, the magician couldn't pull an NBA career out of his sleeve. He was drafted by the St. Louis Hawks, but the team wouldn't guarantee his contract. He eventually went to work for a living, but not before keeping his dream alive by playing in the National Industrial Basketball League and the Eastern League.

Case thought enough of Pucillo to hire him as an assistant coach in 1961. When Pucillo received his first paycheck, he celebrated by taking Case out to dinner. Besides being old and gray, Case was also known as one of the thriftiest foxes ever. When one of the program's big boosters happened by and insisted on picking up the check, Pucillo felt a nudge under the table.

"Let him do it," Case whispered to Pucillo. "And then you can take me out again."

Pucillo remained on N.C. State's staff for three seasons before accepting a job with a friend of Case's who owned a liquor distribution business. He eventually owned and operated his own beverage company, which he ran until his retirement in 2001.

"I am a big believer in destiny," Pucillo said in *Legends of N.C. State Basketball*. "The odds of me ever playing big-time basketball and getting some regional and national awards were crazy. You don't just not play high-school basketball and score just four points a game, and then have one scout see you against a deaf-and-mute team, if there wasn't some kind of reason somewhere.

"You can call it spiritual, or whatever you want to call it. But it happened."

PETE BRENNAN

6-6 Forward | North Carolina | 1955–58 | No. 35

1957	Second-team All-ACC, seventh-most votes	250
	First-team All-Tournament	75
1958	First-team All-ACC, unanimous	425
	First-team All-Tournament	75
	ACC POY	200
	Second-team All-American	150
Awards Points		**1,175**

New York City had seven daily newspapers in the mid-1950s, so it's not surprising two of them came up with the same idea. Cartoons ran in both the *New York Sun* and *New York World Telegram* of a Chapel Hill stop on the NYC subway.

"New York is my personal territory," Coach Frank McGuire of North Carolina told *Sports Illustrated*. "Duke can scout in Philadelphia and North Carolina State can have the whole country. But if anybody wants to move into New York, they need a passport from me."

Not until the train pulled into the Chapel Hill station loaded with Pete Brennan and Joe Quigg of Brooklyn, Bob Cunningham of All Hallows High, and Tommy Kearns from across the Hudson in Bergenfield, New Jersey, did McGuire have the manpower to wrest the mantle of supremacy from Everett Case and N.C. State. The players were strangers in a strange land—Catholics in the bedrock Protestant South. They joined forces with a Jewish star who had made the trek down the year before, Lennie Rosenbluth, to form the nucleus of the ACC's first team for the ages.

Once, in the dying seconds of a close game, McGuire told Rosenbluth to say a Hail Mary and hit a clutch free throw. When Rosenbluth explained he didn't know how, Brennan was quick with a rejoinder: "We'll say the Hail Mary. You make the shot."

Brennan's original conveyance to Chapel Hill was actually a car he rode in with another NYC schoolboy star, Johnny Lee, who, like Brennan, was also considering Yale. When they passed the DuPont Plant in Delaware, Lee's mother surmised that the head man there was more likely to be a Yale man

Pete Brennan

than a Carolina man. Her son chose Yale, but Brennan fell for the charms of the loquacious McGuire and cast his lot with the Tar Heels.

One of 10 children born to immigrant parents, Brennan was the first of his family to graduate from college. He eventually settled in North Carolina and made a good living from an apparel business and later by selling real estate in the Kitty Hawk area.

The only time I was around Brennan was during the 2006–7 season, when North Carolina staged a 50-year reunion for the 1957 national champions and a 25-year reunion for the 1982 champs. I happened to be at the Smith Center that day because the Tar Heels were playing the team I cover, Wake Forest. I was taken by how gracious and articulate Brennan came off while fielding questions alongside Rosenbluth. I wish I had known then to ask him about an incident I came across late in the research for this book, from another time the Tar Heels faced off against the Deacons.

The year was 1956, Brennan's sophomore season. He was at the free-throw line late in a close game when he heard a voice from the Deacons' bench chirping, "Brennan's going to choke. Brennan's going to choke."

Brennan recognized his heckler to be the irrepressible Bones McKinney, then an assistant to Coach Murray Greason. He hit the two free throws to nail down the Tar Heels' 77–73 comeback victory and on his way back downcourt dropped his chewing gum into the pail of water McKinney always kept beside him during games.

"Coach," he said, "Brennan doesn't choke."

Even if he hadn't developed into the ACC's best player as a senior, Brennan would be remembered for two reasons.

The first came during the final 11 seconds of the first overtime in the 1957 national semifinal, against Michigan State. The Spartans led the undefeated (30–0) Tar Heels 64–62 and had star Jumping Johnny Green at the line. One of the Michigan State players walked over to Kearns.

"Thirty and one," the Spartan said.

Green, as fate would have it, missed the free throw. Brennan rebounded, drove the ball upcourt, and pulled up for a 20-foot jumper. The ball swished through the net as the buzzer sounded. The Tar Heels prevailed 74–70 two overtimes later.

After the Tar Heels shot the moon by beating Wilt Chamberlain and Kansas 54–53 in three overtimes to win the national championship, Brennan returned to his Brooklyn tenement home for a hero's welcome. Or so he thought until a neighbor (whose knowledge of college basketball was sorely lacking) saw him climbing the stairs.

"Hey, everybody, come look!" the neighbor yelled out her apartment window. "Petey's back from the service."

Then there was the Tar Heels' lucky charm, a used gray Chrysler that Brennan was given his sophomore season. The only snag was that the car was missing first gear. Brennan improvised by parking it on a hill in front of the Monogram Club on campus. When he left Chapel Hill for the summer, he pinned a note on the car saying he would make the necessary repairs in September, a statement to which he signed his name.

Upon returning for the fall semester, he was greeted with a stack of parking tickets. Told by McGuire to deal with the distraction, Brennan explained it was the team's good-luck car. So McGuire got police permission for Brennan to park the car on the hill until the end of basketball season.

Raleigh's *News & Observer* wrote a story on the hoopla surrounding the ride, which prompted students from N.C. State to slip onto campus, push the car down the hill, and splash it with red paint. Not having any of it, North Carolina students shouldered the car back up the hill and painted it light blue.

"That car hadn't been painted in 20 years," Brennan recounted in *The Best Game Ever* by Adam Lucas. "And then in the span of two days, it got two paint jobs."

LENNIE ROSENBLUTH

6-5 Forward | North Carolina | 1954–57 | No. 10

1955	First-team All-ACC, fourth-most votes	325
1956	First-team All-ACC, unanimous	425
	First-team All-Tournament	75
1957	First-team All-ACC, unanimous	425
	ACC Tournament MVP	100
	ACC POY	200
	First-team All-American (with Wilt Chamberlain of Kansas, Rod Hundley of West Virginia, Chet Forte of Columbia, and Jim Krebs of Southern Methodist)	200
Awards Points		**1,750**

As revered as the memory of Everett Case remains at N.C. State, it might even be more exalted if not for his practice of holding tryouts.

First of all, the NCAA deemed tryouts to be illegal, which landed Case's program on probation after he insisted on having them. And second, he will always be remembered, among his more hallowed achievements, as the man who passed on Lennie Rosenbluth.

Mitigating circumstances factored into his decision not to offer Rosenbluth a free ride.

Case was hot on Rosenbluth's trail, as was evident when he had Rosenbluth's father down from the Bronx for the 1951 Dixie Classic. But by the time Rosenbluth showed up for the tryout in April 1952, he had played precious little high-school basketball. A classic late bloomer, he had failed to make the high-school varsity as a sophomore and junior. And when he finally cracked the roster as a senior, a lengthy teachers' strike in New York City truncated the season after a total of seven games. Rosenbluth played instead for the otherwise all-black Carlton YMCA team in Brooklyn, coached by Hy Gotkin, whose cousin Harry Gotkin was a scout who supplied talent to Case.

Invited to Raleigh, Rosenbluth arrived to find himself pitted against around 100 candidates, all vying for one spot on the roster. He was not in peak shape—nor was his academic transcript.

Utterly dashed by the rejection, Rosenbluth returned home to work out

Lennie Rosenbluth
UNC Athletic Communications

with Buck Freeman, who had coached Frank McGuire at St. John's in the 1930s and was destined to become McGuire's assistant at North Carolina. That was about the time the Gotkins happened to mention to Rosenbluth that McGuire was contemplating leaving his position as St. John's head coach for the same job at North Carolina.

McGuire indeed headed south, and he was determined to take Rosenbluth with him. But Rosenbluth first had to spend a year at Staunton Military Academy in Virginia gussying up his grades for admission to North Carolina. As the story goes, Rosenbluth's mother hocked her fur coat to pay the tuition at Staunton. In the end, it was worth it, especially for McGuire, who considered Rosenbluth the recruit who got his "Underground Railroad" from NYC to Chapel Hill up and running. Rosenbluth was enough of a sensation at Staunton to draw interest from programs throughout college basketball. But McGuire had stood by Rosenbluth, and Rosenbluth felt duty-bound to stand by McGuire.

Another boxcar load of talent arrived from New York a year later. Unlike Rosenbluth, who was Jewish, this one was filled with Catholics Pete Brennan, Bob Cunningham, Joe Quigg, and Tommy Kearns. The five kids from the big city started for the 1956–57 team that finished 32–0 by beating Wilt Chamberlain and Kansas for the national championship.

Listed at 195 pounds, Rosenbluth—who grew up watching Joe DiMaggio in Yankee Stadium—was a rail-thin wing forward with a velvet touch and no semblance of a conscience. He scored so many points his first year on campus that the gym would be packed for the freshman game but would pretty much empty out by the time the varsity tipped off.

Believing that practically everyone in this strange part of the country sported three names, Rosenbluth introduced himself as Lennie Shootalot Rosenbluth. He hated to practice and, according to teammate Cunningham, was quite honest about it. The seat his girlfriend and wife-to-be, Pat, got at home games—right under the Woollen Gym basket next to McGuire's wife—exemplified Rosenbluth's special status on the team.

He rode to games with Quigg, Ken Rosemond, and team manager Joel Fleishman, so they could smoke cigarettes out of sight of McGuire, who rode shotgun in the lead car. Quigg, as Ron Morris noted in *ACC Basketball*, was the Phillip Morris Tobacco representative on the campus and got all the free cigarettes he, Rosemond, and Rosenbluth needed.

Rosenbluth loved movies so much McGuire would send Freeman into the Varsity Theatre on Franklin Street to flush the star player back to class. Morris wrote about how Freeman once became so engrossed in a movie himself that he sat down next to Rosenbluth and watched until the credits rolled.

A finicky eater, Rosenbluth customarily passed up the pregame steak at The Pines so he could order a pastrami sandwich at the Goody Shop afterward. When he had to have some fuel for the game, he stuck to shrimp cocktails.

Before a game against Wake Forest in Winston-Salem, as Gerald Holland recounted in the December 9, 1957, edition of *Sports Illustrated*, Rosenbluth coughed so long and loud that McGuire couldn't give the Tar Heels their marching orders.

"Lennie, that's the worst cough I've ever heard," McGuire observed. "You're obviously dying. Now I don't want you to die anyplace but in Chapel Hill. Get dressed, Lennie, and we'll call off the game and drive you home."

"My boy, I can't promise you that you will live to see the old school again, but I do promise that you'll have the finest three-day Irish wake in the history of North Carolina."

But when Rosenbluth was right, few who ever played the game were better. And he was never more right than during the 1957 ACC Tournament, when he laid 45 points and 12 rebounds on Clemson in the first round, 23 points and 10 rebounds on Wake Forest in the semifinals, and 38 points and 11 rebounds on South Carolina in the championship victory. The record of

106 points stood until Randolph Childress's epic 107-point performance in the 1995 tournament.

Rosenbluth's game and lack of strength didn't translate well to the NBA. He played only two seasons with the Philadelphia Warriors, averaging 4.2 points a game. After completing his degree at North Carolina, he moved to Miami, where he taught American history and coached high-school basketball.

RONNIE SHAVLIK

6-9 Center | N.C. State | 1953–56 | No. 84

1954	First-team All-Tournament	75
1955	First-team All-ACC, unanimous	425
	ACC Tournament MVP	100
	ACC POY, runner-up	100
	Second-team All-American	150
1956	First-team All-ACC, unanimous	425
	Second-team All-Tournament	50
	ACC POY	200
	First-team All-American (with Robin Freeman of Ohio State, Sihugo Green of Duquesne, Tom Heinsohn of Holy Cross, and Bill Russell of San Francisco)	200
Awards Points		**1,725**

Many is the man described as a great player on the court and an even better person off it. Few, if any, have gone to such lengths to prove it as Ronnie Shavlik.

On the court, he transformed the way the game was played. Before Shavlik's arrival from Denver as the first ACC recruit west of Chicago, the conference was known for its physical low-post play and sluggish pace. But Everett Case needed a center fast enough to run with his "M-Twins" guard tandem of Vic Molodet and John Maglio. He found his man playing for an AAU team way out west.

Shavlik received scant attention for being a two-time all-state player in Colorado and leading East High School to consecutive state titles. It took fate to thrust him into the limelight.

Ronnie Shavlik
N.C. STATE ATHLETICS

The national AAU Tournament was played in Denver in 1952. Shavlik's local team was invited to participate mostly as a courtesy. But by the time his scoring and rebounding carried the team all the way to the semifinals and himself to center court to receive MVP honors, national powers like Kentucky were all over him.

Case won the recruiting battle. His efforts did not, as has been widely reported, land the Wolfpack on probation. N.C. State was sanctioned by the ACC and the NCAA for illegally trying out a total of 14 players, but investigations by both the school and the conference determined that Shavlik was not involved. The Wolfpack was on probation for the 1954–55 season, which was why N.C. State couldn't represent the ACC after beating Duke for the conference title in Reynolds Coliseum. The invitation instead went to the Blue Devils, who lost to Villanova 74–73 in the first round of the national tourney.

"For his size that boy moved up and down the court pretty well," Molodet told Tim Peeler in *Legends of N.C. State Basketball*. "He was always around the hole. He was always where the ball was.

"When you can pick up 22, 23 rebounds a game, that's pretty damned good, isn't it?"

Shavlik padded his rebounding and scoring by being the ACC's first noted practitioner of the tap shot, which helped him average 18.5 points and 16.8 boards over his three seasons.

"I worked hard on the timing of getting the ball back through the net," Shavlik told Ron Morris in *ACC Basketball*. "Nobody suggested it to me. It was the easy way to score and it came natural to me."

But it was what Shavlik did when he wasn't playing basketball that prompted Case to declare, "I have never had a better player or better boy in my 36 years of basketball."

The grandson of Czechoslovakian immigrants, Shavlik was a Big Brother to an eight-year-old. He could often be found at the Governor Morehead School for the Blind, across from the N.C. State campus. He married his wife, Beverly, while in school. The two launched a janitorial service, Carolina Maintenance Company, that grew into a $250 million enterprise. In time, Carolina Maintenance became one of North Carolina's largest employers of the handicapped. In 1965, it received a Meritorious Award from President Lyndon Johnson. Shavlik returned to his business after a brief, uninspired fling with the NBA and became ever more active in the community, working with the Boys Clubs of America, the Raleigh Chamber of Commerce, and N.C. State's Student Aid Foundation.

His consideration for others did not surprise those who played against him. After inadvertently smashing the glasses of an opponent during one on-court collision, Shavlik helped search the floor for the shards.

"Shavlik is one of the truly great players of our time, and he's my candidate for all sportsmanship awards," Case said. "I never saw him lose his temper in four years, and I never heard anybody talk against him. He is always the same, giving his best and trying to win."

Such a good person deserved a better ending to his college career. Shavlik played in the 1956 ACC Tournament and NCAA Tournament with a makeshift leather brace to help stabilize his broken wrist. Though N.C. State won its third-straight conference title, the Wolfpack was upended by Canisius 79–78 in four overtimes in the national tourney. Ranked number two, the Wolfpack had been eyeballing a meeting with Bill Russell and his number-one San Francisco Dons, the eventual national champions.

Unlike Russell, Shavlik never established himself in the NBA. He was picked fourth by the New York Knicks, who gave him a $5,000 signing bonus plus an annual salary of $14,000. But for whatever reason, Shavlik was a bust, playing only seven games in 1956–57 and one in 1957–58. His career NBA totals were 10 points, four field goals on 22 attempts, 23 rebounds, and 12 personal fouls.

Joe Belmont, who played against N.C. State as a guard for Duke, suspected Shavlik's problem as a pro.

"He was probably not aggressive enough," Belmont said in *ACC Basketball*. "This is going to sound crazy, but if he would have grown up on the East Coast where he would have understood the game better and played 365 days a year, Shavlik would probably be in the Hall of Fame.

"Ronnie could play. He could handle the ball, hook, go outside and shoot the jumper. But he happened to go to New York and the Knicks were hurting for bangers. It was a survival test and I don't think Ronnie was prepared to go in and have a fistfight every night."

He played later for the Baltimore Bullets of the Eastern League, commuting from Raleigh while Beverly remained home to tend the business.

Shavlik died of cancer in June 1983, just three months after N.C. State won its second national championship.

His grandson and namesake, Shavlik Randolph, brought his memory back to the minds of many when he signed with Duke in 2002 after a hammer-and-tongs recruiting battle that included N.C. State and his parents' alma mater, North Carolina.

VIC MOLODET

6-0 Guard │ N.C. State │ 1953–56 │ No. 73

1954	Second-team All-ACC, sixth-most votes	275
1955	Second-team All-ACC, eighth-most votes	225
	Second-team All-Tournament	50
1956	First-team All-ACC, third-most votes	350
	ACC Tournament MVP	100
Awards Points		**1,000**

A case—so to speak—can be made that ACC basketball wouldn't have been as good in the early years of the mid-1950s if shoe salesman *extraordinaire* Chuck Taylor hadn't convinced N.C. State that Everett Case was its man, and if State hadn't persuaded Case to migrate south from Indiana to coach the Red Terrors in 1946.

And absolutely no way would it have been as much fun.

As good a coach as he was—and he was good enough to win 337 games (against 134 defeats) and 10 conference championships in his 17 seasons at

Vic Molodet

State—Case might have been an even better promoter of the game. He loved tournament basketball and knew how to stage it. He loved packed houses and knew how to entertain them.

And he loved a fast-paced, get-up-and-go brand of ball and knew how to coach it.

Nobody, according to ex-assistant Vic Bubas, could coach the fast break better.

"I have not seen anyone as good," Bubas told Dick Herbert for the profile on Case in Ron Morris's *ACC Basketball.* "He explained as he taught, and it was a sight to behold.

"The emphasis was on the wing men crossing with stops and pivots and never throwing the ball away. If you ran the break the way he wanted, it was almost impossible to throw the ball away."

To find players fast and sure-handed enough to execute the break, Case had to return time and again to Indiana, where he had won 765 games as a high-school coach. His grand design was to have a basketball goal in every driveway in North Carolina, but as they were being erected one by one, he relied on his Hoosier pipeline to win the first three ACC Tournaments played.

His first N.C. State team, which improved to 26–5 from 6–12 the season before, boasted six "Hoosier hotshots," including all-conference guard Dick Dickey and a future ACC coach named Norm Sloan. His second team added Bubas and Sam Ranzino, a Gary, Indiana, product destined to be a first-team All-American.

The play of Ranzino caught the fancy of a budding star from East Chicago, Indiana.

"When I was in high school I used to listen to N.C. State on the radio," Vic Molodet told Dave Droschak in *Legends of N.C. State Basketball*. "They would always say, 'Ranzino just steps over the 10-second line and lets it fly. Ladies and gentlemen, there it goes.' I said, 'I want to do that.' It was amazing to hear."

Molodet turned out to be as good as most any guard ever in the ACC. At least that was the opinion of Irwin Smallwood, longtime sports editor of the *Greensboro News and Record* and a member of the North Carolina Sports Hall of Fame. Smallwood waxed enthusiastic over Molodet to Droschak in 2010: "I'm an unabashed fan of his. When I get in arguments with younger guys talking about backcourt guys I tell them, 'Give me Molodet and you can have anybody else but Phil Ford. Give me the two of them and I'll beat everybody.' "

A six-foot point guard, Molodet was so known for his speed that Case dubbed him "the fastest player I ever coached." Before Lou Pucillo was there to feed John Richter in the post, before Monte Towe got the ball to David Thompson and Tommy Burleson, and long before Chris Corchiani was always on the lookout for Rodney Monroe on the wing, Molodet helped make center Ronnie Shavlik one of the most dominant forces in the early days of the ACC.

It can be argued that Shavlik's star overshadowed Molodet's. What fame Molodet accrued during his playing days was as one of the "M-Twins," along with John Maglio. But that was enough for his jersey to hang today in the rafters of N.C. State's home arena.

"I match my guards against any in the country," Case crowed.

Molodet struggled with his aim as a sophomore, shooting only 29 percent, but found the range to make 41 percent as a junior and 43 percent as a senior—more than respectable for the era. And he did so with a wide range of shots that included, believe it or not, the hook.

"For a guy my size I had a deadly hook," Molodet told Droschak. "That's the truth.

"Anywhere around the circle, I was really effective, either left or right. You see, in high school they set me up underneath and wanted me to go one-on-one, and that's where I developed my hook shot."

Molodet might also be more widely remembered if the Wolfpack, ranked number two behind San Francisco, hadn't been upset by Canisius 79–78 in the 1956 NCAA Tournament, in a game in Madison Square Garden that Case called "the greatest disappointment I've suffered in my 36 years of basketball."

Shavlik played with a leather brace on his broken left hand, and Maglio missed a key free throw down the stretch. But the real blow came when Molodet, who had been called for three charges in the first half, fouled out early in the first of four overtimes.

"I hate to end like this," Molodet said. "I thought we were going all the way."

Regardless, those who were around to watch Molodet play will never forget what they saw.

"This guy would eat the lunch of a lot of these guys today that are touted as extraordinary point guards," Smallwood said. "He knew how to play north and south. He knew where the basket was. He knew that the game hinged on how many times the ball went through the basket, and he knew how to get to it.

"He's got to be one of the top five guards in ACC history."

DICKIE HEMRIC

6-6 Center | Wake Forest | 1953–55 | No. 24

1954	First-team All-ACC, unanimous	425
	ACC POY, contested	175
	ACC Tournament MVP	100
1955	First-team All-ACC, unanimous	425
	First-team All-Tournament	75
	ACC POY, contested	175
	Second-team All-American	150
Awards Points		1,525

Nobody, least of all Dickie Hemric, knew what to expect from Dickie Hemric when he showed up at Wake Forest in the fall of 1951.

"My first choice was Appalachian," Hemric explained years later. "I had a lot of friends there, and I just felt the caliber of play in the old Southern Conference [before the formation of the ACC in 1953] was a little beyond me. I was a junior before I played an appreciable amount of high-school ball."

The ACC's original diamond in the rough grew up the ninth of 10 children of a carpenter in the foothills town of Jonesville in rural Yadkin County.

Dickie Hemric with
Coach Bones McKinney
Courtesy of Irvin Grigg

The family was so poor that Hemric delivered papers to help buy the one pair of overalls each child wore during the week and the one suit or dress for church. When the overalls wore out at the knees, they were cut off to wear in the tobacco fields that provided the family's means of sustenance.

Coach Murray Greason was on his way to recruit Hemric at Jonesville High School when he stopped by a general store to ask directions. The broad-shouldered teen behind the counter asked the coach why he was visiting the school. Greason replied that he wanted to meet Dickie Hemric.

"Well, you don't need directions," the youth replied. "I'm Dickie Hemric."

For a man considered to have one of the keenest eyes for talent in ACC history, Everett Case of N.C. State whiffed at least a couple of times. Four years before Case passed on Lennie Rosenbluth, he took a look at Hemric and decided he wasn't Wolfpack caliber.

Hemric proved otherwise, setting national records for career points (2,587), most career free-throw attempts (1,359), most career free throws made (905), and most free throws made in a season (302).

What an ordeal it must have been to play against Hemric on the Deacons' tiny home court of Gore Gym on the old campus north of Raleigh, where Wake Forest was located from its founding in 1834 until its move to Winston-Salem in 1956.

First off, Hemric worked for every home-court advantage he could get.

Skeeter Francis, the legendary media relations director for Wake Forest (and later the ACC), recounted Hemric's practice of stopping by the officials' locker room before every home game.

"I just want to welcome you gentlemen to the game tonight," Hemric would say. "I'm just so glad you fellows are officiating this game. You're the best officials in the league."

Francis chuckled at the memory.

"And then he'd go back upstairs and ram everybody's head into the wall," Francis said. "And they wouldn't call any fouls on Dickie."

As good as he was as a freshman, Hemric got even better when Greason hired an ex-NBA center named Bones McKinney as an assistant coach before the 1952–53 season. McKinney, as colorful a character as the ACC has ever known, worked diligently with Hemric as the two battled one-on-one in the tight confines of Gore.

"Dickie learned more in a month than any man I ever saw," McKinney said. "I don't know of any man who ever progressed as quickly as he did. When he came, he did not have a hook and he could not shoot a foul shot."

By all accounts a warrior, Hemric had to play his home games on a court built on an unyielding cement base. In one legendary performance in 1954, he scored 44 points against Duke while limping around on what was later diagnosed as a broken ankle.

Wake Forest had plenty of talent in the league's earliest days, boasting the likes of Lefty Davis, Jackie Murdock, and Ernie Wiggins. But that didn't keep opposing coaches from following Frank McGuire's advice on how to play the Deacons.

"That guy [Hemric] is going to score about 30 or more points against you regardless, so why bother to concentrate on him?" McGuire said. "We just try to stop other guys on the team."

Cynics might say the rules of basketball at the time—which mandated a six-foot-wide lane that allowed powerful post players to camp out under the basket—distorted Hemric's accomplishments. Further enhancing his advantage in strength was an experimental rule the ACC instituted in 1954–55 that allowed each team an inside spot on free throws. How many of Hemric's rebounds came off missed free throws by teammates, and how many of those did he put back in the basket?

Hemric's defense, if he needs any, is that the ACC in 1954–55 had 14 players as tall as he was and eight even taller. And none came within a country mile of the 27.6 points and 19 rebounds he averaged that season.

Hemric played two seasons for the Boston Celtics and was on the team that won the 1957 NBA championship.

Granted, Bones McKinney wasn't the most impartial judge. And granted, he coached at Wake Forest before integration and wasn't on the scene when the likes of David Thompson, John Lucas, James Worthy, and Michael Jordan came along.

Nevertheless, McKinney waxed poetic about the abilities of Dickie Hemric, calling him "the best basketball player North Carolina has ever produced."

He certainly had the numbers.

THE PORTICO OF PROMINENCE

Tree Rollins was a beast. He terrorized ACC centers during his four years at Clemson, which coincided, largely because he was so dominant, with one of the most successful runs in the school's basketball history. Though never a big scorer, he controlled the game with his defensive presence and ability to pound the backboards.

Anyone who doesn't think Tree Rollins belongs in an ACC Basketball Hall of Fame is whacked.

Dennis Scott scared the wits out of every coach who had to face him during his three years at Georgia Tech. How to defend a guard who, at six-eight, could get his shot off from anywhere, anytime he liked? Scott made more three-pointers per game (3.6) than anyone to ever play in the league. He averaged 21.4 points a game, ranking fifth in the ACC as a sophomore and first as a junior. He also holds the record for most points in a season (970).

If Dennis Scott isn't a Hall of Famer, there's no such thing.

Elton Brand was "the Man" in college basketball in 1998–99. Don't take my word for it—he was voted consensus National Player of the Year, and there's only one of those per season. Richard Hamilton of Connecticut was really good, and Michigan State's Mateen Cleaves wasn't bad either. But Brand, who shot 62 percent from the floor while averaging 17.7 points and 9.8 rebounds for a Duke team that tied its own record with 37 victories by an ACC school, was the best of them all.

Any Hall of Fame that doesn't include Brand should be converted into a mental hospital for the drooling sportswriters who voted against him.

Before researching this project, I would have agreed with all the above sentiments. Catch me on the right night, telling the right stories while drinking the right adult beverages around the right table at the right ACC Tournament hospitality suite, and I still might.

Rollins, Scott, and Brand were special players. And so were a number of others who could be considered among the best 100 or so ever in the ACC. Some were as good as, if not better than, players honored in this book. Yet all are outside looking in because when the awards, accolades, and accomplishments of their college careers were tallied, they came up short.

My one regret from two years of researching and writing this book is that readers might feel that not including a Tree Rollins, a Dennis Scott, or an Elton Brand in my Hall of Fame in any way denigrates who those players were and what they accomplished. But I also realized that I couldn't, from my own body of knowledge and experience, pick the absolute best players in the history of ACC basketball. No one can. All I could do was pore over the records and determine who were considered the best players by those who watched them. So that's what I spent those many months doing. Mistakes were made in the original record, but that record is still the best guide for peering through the haze of remembered and misremembered deeds of days gone by.

Along the way, I began thinking of ways to recognize those players who may have been as good as some in the Hall of Fame but never accumulated the accolades to prove it. What I arrived at, honestly and with no tint of sarcasm, is what I call "the Portico of Prominence." The path through the grounds into the Hall goes through the Portico. Visitors have no way to enter the hallowed halls without passing the life-sized statues of those who, in the minds of many, might belong inside as well.

Sean Singletary
6-0 Guard | Virginia | 2004–8 | No. 44
975 Awards Points

Why he should be in: Of the 24 players who made first-team All-ACC three times, 23 are in my ACC Basketball Hall of Fame. The only one who is not is Singletary, who finished fifth in the voting as a sophomore, fourth as a junior, and third as a senior—the season only Tyler Hansbrough and Tyrese Rice received more votes.

Why he's not: Singletary never made All-Tournament, either first- or second-team. He was never named an All-American, first- or second-team. And he never made a serious run at ACC Player of the Year, finishing no higher than fourth in the balloting with 12 votes as a junior. That year, Jared Dudley won with 45, Al Thornton got 30, and Tyler Hansbrough received 19.

Chris Paul
6-0 Guard | Wake Forest | 2003–5 | No. 3
875 Awards Points

Why he should be in: As he has proven during his brilliant NBA career, Paul is one of the greatest point guards to ever break an ankle or lay a lob on the rim for an arena-rattling dunk. He was really good as a Wake Forest freshman, when he averaged 14.8 points and 5.9 assists, and even better as a sophomore, when he contributed 15.3 points and 6.6 assists. In his 63 college games, he shot 47 percent from three-point range and had 395 assists against 171 turnovers.

Why he's not: The short answer is he left Wake Forest after his sophomore season. But despite his early departure, he might have made the cut with a bigger finish that year. He made first-team All-American but came in second behind J. J. Redick in the All-ACC voting and a distant third (behind Redick and Sean May) for conference POY. Lest it be forgotten, he was suspended for the first game of the ACC Tournament for hitting Julius Hodge of N.C. State in a sensitive area in the regular-season finale. The Deacons lost to the Wolfpack in the tournament opener and were eliminated from the NCAA Tournament in the second round by West Virginia.

Lonny Baxter
6-8 Center | Maryland | 1998–2002 | No. 35
950 Awards Points

Why he should be in: Baxter was the inside anchor of the only Maryland teams to ever make the Final Four. The Terps lost to Duke in the national semifinals Baxter's junior season and beat Indiana for the title his senior season. He was named East Regional MVP in 2002 after he abused Connecticut's Emeka Okafor in a 29-point, nine-rebound performance while holding Okafor to six points and six rebounds.

Why he's not: Although he made first-team All-ACC twice and second-team once, Baxter was never considered one of the four best players in the league. He finished fifth in the voting as a sophomore and senior and eighth as a junior. To make the cut, he would have needed national honors that were never forthcoming.

Elton Brand
6-9 Center | Duke | 1997–99 | No. 42
975 Awards Points

Why he should be in: Brand was the best player in college basketball in 1998–99. I wish I could award points for his classic response to the Duke coed who upbraided him for the "disloyalty" he showed by leaving school after his sophomore season for the NBA. "People like you can not and will not ever understand my situation," Brand wrote her in part. "Never being considered a part of your posh group of yuppies really hurts me to the heart. Yeah, right."

Why he's not: He played only 60 games during his time in the ACC. He hurt his foot as a freshman and participated in just 21 of Duke's 35 games. So his time in the league lasted barely a season and a half. But what a hellacious season and a half it was.

Ed Cota
6-1 Guard | North Carolina | 1996–2000 | No. 5
975 Awards Points

Why he should be in: One of the ACC's greatest playmakers, Cota dished out more assists (1,030) than any college player ever except Bobby Hurley (1,076) and Chris Corchiani (1,038). Although never a prolific scorer, he was named ACC Rookie of the Year in 1997 and second-team All-ACC as a sophomore, junior, and senior.

Why he's not: Cota never made first-team All-ACC and in fact never finished above seventh in the voting.

Vince Carter
6-6 Forward | North Carolina | 1995–98 | No. 15
700 Awards Points

Why he should be in: One of the most dynamic athletes in ACC history, Carter was something to see in his three years at North Carolina, during which the Tar Heels compiled a record of 83–22, won two ACC titles, and reached the 1998 Final Four, where they lost to Utah in the semifinals. If I allotted Awards Points for *SportsCenter* highlights, Carter would be a lock for the Hall of Fame.

Why he's not: It took too long for his production to catch up with his ability, and then he was gone. He made third-team All-ACC as a sophomore (11th-most votes), then rose to first-team as a junior (third-most votes), the season he also made second-team All-American. A big senior season would have put him across the threshold, but he departed for the NBA as the fifth overall pick by the Golden State Warriors.

Bob Sura
6-5 Guard | **Florida State** | **1991–95** | **No. 3**
925 Awards Points

Why he should be in: Florida State joined the ACC in 1991. Being the most decorated Seminole player during that time is a great honor. Sura easily out-polled his strongest competition, Al Thornton, 925 Awards Points to 875. He was All-ACC three seasons and was considered one of the seven-best players twice and one of the three best (after Grant Hill and Randolph Childress) as a junior in 1994. "Oh, he got after it, man," Childress said. "He didn't back down from anybody. He was a tough guard. He was good at everything. He shot off the dribble. He would get after you a little bit. He wasn't afraid of the big moment, the big stage—at Carolina and Duke, anywhere. He definitely was a heck of a player."

Why he's not: Sura's career peaked his junior year, when he led the ACC with 21.2 points a game. He wasn't among the top five as a senior, when he slipped back to second-team. His field-goal accuracy also tumbled from 46.9 percent as a junior to 41.7 percent as a senior. The Seminoles finished second in the ACC Sura's first two seasons—when he played alongside Sam Cassell, Charlie Ward, and Douglas Edwards—but had losing records (13–14 and 12–15) his final two years. Wide-open but error-prone, Sura hurt his team almost as often as he helped it. "He's so competitive sometimes, he gets too emotional, and as a result he sometimes makes poor decisions on the court," Coach Pat Kennedy told Barry Jacobs in *A Fan's Guide to ACC Basketball*.

Eric Montross
7-0 Center | **North Carolina** | **1990–94** | **No. 00**
975 Awards Points

Why he should be in: Not only was Montross a two-time All-ACC performer, he was twice named consensus second-team All-American. As a junior, he got more All-ACC votes (308) than anyone other than Rodney Rogers (348) and Bobby Hurley (347). He also made first-team All-Tournament as a junior and second-team as a senior, the season the Tar Heels beat Georgia Tech 73–66 for the conference title.

Why he's not: Montross is one of three ACC players named second-team All-American the same season he didn't make first-team All-ACC. The others were Mike O'Koren in 1979 and Jeff Teague in 2009. As a senior, Montross received his national honor despite finishing ninth in the All-ACC balloting. Those who watched him play game in and game out recognized him as one of the top eight players in the league only once.

Tom Gugliotta
6-10 Forward | N.C. State | 1988–92 | No. 24
550 Awards Points

Why he should be in: Gugliotta was clearly a Hall of Fame–caliber player his senior season, when he led the conference with 9.8 rebounds a game, ranked second with 22.5 points a game, and made first-team All-ACC with the third-most votes (behind Christian Laettner and Walt Williams).

Why he's not: It took him too much time to reach that level. A late-bloomer, he never scratched the All-ACC voting until he made the second team (ninth-most votes) as a junior.

Rick Fox
6-7 Forward | North Carolina | 1987–91 | No. 44
550 Awards Points

Why he should be in: By his senior season, Fox was easily the best player on a team that won 29 games, finished second in the ACC regular season, beat Duke for the conference title, and lost to Kansas in the national semifinals.

Why he's not: Before he made first-team All-ACC as a senior (fifth-most votes), Fox's only Awards Points came from making third-team All-ACC (12th-most votes) as a junior and being named second-team All-Tournament as a sophomore and first-team All-Tournament as a senior.

Dennis Scott
6-8 Guard | Georgia Tech | 1987–90 | No. 4
950 Awards Points

Why he should be in: Not only is Scott the ACC's all-time leader in three-pointers per game, he's eighth in career three-point accuracy at 42.2 percent and 19th in scoring per game. The 27.7 points he averaged as a junior were the most by an ACC player since David Thompson's 29.9 in 1975, and no one has scored more since. And his record for points in a season has stood for more than two decades. National writers were impressed enough to name him consensus second-team All-American in 1990, the season he was honored as ACC Player of the Year and led Georgia Tech's "Lethal Weapon 3" outfit to the conference championship and the Final Four.

Why he's not: Even though he left for the NBA a year early, Scott still would have waltzed into the Hall of Fame if he had received any recognition at all for his standout sophomore season, when he ranked fifth in the conference with 20.3 points a game. But he was left off not only first- but second-team All-ACC, as writers saw fit to bestow second-team honors on two players from—surprise, surprise—North Carolina. Remember Steve Bucknall and Kevin Madden? Both were picked instead of Scott, the league's Rookie of the Year in 1988 and Player of the Year as a junior.

Tom Hammonds
6-9 Forward | Georgia Tech | 1985–89 | No. 20
925 Awards Points

Why he should be in: The ACC Rookie of the Year in 1986, Hammonds was considered one of the three best players in the conference his final two seasons. As a senior, he got every vote, as he and Danny Ferry were the two unanimous picks. As a junior, he finished third with 221 votes, which placed him much closer to the 239 Ferry and J. R. Reid received as unanimous selections than to the 175 Vinny Del Negro got at fourth in the pecking order. He made second-team All-Tournament as a freshman, the season the Yellow Jackets lost to Duke in the title game.

Why he's not: He probably should have been at least second-team All-ACC as a sophomore, when he averaged 16.2 points and 7.2 rebounds while shooting 56.9 percent from the field. But the five spots went instead to Reid, Ferry, Andrew Kennedy, Tommy Amaker, and Duane Ferrell. If Ferrell, who finished more than 300 points shy of enshrinement, could allot his second-team All-ACC points to Tech teammate Hammonds, then Hammonds would be in with 100 points to spare.

Horace Grant
6-10 Center | Clemson | 1983–87 | No. 54
750 Awards Points

Why he should be in: No player ever in the conference has a stronger grievance with those who select All-ACC teams. To lead the league with 10.5 rebounds a game (1.5 more than runner-up Brad Daugherty) and not even make second team is a gross oversight. Even the recognition Grant received the next season as ACC Player of the Year doesn't make up for that.

Why he's not: He was a dominant player for only two seasons and got screwed out of All-ACC in one of those—the same year Steve Hale, who averaged 11.3 points and 4.9 assists a game for North Carolina, made the second team. Again, surprise, surprise.

Brad Daugherty
7-0 Center | North Carolina | 1982–86 | No. 42
900 Awards Points

Why he should be in: I was stunned when Daugherty came up short, given what I remember of him as a player. He was, after all, a two-time first-team All-ACC performer who received national recognition as a consensus second-team All-American in 1986. He got every vote but one for All-ACC that season, finishing second in the balloting to unanimous pick Len Bias. And he made first-team All-Tournament as a junior, when the Tar Heels lost to Georgia Tech in the title game. This one hurts because Big Brad was one of my favorite guys ever in the league.

Why he's not: Maybe if he had been older when he showed up, he could have contributed more early in his career. Playing ACC basketball at 16 is tough, especially when you're competing with the likes of Sam Perkins and Warren Martin for playing time. Daugherty spent his sophomore year of high school as a manager on the basketball team, so he was a project. He averaged 8.2 points and 5.2 rebounds as a college freshman and 10.5 points and 5.6 rebounds as a sophomore, so he didn't crack an All-ACC team until his junior season, when he finished fifth in the voting.

John Salley
6-11 Center | Georgia Tech | 1982–86 | No. 22
500 Awards Points

Why he should be in: Salley provided the inside prowess to complement guard Mark Price on the Georgia Tech teams that first attained ACC prominence.

Why he's not: He never came close to making first-team All-ACC. He was named second-team twice, garnering the eighth-most votes as a junior and the 10th-most as a senior.

Lorenzo Charles
6-7 Forward | N.C. State | 1981–85 | No. 43
925 Awards Points

Why he should be in: It may be argued that Charles should be in the Hall of Fame based solely on his winning dunk for the 1983 national championship. But he was far more than a one-shot wonder, as he proved his junior and senior seasons, when he was recognized as one of the three best players in the conference. He made the first team with the third-most votes as a junior and was a unanimous selection as a senior, the season he made a strong run at Player of the Year, only to come up short of Len Bias, 54 votes to 28.

Why he's not: Charles took too long to start accumulating Awards Points. Through his first two seasons, he pocketed only the 50 that came from making second-team All-Tournament as a sophomore. Also, the national recognition that could have pushed him over the top just wasn't there.

Thurl Bailey
6-11 Forward | N.C. State | 1979–83 | No. 41
550 Awards Points

Why he should be in: Bailey, along with Sidney Lowe, Dereck Whittenburg, and Lorenzo Charles, will always hold an exalted place at N.C. State for helping carry the Cardiac Pack to the national championship.

Why he's not: If any ACC team has ever attained synergy, it was the 1983 Wolfpack. Of the team's three senior leaders, Lowe finished with 575 Awards Points, Bailey with 550, and Whittenburg with 325. None ever finished higher than fourth in the All-ACC voting, none ever received a vote for conference POY, and none ever made an All-American team.

Buck Williams
6-8 Forward | Maryland | 1978–81 | No. 52
725 Awards Points

Why he should be in: An honoree on the ACC's 50th-anniversary team, Williams averaged at least 10 rebounds all three seasons he played, led the ACC in boards as a freshman and junior, scored 15.5 points a game both his sophomore and junior seasons, and shot 61.5 percent from the floor.

Why he's not: Williams is easily one of the best-regarded players never to make first-team All-ACC, finishing eighth in the voting in 1980 and sixth in 1981. The two seasons he led the conference in rebounding, he won little recognition for it. He was never an All-American, though he might have been had he returned for his senior season. Instead, he made himself eligible for the NBA draft and was picked third overall by the New Jersey Nets.

Frank Johnson
6-1 Guard | Wake Forest | 1976–81 | No. 14
875 Awards Points

Why he should be in: "The Smiling Deacon," as he was known around Wake Forest for his effervescent nature, Johnson made first-team All-ACC once and second-team twice. He began his college career as an integral cog in the Deacons' run to the Elite Eight in 1977 and closed it as the unquestioned leader of a team good enough to finish 22–7 overall and 9–5 in ACC play in 1981. He was still at Wake Forest as a fifth-year senior after tearing a knee ligament early in his junior season.

Why he's not: Johnson was never deemed to be one of the three best players in the conference. He received the eighth-most votes as sophomore, the ninth-most as a junior, and the fourth-most as a senior. He never received more than nominal support for ACC POY and never made an All-American team.

Tree Rollins
7-1 Center | Clemson | 1973–77 | No. 30
775 Awards Points

Why he should be in: Rollins provided an inside presence Clemson had never before known. The Tigers won a total of 11 ACC games the four years before he arrived and 24 while he was on the floor blocking shots and dominating the boards. He ranks first all-time in the ACC with 4.09 blocks per game and fifth with 1,311 total rebounds.

Why he's not: Rollins never made first-team All-ACC. He came close twice, finishing sixth in the voting in both 1975 and 1977, two of the three seasons he was named second-team all-conference. And he never made All-Tournament and never received more than nominal support for ACC Player of the Year.

I can't help wondering what Rollins's legacy might be if his short hook shot at the end of regulation in the 1975 tournament semifinal against North Carolina had gone in. The Tigers would have won the game and—who knows?—maybe even beaten N.C. State the next day (they routed the Wolf-pack 92–70 that season in Littlejohn) for their first and, to date, only ACC championship. But it rimmed out, the Tar Heels won in overtime, and Rollins is still remembered for stretching his seven-one body out in the lane, prostrate in disappointment.

Walter Davis
6-6 Forward | North Carolina | 1973–77 | No. 24
675 Awards Points

Why he should be in: Davis was one of the most popular players in North Carolina history, for good reason. Not only was he so warm and easygoing that he was nicknamed "Sweet D," he was also the prototypical college wing forward, averaging 15.7 points and 5.6 rebounds over his career. Consistency was his calling card, in that he never averaged fewer than the 14.3 points a game he scored as a freshman and never shot worse than 50 percent from the floor. He topped out at 57.8 percent as a senior, the season the Tar Heels made it to the NCAA championship game before losing to Marquette.

Why he's not: For all the plays and friends he made, Davis was surprisingly undecorated in college. Part of that may have resulted from being overshadowed by two more heralded teammates, Phil Ford and Mitch Kupchak, and part might have been that he played at a time the conference was so loaded that players as good as Clemson's Tree Rollins and Virginia's Wally Walker never made first-team All-ACC. Davis did make the first team as a senior, though with the fifth-most votes. He made the second team as a junior with the eighth-most votes. It's also worth noting that he never made an All-American team, not even second- or third-team. And he never made first-team All-Tournament, though he was second-team as a sophomore, junior, and senior.

Bobby Jones
6-9 Forward | North Carolina | 1971–74 | No. 34
800 Awards Points

Why he should be in: Named by a panel of sportswriters one of 50 members on the ACC's 50th-anniversary team, Jones shot 60.8 percent from the floor for his career, averaged 15 points and 10.5 rebounds as a junior and 16.1 points and 9.8 rebounds as a senior, and was considered one of the best defensive forwards in the nation. A consummate team player, he excelled in the less-glorified aspects of the game, such as setting screens, moving the basketball, and playing lock-down defense.

Why he's not: Points have always been given heavy consideration in awards voting, and Jones never finished in the top seven among ACC scoring leaders. His 16.1 points as a senior ranked him eighth in the conference. That season, he made first-team All-ACC (fourth-most votes) and second-team All-American. He was named second-team All-ACC as a junior (sixth-most votes). None of that was enough to overcome a lack of points early in his career. He was not eligible as a freshman and received no recognition after averaging 10.2 points and 6.3 rebounds as a sophomore.

Len Elmore
6-9 Center | Maryland | 1971–74 | No. 41
950 Awards Points

Why he should be in: Elmore should have received greater recognition for his signature ability, which was rebounding the basketball. Of all the great players at Maryland, none pulled down as many rebounds (1,053). He ranked third in the conference as a sophomore (11 per game), second as a junior (11.2), and first as a senior (14.7). Over the 38 seasons since, only Tim Duncan in 1997 has averaged as many rebounds, and no one has averaged more. He was also a formidable defensive presence in the post. "He blocks shots," Coach Norm Sloan of N.C. State said. "He shoots. They play a zone press, and I don't think they even care if you beat it, because if you do they've got Elmore back there waiting."

Why he's not: I was surprised to learn that Elmore only once averaged more than 10.8 points a game, and never averaged more than 14.6, and that he only once (as a senior) shot better than 46.9 percent from the floor, despite making the bulk of his attempts from relatively close range. He ranked third on his team in points per game as a sophomore, fourth (behind Tom McMillen, Jim O'Brien, and John Lucas) as a junior, and third as a senior. Scoring average has always been a prime consideration for All-ACC voting, which is probably why Elmore was never considered one of the seven best players in the conference until his senior season, when he finally made first-team All-ACC with the fifth-most votes.

George Karl
6-3 Guard | North Carolina | 1970–73 | No. 22
925 Awards Points

Why he should be in: Karl, like many in the Portico of Prominence, made All-ACC three times. He was named to the second team as a sophomore (accumulating the seventh-most votes) and junior (ninth-most votes) before cracking the first team as a senior (third-most votes). He received 232 votes as a senior, more than anyone not named David Thompson (248) or Tommy Burleson (238). He also, curiously, got four votes for ACC Player of the Year, fanning the flames of resentment over what many in the ACC—especially those 30 miles east in Raleigh—felt was an undue North Carolina bias among the media. Karl padded his resume by making second-team All-Tournament as a sophomore and first-team as a junior.

Why he's not: He needed a breakout senior season—when he made 50 percent of his field-goal attempts and averaged 17 points and 5.8 assists on a 25–8 team that finished second in the regular season—to even get in the running. That was the only season he was considered one of the top six players in the conference.

Billy Packer
5-10 Guard | Wake Forest | 1959–62 | No. 34
650 Awards Points

Why he should be in: Packer was the point guard and spark plug of the only Wake Forest team to ever make the Final Four, the 1962 squad featuring Hall of Famer Len Chappell at center. The Deacons won back-to-back ACC titles with Packer running the show.

Why he's not: After making second-team All-ACC as a sophomore (ninth-most votes) and first-team as a junior (fourth-most votes), Packer experienced enough of a senior slump to get snubbed in the all-conference voting. His scoring average slid from 17.2 points as a junior to 14.1 as a senior—though, being the competitor he was, he responded by making first-team All-Tournament for the second-straight season.

John Richter
6-8 Center | N.C. State | 1956–59 | No. 24/25
975 Awards Points

Why he should be in: The first N.C. State player to lead the ACC in scoring, Richter made All-ACC the three years he was eligible. As a senior, he teamed with Lou Pucillo to carry Everett Case's last great Wolfpack team to the conference championship. His main claim to fame was being named MVP (over Oscar Robertson of Cincinnati, Jumping Johnny Green of Michigan State, Pucillo, and Doug Moe and York Larese of North Carolina) of the star-studded 1958 Dixie Classic. Case, in Bethany Bradsher's *The Dixie Classic*, called Richter's 26-point, 16-rebound semifinal performance against Robertson's Bearcats "his greatest effort ever for us. Richter played those last 10 minutes on guts alone."

Why he's not: Richter's only Hall of Fame–caliber season was 1958–59, when he narrowly finished second to Pucillo in the voting for ACC Player of the Year, 43 votes to 25. Otherwise, he finished ninth in the voting as a sophomore and seventh as a junior. Even so, he might have received the national recognition he needed to cross the threshold if the Wolfpack, after winning the 1959 ACC title, had been eligible to compete in the NCAA Tournament.

Lefty Davis
6-1 Guard | Wake Forest | 1953–56 | No. 13/43
900 Awards Points

Why he should be in: The ACC's first famous Lefty, Davis emerged as the Deacons' go-to guy after Dickie Hemric graduated before the 1955–56 season. As a senior, Davis made first-team All-ACC with the fourth-most votes, needing just one more to tie Vic Molodet of N.C. State for third-most.

Why he's not: He never made a serious run at first-team All-ACC until his senior season. He did finish tied for sixth in the voting with Molodet as a sophomore, but the two got only 91 votes—57 shy of the first team. He actually slid to 10th in the voting as a junior, even though his scoring average climbed from 17.4 points a game to 19.3.

Buzz Wilkinson
6-2 Guard | Virginia | 1953–55 | No. 14
875 Awards Points

Why he should be in: Wilkinson is the ACC's all-time leader in career scoring average at 28.6 points a game. He scored 30 or more 20 times as a senior. No one else has done so more than 15 times in a season. He scored 30 or more 33 times in his two-year ACC career, which ties him with David Thompson at the top of the list.

Why he's not: Like Dickie Hemric, Wilkinson was already a star when the ACC was formed his junior season. Unlike Hemric, he didn't do quite enough in two years to make the cut. For all the points he scored, he was only once considered one of the three best players in the league—as a senior, when he finished third in the balloting, garnering two votes fewer than unanimous selections Hemric and Ronnie Shavlik. As a junior, he also made first-team All-ACC but finished fifth in the balloting. Perhaps his field-goal accuracy of 39.5 percent was held against him.

ACKNOWLEDGMENTS

Contrary to how it often feels, I've not covered ACC basketball forever. Nor will I. When I turn in my laptop and pack up my pads and pens, what I'll miss more than the games, athletes, and coaches will be the scores of great friends who have been on press row with me, and all the times and experiences we have shared.

This book was a labor of love, and nothing made it more so than the way so many pitched in to help me write it. I have three great friends without whom I really couldn't have written the book—Gary Strickland, Al Featherston, and Barry Jacobs. All know about as much about ACC basketball as there is to know, and they were with me from the start of this endeavor, reading rough drafts, floating ideas, shooting down misconceptions, and setting me straight the many times I needed it.

Dozens of others made the project easier and more fun. I'm especially proud of my daughter, Rebecca Collins, a 2012 graduate of the journalism school at UNC–Chapel Hill, who helped gather material for a number of the Tar Heel players enshrined in *The ACC Basketball Book of Fame.* Along with my wife, Tybee, and son, Nate, Rebecca provided the necessary encouragement and support.

I would be painfully remiss not to mention and give thanks for the assistance and support I received from Brian Morrison, Dave Odom, Ron Morris, Lenox Rawlings, Steve Kirschner, Charlie Bryant, Billy Packer, Steve Shutt, Vic Bubas, Lou Pucillo, Ed Hardin, Randolph Childress, Jim Daves, Darlene Craig, Chris Capo, Tom Collins, Jenny Collins, Joe Collins, Kim Hawks, David Zucchino, Moose Pulley, and Crag T. Perry.

Thanks to the following people who helped me procure photos: Robert Crawford, Tim Peeler, Matt Bowers, Mike Stamus, Matt Plizga, Scott Wortman, and Zack Bolno.

BIBLIOGRAPHY

Barrier, Smith. *On Tobacco Road: Basketball in North Carolina.* Leisure Press, 1988.

Bradsher, Bethany. *The Classic: How Everett Case and His Tournament Brought Big-Time Basketball to the South.* Whitecaps Media, 2011.

Brill, Bill. *An Illustrated History of Duke Basketball: A Legacy of Achievement.* Sports Publishing, 2012.

————. *A Season Is a Lifetime: The Inside Stories of the Duke Blue Devils and Their Championship Seasons with Mike Krzyzewski.* New York: Simon and Schuster, 1993.

Carry, Peter. "The Best High School Player in America." *Sports Illustrated* (Feb. 16, 1970).

Chansky, Art. *Blue Blood: Duke-Carolina—Inside the Most Storied Rivalry in College Hoops.* New York: St. Martin's Griffin, 2006.

————. *Light Blue Reign: How a City Slicker, a Quiet Kansan and a Mountain Man Built College Basketball's Longest-Lasting Dynasty.* New York: Thomas Dunne Books, 2009.

Collins, Dan. *Tales from the Wake Forest Hardwood.* Sports Publishing, 2004.

Conroy, Pat. *My Losing Season.* New York: Bantam Books, 2003.

Crothers, Tim. "No More Mr. Nice Guys." *Sports Illustrated* (Feb. 22, 1999).

————. "The Players' Player." *Sports Illustrated* (Nov. 20, 2000).

Deford, Frank. "Chapel Hill's Tobacco Rogues." *Sports Illustrated* (Feb. 20, 1967).

————. "They're the L&M Kids." *Sports Illustrated* (Feb. 20, 1967).

Dohrmann, George. "International Connection." *Sports Illustrated* (March 22, 2010).

Durkin, Duff. "Maryland's Juan Dixon Is a Survivor." *Theacc.com.* Feb. 16, 2000. http://www.theacc.com/sports/m-baskbl/spec-rel/021600aaa.html. Accessed June 11, 2012.

Featherston, Al. *Duke: Memorable Stories of Blue Devil Basketball (Game of My Life).* Sports Publishing, 2007.

————. "The Fight." *Goduke.com.* Feb. 11, 2009. http://www.goduke.com/ViewArticle.dbml?DB_OEM_ID=4200&ATCLID=3666904. Accessed March 22, 2012.

————. "Good Move." *Goduke.com.* Oct. 19, 2007. http://www.goduke.com/ViewArticle.dbml?DB_OEM_ID=4200&ATCLID=1283675. Accessed June 23, 2012.

————. "Retired Jerseys & Standards." *Dukebasketballreport.com.* Dec. 27, 2005. http://www.dukebasketballreport.com/articles/?p=20528. Accessed May 22, 2012.

————. *Tobacco Road: Duke, Carolina, N.C. State, Wake Forest and the History* of the Most Intense Backyard Rivalries in Sports. Lyons Press, 2006.

Feinstein, John. *Forever's Team*. New York: Villard, 1989.

———. *A March to Madness: A View from the Floor in the Atlantic Coast Conference*. Back Bay Books, 1999.

———. *A Season Inside: One Year in College Basketball*. Fireside, 1989.

Forde, Pat. "The Other Side of J. J. Redick." *Espn.com*. Feb. 22, 2006. http://sports. espn.go.com/espn/columns/story?columnist=forde_pat&id=2339265. Accessed May 14, 2006.

Fowler, Scott. *North Carolina's Tar Heels: Where Have You Gone?* Sports Publishing, 2005.

Friend, Tom. "With Honors." *ESPN: The Magazine* (March 27, 2006).

Golenbock, Peter. *Dynasty: The New York Yankees, 1949–64*. Dover Publications, 2010.

———. *Personal Fouls: The Broken Promises and Shattered Dreams of Big Money Basketball at Jim Valvano's North Carolina State*. New York: Carroll and Graf, 1991.

Hannon, Kent. "Brooklyn High School Star Albert King Is the College Recruiters' Most Wanted Man." *Sports Illustrated* (Feb. 7, 1977).

———. "You Don't Know Them, Al." *Sports Illustrated* (Feb. 13, 1978).

Herakovich, Douglas. *Pack Pride: The History of N.C. State Basketball*. Yesterday's Future, 1994.

Hoffer, Richard. "Sam the Man." *Sports Illustrated* (Nov. 5, 1990).

Holland, Gerald. "Dixie's Yankee Hero." *Sports Illustrated* (Dec. 9, 1957).

Jacobs, Barry. *Barry Jacobs' Fan's Guide to ACC Basketball*. 11th annual. 1995.

———. *Three Paths to Glory: A Season on the Hardwood with Duke, N.C. State and North Carolina*. New York: Macmillan, 1993.

James, Bill. *Whatever Happened to the Hall of Fame? Baseball, Cooperstown and the Politics of Glory*. Free Press, 1995.

Katz, Andy. "Sophomore 'Find' Helps Eagles Stay Unbeaten." *Espn.com*. Jan. 19, 2005. http://sports.espn.go.com/ncb/columns/story?columnist=katz_ andy&id=1970905. Accessed June 25, 2012.

Kirkpatrick, Curry. "David Goes After Goliath." *Sports Illustrated* (Nov. 26, 1973).

———. "Everyone Has a Shot This Year." *Sports Illustrated* (March 2, 1987).

———. "The Toughest Kid on Anybody's Block." *Sports Illustrated* (Jan. 4, 1971).

Lake, Thomas. "Did This Man Really Cut Michael Jordan?" *Sports Illustrated* (June 16, 2012).

Lazenby, Roland. *Sampson: A Life Above the Rim*. Full Court Press, 1983.

Lerner, Rich. "Johnson a Slam Dunk Talent." *Golfchannel.com*. Feb. 13, 2010.

"Lonely and Lively Hours of a Star." *Sports Illustrated* (Dec. 6, 1965).

Lostlettermen.com. Interview with Jay Bilas. Feb. 4, 2010. http://www.lostlettermen.com/jay-bilas-/. Accessed June 11, 2012.

Lucas, Adam. *The Best Game Ever: How Frank McGuire's 1957 Tar Heels Beat Wilt and Revolutionized College Basketball.* Lyons Press, 2006.

———. *Carolina Basketball: A Century of Excellence.* Chapel Hill: University of North Carolina Press, 2010.

———. *One Fantastic Ride: The Inside Story of Carolina Basketball's 2009 Season.* Chapel Hill: University of North Carolina Press, 2009.

McCallum, Jack. "The Cruelest Thing Ever." *Sports Illustrated* (June 30, 1986).

McDermott, Barry. "A Man for Two Seasons." *Sports Illustrated* (Dec. 1, 1975).

McLernon, Sean. "Last Ball in U-Hall: Jeff Lamp Lit It Up." *Thesabre.com.* Feb. 9, 2006. http://www.thesabre.com/php-bin/news/printerFriendly.php?id=1787.

———. "Last Ball in U-Hall: Parkhill Raised UVA's Profile." *Thesabre.com.* http://www.thesabre.com/php-bin/news/printerFriendly.php?id=2098. Accessed May 3, 2012.

McMullen, Paul. *Maryland Basketball: Tales from Cole Field House.* Baltimore: John Hopkins University Press, 2002.

Menzer, Joe. *Four Corners: How UNC, N.C. State, Duke and Wake Forest Made North Carolina the Crossroads of the Basketball Universe.* New York: Simon and Schuster, 1999.

Morris, Ron. *ACC Basketball: An Illustrated History.* Four Corners Press, 1988.

Newman, Bruce. "Opposite Sides of the Tracks." *Sports Illustrated* (Nov. 20, 1985).

———. "Rich, But Not Spoiled." *Sports Illustrated* (Nov. 23, 1981).

Peeler, Tim. "Hawkeye's Difficult Path Winds Back Home." *Gopack.com.* http://www.gopack.com/sports/m-baskbl/spec-rel/091806aaa.html. Accessed May 13, 2012.

———. *Legends of N.C. State Basketball.* Sports Publishing, 2004.

———. *N.C. State Basketball: 100 Years of Innovation.* Chapel Hill: University of North Carolina Press, 2010.

Price, Tom. *Tales from the Gamecocks' Roost.* Sports Publishing, 2001.

Prouty, John. *The ACC Basketball Stat Book: Complete Player Register.* Willow Oak Publishing, 2008.

Rappoport, Ken. *Tales from the North Carolina Locker Room: A Collection of the Greatest UNC Basketball Stories Ever Told.* Sports Publishing, 2012.

Roth, John. *The Encyclopedia of Duke Basketball.* Durham, N.C.: Duke University Press, 2006.

Schaap, Richard. "Basketball's Underground Railroad." *Sports Illustrated* (Feb. 4, 1957).

Smith, Dean. *Basketball: Multiple Offense and Defense*. Prentice Hall, 1982.

Smith, Dean, with John Kilgo and Sally Jenkins. *A Coach's Life*. New York: Random House, 1999.

Sumner, Jim. "Looking Back: Barry Parkhill Leaving a Legacy at Virginia." *Theacc.com*. Dec. 6, 2006. http://www.theacc.com/sports/m-baskbl/spec-rel/120606aab.html. Accessed Feb. 20, 2012.

———. "Looking Back: The Building of Georgia Tech in the ACC." *Theacc.com*. Jan. 18, 2007. http://www.theacc.com/sports/m-baskbl/spec-rel/011807aaa.html. Accessed July 7, 2012.

———. "Looking Back: The Career of Maryland's Tom McMillen." *Theacc.com*. March 6, 2009. http://www.theacc.com/sports/m-baskbl/spec-rel/030609aab.html. Accessed April 25, 2012.

———. *Tales from the Duke Blue Devils Locker Room: A Collection of the Greatest Duke Basketball Stories Ever Told*. Sports Publishing, 2012.

Tarkanian, Jerry. *Runnin' Rebel: Shark Tales of "Extra Benefits," Frank Sinatra and Winning It All*. Sports Publishing, 2005.

Telander, Rick. "Greetings from New Jersey." *Sports Illustrated* (Nov. 23, 1992).

Wahl, Grant. "Boo Devil." *Sports Illustrated* (Jan. 24, 2005).

Walker, Samuel J. *ACC Basketball: The Story of Rivals, Traditions and Scandals of the First Two Decades of the Atlantic Coast Conference*. Chapel Hill: University of North Carolina Press, 2011.

"Where There's a C-Well, There's a Way." *Dukebasketballreport.com*. Oct. 24, 2011. http://www.dukebasketballreport.com/articles/?p=42600. Accessed March 22, 2012.

Wilkinson, Jack. "Hall of Fame Profile—Matt Harpring: Basketball Forward from Atlanta One of the Hardest-Working Players in Tech History." *Ramblinwreck.com*. Aug. 29, 2008. http://www.ramblinwreck.com/sports/m-baskbl/spec-rel/082908aab.html. Accessed June 20, 2012.

Williams, Roy, with Tim Crothers. *Hard Work: A Life On and Off the Court*. Chapel Hill, N.C.: Algonquin Books, 2009.

Wolff, Alexander. "Getting Right to the Point." *Sports Illustrated* (Jan. 23, 1984).

———. "No Question." *Sports Illustrated* (Feb. 16, 1998).

———. "To Find Out Why I'm Here." *Sports Illustrated* (Sept. 22, 1986).

(opposite page)
Len Bias
UNIVERSITY OF MARYLAND ARCHIVES

INDEX